Kierkegaard and Literature

KIERKEGAARD
and LITERATURE

IRONY, REPETITION, and CRITICISM

Edited by Ronald Schleifer
and Robert Markley

UNIVERSITY OF OKLAHOMA PRESS   NORMAN

By Ronald Schleifer

The Genres of the Irish Literary Revival (editor) (Dublin and Norman, 1980)
Kierkegaard and Literature: Irony, Repetition, and Criticism (coeditor) (Norman, 1984)

By Robert Markley

From Renaissance to Restoration: Metamorphoses of the Drama (coeditor) (Cleveland, 1983)
Kierkegaard and Literature: Irony, Repetition, and Criticism (co-editor) (Norman, 1984)

Library of Congress Cataloging in Publication Data

Main entry under title:

Kierkegaard and literature.

Includes bibliographical references and index.
1. Kierkegaard, Søren, 1813-1855—Aesthetics—Addresses, essays, lectures. 2. Literature—Philosophy—Addresses, essays, lectures. 3. Literature—History and criticism—Addresses, essays, lectures. I. Schleifer, Ronald. II. Markley, Robert, 1952-   .
B4378.A4K54 1984   801   84-40276
ISBN 0-8061-1879-2 (alk. paper)

Publication of this book has been made possible in part by grants from the Andrew W. Mellon Foundation and from the Office of the Vice-Provost for Research Administration, University of Oklahoma.

The paper in this book meets the guidelines for permanence and durability of the Committee on Production Guidelines for Book Longevity of the Council on Library Resources, Inc.

To Our Parents

Contents

Contents

Editors' Preface

IN 1980, when we first began collecting the essays that appear in this volume, Anglo-American literary criticism was in the midst of a crisis of self-confidence. A younger generation of scholars in England and America had done much to assimilate at least some of the major tenets of French structuralism and, in the process, was beginning to question many of the goals and strategies of New Criticism and the academic departmentalization of what the French had come to call the human sciences. Claude Lévi-Strauss, Roland Barthes, A. J. Greimas, Jacques Lacan, and others had found in linguistics, we were discovering, a science and a method that could link the sciences of man by interrogating the nature of meaning—of "signification"—altogether. This new "science" of signification, sometimes called "semiotics," sometimes "semiology," almost immediately gave rise to its philosophical critique as it both informed and occasioned a philosophical response to its claims to be the science of meaning. Thus Jacques Derrida published *Of Grammatology* (1967), a full-length philosophical "deconstruction" of Lévi-Strauss based, as Gayatri Spivak notes in her translator's introduction, on the work of Heidegger, Nietzsche, Marx, Freud, and others, almost simultaneously with Greimas's rigorous extension of Lévi-Strauss's structural anthropology to semantics in *Structural Semantics* (1966). In Anglo-American studies in the middle and late 1970s, "introductions" to semiotics (by Terence Hawkes, Jonathan Culler, and Philip Pettit, among others) were all the rage. By the early 1980s these books had given way to primers on poststructuralism (by Catherine Belsey, Culler again, Christopher Norris, and Vincent Leitch, among others).

The movement here is from "scientific" to "philosophical" approaches to literature. Yet what is clear from these approaches and this movement is that the autonomous "literary" treatment of literary texts—the conception of literature as somehow "pure" with its corollary of literary criticism as both an independent discipline and a secondary discourse directed at the works of the "great tradition"—is, at best, a problem. It was a difficult and seemingly foreign problem: all of us needed these introductions to a new and wider world of literary studies that sometimes seemed too literary (as criticism attempted to marshal the same rhetorical techniques in its discourse that in former times it had calmly analyzed) and sometimes not literary at all (as it exploded the tradition to examine "discourse" in myth, popular culture, philosophical texts, psychoanalysis, economics, and so forth). Thus these intriguing, controversial, and sometimes difficult books—both the introductions and the texts they introduced to Anglo-American literary criticism—raised fundamental questions about the nature of criticism. "Why the gulf," Geoffrey Hartman asked in *Criticism in the Wilderness* (1980), "between *philosophic* criticism and *practical* criticism, the former flourishing in Continental Europe, the latter insulating the writings of English and American teachers?"

Kierkegaard and Literature is one attempt to answer this question with its assertion that such a gulf cannot, in fact, exist, that interpretation always presents (more or less explicitly) a philosophical stance just as philosophical discourse is always (more or less explicitly) literary. This volume, then, is an indirect result of the ongoing self-questioning of literary criticism inaugurated by the crossing of criticism with seemingly extraliterary disciplines. That is, the work of the last decades has taught us to reconceive what used to be called the comparative studies, such as those in our book, in terms of *intertextuality.* Comparative literature has often found itself in the paradoxical position of not being literary at all: often it has compared "ideas" and concepts through simple juxtaposition. What the last decades have taught us is to discern and interchange textual and rhetorical strategies, to discover the place of rhetoric in philosophical discourse so that the texture and textuality of such discourse can be seen for what it is, discourse inconceivable outside the context of other discourse. At the same time it has taught us that rhetoric always bears philosophical import.

In this regard Sören Kierkegaard, with his polemical pseudonymous writing, has much to teach us. That teaching, however, could not be achieved without the polemics and crises that contemporary criticism has experienced and continues to engage in. What the crisis of criticism has offered us is the implied but often polemical assumption that criticism, even Hartman's "*practical* criticism," *is* philosophic: that to question meaning, even in the confines of a particular "autonomous" poem and even in the expanse of "world-historical" events, is to raise the basic questions that philosophy has always addressed. The polemics and the bewilderment of the last decades have brought us to a place where neither introductions nor arguments need overwhelm our reading and where the work of resituating rhetoric at the center of the human sciences both in France and in America is no longer a strained polemics of "foreign" discourses, whether they be French vocabularies, the neologisms of contemporary theory, or what had seemed the scandal of bringing to bear on literature the language of philosophy. We have learned that no discourse can be "foreign" and that even polemic and scandal can become institutionalized discourse.

Thus *Kierkegaard and Literature* takes its place self-consciously in a poststructuralist world. It assumes explicitly what has been the occasion of the passionate critical debate of our time: that literary criticism, whether theoretical or practical, is a philosophic enterprise. It assumes, that is, that the "introductions" have been made: that the interdisciplinary crossing of criticism and philosophy is a necessary gesture of understanding, that it takes place in the larger rhetorical context of intertextuality, and that the interplay of both analysis and polemic is a fact. To accentuate this interplay, we have divided the essays of the book into two sections: "Kierkegaard and Literature," which explores the literary criticism implicit in Kierkegaard's work, and "Literary Studies," which explores in practical literary studies the usefulness of the philosophical rhetoric of Kierkegaard's work to literary criticism. In the Editors' Introduction we examine that rhetoric as well as the rhetoric of these essays, and the final essay attempts to bring together, as Kierkegaard himself does, the two "interests" of this project.

Still, as we originally intended, *Kierkegaard and Literature* is a provisional work, one that explores possibilities rather than argues for a single interpretation or "revaluation" of Kierkegaard's work. This provisionality, we think, seems particularly suited to Kierkegaard, whose extended discourse parodies, questions, challenges, and often subverts philosophical traditions of his time and ours. As several essays in this volume suggest, Kierkegaard's fascination with "indirect communication" reflects his characteristic questioning of temporal authority—including his own claims to speak "authoritatively." In this regard, *Kierkegaard and Literature* addresses, with several voices, the questions that arise from the conjunction of the two subjects of this collection: Is a Kierkegaardian aesthetics, a Kierkegaardian criticism, possible? If it is, how does this crossing of philosophy and literature change our usual perceptions of literature?

These questions cannot be readily answered. As a result, many of the essays in this volume are studies in the possibility—the potentiality—of a Kierkegaardian rhetoric, a Kierkegaardian poetics of irony or of repetition. More generally, the articles we have collected investigate the range of Kierkegaard's significance for poststructuralist movements in criticism. In this respect they are concerned with several historical moments: that of Kierkegaard's own writing, that of the various works of literature they investigate, and that of their own compositions in the early 1980s. They explore alternative modes of criticism, from Kierkegaardian interpretations of individual texts to polemical views of Kierkegaard's own work. These essays evidence their historical situations in several ways: a renewed attention to the role of language in Kierkegaard's thought, an emphasis on the literary rather than conceptual aspects of his work, and a desire to pursue parallels between Kierkegaard and contemporary thinkers, notably Derrida and Michel Foucault.

The "readings" of Kierkegaard and literary works that appear in this collection, then, should perhaps be seen as seminal rather than authoritative. They are explorations and participate consciously in the continuing debate about the assumptions, methods, and values of contemporary criticism and the place of philosophy in criticism. They are also, of course, concerned with—"interested" in—the place of criticism in philosophy. The Kierkegaard who emerges in all of this is less a traditional philosopher than an inherently problematic writer whose contributions to aesthetics, literature, and criticism are yet to be explored fully.

The editors of this book have benefited from the generous support of many in this project. Chief among these, of course, are the contributors to the volume, whose cheerful patience equaled the quality of their work. There were many others with whom we corresponded about this volume whose encouragement sustained us in the early stages of the collection. In this regard we owe special thanks to Hillis Miller, Alan Hager, Avrom Fleishman, and Arthur Scouten. Also, simply working together—on our introduction, our individual contributions, and in the editorial process—produced a kind of Kierkegaardian dialectical exhilaration which we hope informs our work and which we know fulfilled our best hopes about the collaborative nature—again a Kierkegaardian notion—of intellectual endeavor. The collection, however, benefited from more than our collaboration. Portions of this book received careful readings from Robert Con Davis, Richard Macksey, Nancy Mergler, and David Gross. We also received both moral and financial support from Kenneth Hoving, Dean of the Graduate College of the University of Oklahoma, at a crucial juncture in this project.

A substantially different version of Paul Bové's essay appeared in *boundary 2;* Part One of Ronald Schleifer's article originally appeared in *Sub-Stance.* The editors gratefully acknowledge these journals for permission to reproduce the articles.

While working on this book, both editors learned about Kierkegaard's "maieutic" function that we speak of in our introduction more literally than either we or Kierkegaard speak of it, and we have discovered in our new sons, Cyrus Schleifer and Stephen Markley, the affectionate concern and the temporal and generational understandings that inform the more passionate and mysterious motives within and behind Kierkegaard's discourse. For this, and for much more, we thank our other collaborators, our wives, Nancy Mergler and Laurie Finke.

Ronald Schleifer
University of Oklahoma

Robert Markley
Texas Tech University

Abbreviations

Abbreviations of Works of Kierkegaard Cited in the Text
(in Order of Publication)

Irony	*The Concept of Irony.* Translated by Lee Capel. Bloomington: Indiana University Press, 1965.
Either/Or	*Either/Or.* Translated by David F. Swenson and Lillian Marvin Swenson. New York: Anchor Books, 1959.
Edifying Discourses	*Edifying Discourses.* Translated by David F. Swenson and Lillian M. Swenson. Minneapolis: Augsburg Publishing House, 1943.
Repetition	*Repetition: An Essay in Experimental Psychology.* Translated by Walter Lowrie. New York: 1964.
	Fear and Trembling: A Dialectical Lyric. Translated by Walter Lowrie. New York: Anchor Books, 1954.
Fragments	*Philosophical Fragments or a Fragment of Philosophy.* Translated by David Swenson, revised by Howard Hong. Princeton, N.J.: Princeton University Press, 1962.

Dread	*The Concept of Dread.* Translated by Walter Lowrie, revised by Howard Hong. Princeton, N.J.: Princeton University Press, 1962.
Postscript	*Concluding Unscientific Postscript.* Translated by D. F. Swenson and Walter Lowrie. Princeton, N.J.: Princeton University Press, 1968.
Two Ages	*The Two Ages: The Age of Revolution and the Present Age.* Translated by Howard Hong and Edna Hong. Princeton, N.J.: Princeton University Press, 1978.
Point of View	*The Point of View for My Work as an Author.* Translated by Walter Lowrie. New York: Harper Torchbook, 1962.
Climacus	*Johannes Climacus, or De Omnibus Dubitandum Est.* Translated by T. H. Croxall. Stanford, Calif.: Stanford University Press, 1958.
Journals	*Sören Kierkegaard's Journals and Papers.* Translated by Howard Hong and Edna Hong. 2 vols. Bloomington: Indiana University Press, 1967.
Letters	*Kierkegaard: Letters and Documents.* Translated by Henrite Rosenmeier. Princeton, N.J.: Princeton University Press, 1978.
Last Years	*The Last Years: Journals, 1853-1855.* Translated by R. G. Smith. New York: Harper Torchbooks, 1965.

Kierkegaard and Literature

RONALD SCHLEIFER and ROBERT MARKLEY

Editors' Introduction: Writing Without Authority and the Reading of Kierkegaard

THERE is something altogether appropriate in a collection of essays by various hands on the subject of Sören Kierkegaard and literature. Kierkegaard is the most "literary" of philosophical writers—he is so, we suspect, because he sees, as Louis Mackey suggests in his essay on *Repetition,* that "the temporalizing of essence makes metaphysics interesting"—and throughout his "whole authorship," as he calls it, Kierkegaard is interested, as literature is, in various and particular occasions for discourse which generate their signification as much from their contrasting juxtapositions as from their positive content. For this reason Kierkegaard is interested in narrative, literary tropes, the relations between what Paul Bové calls "a particular individual and cultural type," and, subsuming all of these, the relation between experience—temporality—and meaning. That is, as George Stack demonstrates below, Kierkegaard's philosophical career argues "that true or authentic existence combines thinking with experience. But thought, of course," Stack goes on, "pertains to the universal or is concerned with ideality or conceptual-linguistic ideals. The paradox of ethical existence is found in the attempt to relate conceptual-linguistic ideals to one's own concrete actuality." The combination of thinking and existence, especially when "thinking" is understood as in some sense "linguistic" and "existence" as above all particular,

3

does indeed define literature; one can see how this conception of Kierkegaard's philosophic project, as Ronald Schleifer says, "implicates his 'whole authorship'—his 'philosophy' itself—in literature and language."

For this reason, then, in addition to the "philosophical" studies in our volume, our collection offers "Kierkegaardian" readings of medieval narrative poetry, a Restoration play, Thoreau's nineteenth-century autobiographical prose, and a novel by George Eliot. Moreover, even the "philosophical" studies border on the "literary": Mackey's essay reads *Repetition* as if it were a (problematical) novel, Bové explores Kierkegaard's own "literary criticism" of *Two Ages,* and the first part of Schleifer's essay, the "reading" of *The Concept of Irony,* attempts to repeat the parodic aspect of Kierkegaard's text. There is, then, a method in the unmapped events of these essays: they present multiple, "dialectical" views of the philosopher as novelist, thinker, critic, and—perhaps in the same way Kierkegaard claims to have "secured the possibility of being able to explain the disparity among these three conceptions [of Socrates] by another conception of Socrates corresponding to this disparity" (*Irony,* pp. 183-84)—finally as parodist. And the second group of critical essays approaches Kierkegaard's "concepts" (and more important, the experience of reading that his texts make clear) through the genres of poetry, drama, autobiography, and fiction (all genres Kierkegaard appropriates to philosophy) to study and experience literary texts.

In fact, the last essay, with its two parts and the virtual silence of Kierkegaard in the critical reading of *The Mill on the Floss,* attempts a repetition of the bipartite structure of our volume (and of our introduction) that privileges both philosophy and literature, making them, in the manner Robert Markley describes, virtual (and finally "impossible": hence Kierkegaard's final silence) repetitions of one another. Part one of Schleifer's essay, "On *The Concept of Irony,*" uses literature *(Hamlet)* and criticism (T. S. Eliot) to understand Kierkegaard's "concept"; part two, "On the Resistance to Irony," uses philosophy—silently—to develop a read-

4

ing of George Eliot. Literature finally resists the conceptualizations of philosophy; this is a point of the most "philosophical" essay in our volume, Stack's essay on "truth," and the point of Kierkegaard's own literary procedures described in the opening essays. Thus it is our hope that our volume will "end" as a form of reading informed by Kierkegaard, even readings of Kierkegaard himself, and not simply a traditional "explication" of Kierkegaard. This is why "silence" is such an important aspect of what we will argue is a particularly Kierkegaardian rhetoric: it does not impose the authority of assertion and conceptualization, but rather creates the occasion, as literature does, for the drama of interpretation—in a word, an occasion for *reading.*

To this end the essays of our volume do more than "describe" Kierkegaard's literary procedures; they attempt to exemplify his particular rhetoric in their modes of reading. Above all, his rhetoric eschews authority. "In all eternity," Kierkegaard writes, "it is impossible for me to compel a person to accept an opinion, a conviction, a belief. But one thing I can do: I can compel him to take notice" (*Point of View,* p. 35). To make us see, as Conrad said, is the task of literature, and this finally defines the silences that, "repeating" Kierkegaard, inform the juxtapositions in Schleifer's attempt to read *The Mill on the Floss* "against" *Hamlet, The Concept of Irony,* and "Hamlet and His Problems." Reading "against" another text (what Bové calls a *competing* text and Kierkegaard calls the *indirect* text) creates a meaningful silence that calls to the reader's attention the necessity of choice. This is perhaps the most rhetorical of strategies. As the Judge says in *Either/Or,* "it is important to choose and choose in time" (*Either/Or,* 2:169). "I would only bring you to the point," he says later,

where the choice between the evil and the good acquires significance for you. Everything hinges on this. As soon as one can get a man to stand at the crossways in such a position that there is no recourse but to choose, he will choose right. Hence, if it should chance that, while you are in the course of reading this somewhat lengthy dissertation . . . you were to feel that the instant of choice had come, then

5

throw the rest of it away, never concern yourself about it, you have lost nothing. [*Either/Or,* 2:172]

In many ways this passage defines Kierkegaard's rhetorical strategy, which recent criticism has taught us is a *literary* strategy, of not offering authoritative stands. Rather, it defines discourse as both ironical and governed by time. What Schleifer does by offering two seemingly independent essays in his contribution is to *repeat* the Kierkegaardian strategy of pseudonymous writing: the strategy of *repetition.*

But his contribution also "repeats" the internal version of this intertextuality that Mackey offers in the opening section, the strategy of *irony.* Mackey presents a critical reading of *Repetition* that attempts to define that difficult concept discursively, as Kierkegaard himself did, by (again silently) reading Kierkegaard "against" Derrida and Derrida's teacher, Heidegger. That is, its rhetoric assumes a discursive mode, even if it sometimes focuses ironically on particular concepts. "The temporalization of essence," Mackey writes, "makes metaphysics interesting. But since metaphysics is properly disinterested it is also the rock on which metaphysics goes aground." What Schleifer does with texts following Kierkegaard's pseudonymous writing Mackey does with words (here the word "metaphysics") following Kierkegaard's ironical writing. He silently brings together two contrary understandings of a concept to generate significance in juxtaposition. In *Fear and Trembling* Kierkegaard uses language the same way:

Either there is an absolute duty to God, and if so it is the paradox here described, that the individual as the individual is higher than the universal and as the individual, stands in an absolute relation to the absolute, or else faith never existed because it has always existed, or, to put it differently, Abraham is lost. [*Fear and Trembling,* p. 91]

"Or else," Kierkegaard writes, "faith never existed because it has always existed." What can this mean? Kierkegaard presents two contradictory definitions of "faith": if "faith" always existed, then it is not a freely chosen state or act; it is neither temporal nor timely, and then Abraham, as he argues, is not the first faithful man, but rather a murderer. If "faith" always existed, then it is not truly—singly, altogether—"faith": faith *must* be timely; it *must* originate in a moment of choice. But why doesn't Kierkegaard provide us with this logic? Why doesn't he *say* what he means? Why does he choose, rather, the obscurity of his rhetorical question, "either this or that"?

The answer is that he sees logic as a form of rhetoric and both reducible to a crucial, unconditioned choice: faith or faithlessness. "Rhetoric," as the pejorative use of the word suggests, is a form of obscurantism; instead of leading simply, clearly, self-evidently— in a word, "logically"—to its conclusions, it circles and plays; it juxtaposes modes of discourse; it presents voices. Newton Garver discusses this difference between rhetoric and logic in his "Preface" to Jacques Derrida's *Speech and Phenomenon:*

Since Derrida, through his critique of Husserl, is attacking the whole tradition in which language is conceived as founded on logic rather than on rhetoric, it is necessary to try to get a general picture of the common features of this philosophical tradition . . . [which adheres] to a philosophy of language that used logic rather than discourse as the ultimate criterion for meaning.[1]

Logic possesses the authority of language; it is grounded in its self-evident, noncontradictory axioms, just as speech is grounded in the self-evidence of the speaker before us, standing behind his words. Rhetoric is not grounded at all, but rather plays between idea and action, meaning and meaning, just as writing plays between the writer and the writing that precedes him. It is the play of discourses. Kierkegaard and Derrida—in fact, literary criticism itself—are essentially rhetorical; they use discourse rather than logic as the ultimate criterion for meaning. By discourse we mean, primarily, verbal interchange, bringing together (as Kierkegaard

---

[1]Newton Garver, "Preface" to *Speech and Phenomena* (Evanston, Ill.: Northwestern University Press, 1973), p. xiii.

does in the single word "faith" and in the *time* of his whole career of pseudonymous writing) contradictions to present a problem, a difficulty, an obscurity that logic cannot solve, but that nevertheless *must* be acted upon. Derrida creates the same kind of problem for logic—a "scandal" to logic, Kierkegaard might call it. But then so does literature.

Unlike logic, what rhetoric requires is taste and tact, terms that are truly temporal and interesting, undefinable outside the contexts in which they are applied. They deny, as Kierkegaard does, the universal in favor of the particular; they elevate freedom over necessity by making choice (as opposed to what Kierkegaard calls "indifference") self-conscious. By virtue of this denial and elevation, they create the central difficulty of literary scholarship. What is the difference between what we might have called "fruitful obscurity" and barren obscurity? The criteria for distinguishing between these two obscurities—the same criteria, we believe, for the most important choices and judgments we make—are our senses of taste and tact, our assumptions of what is good and what is appropriate. Kierkegaard's rhetoric is excessive, but it is an excess, we think, that fits the case, the question of the eternal salvation of the soul. Derrida's rhetoric is excessive, too, and some think it fits the case and some think it seems a self-indulgent claim on our attention. But what is troubling about his discourse cannot be measured against canons of clarity, simplicity, logic; whatever it is, it is not simply obscurity and rhetoric.

To define discourse in terms of rhetoric defines it as both ironical and governed by time, joining *irony* and *repetition;* it creates *a timely rhetoric of indirection* that is both immediate and mediating, hovering above the world, as Kierkegaard defines the ironical stance, yet interestingly engaged in the world, as he defines repetition. For Kierkegaard, irony is a species of drama, of spectacle. For the ironist, drama *is* existence: he "poetically produces himself as well as his environment with the greatest poetic license. . . . Life is for him a drama, and what engrosses him is the ingenious unfolding of this drama. He is himself a spectator even when performing some act. He renders his ego infinite, volatizes it metaphysically and aesthetically" (*Irony,* pp. 300-301). This description of the ironist as actor and spectator, a description worked out in Markley's Kierkegaardian reading of drama, simultaneously suggests the extent to which Kierkegaard's perception of irony problematizes identity itself in *Repetition* and *Either/Or* as well as in *The Concept of Irony.* The workings of irony become an attempt for the ironist as author and the ironist as spectator to imagine the impossible, to re-create (as Kierkegaard does in *The Concept of Irony*) an ironic Socrates, to construct an ironic identity out of the fictions of the actor's multiple roles. The absurdity of this task, in one sense, is part of Kierkegaard's joke. There is, as Gertrude Stein said of Oakland, no "there" there. But the attempt itself, precisely because it is impossible, is also the ironist's trump, the limit that he dares his audience to cross, the nothingness into which he, as both author and subject, disappears.

Or from which he reappears in the timely, chosen repetitions of faith. Repetition, for Kierkegaard, is essentially a choice, and it counters momentary irony with the movement of significant time: it makes choice in time meaningful by conceiving of language not simply as "play," but as "seriousness," as actions which cannot be undone. Thus in *Philosophical Fragments,* Kierkegaard writes:

Suppose [that] two opposing armies [are] drawn up in the field, and that a knight arrives whom both armies invite to fight on their side; he makes his choice, is vanquished and taken prisoner. As prisoner he is brought before the victor, to whom he foolishly presumes to offer his services on the same terms as were extended to him before the battle. Would not the victor say to him: My friend, you are now my prisoner; there was indeed a time when you could have chosen differently, but now everything is changed. Was this not strange enough? Yet if it were not so, if the moment had no decisive significance, . . . the captive knight must really have fought on the other side, the facts having been obscured by the fog, so that at bottom he had fought on the side of the leader whose prisoner he now imagined himself to be. [*Fragments,* pp. 20-21]

Here Kierkegaard makes choice decisive by making time not simply the "stage" for the "play" of contraries, but the occasion for activity with temporal significance—significance, that is, for the future. Repetition is the choice of the future, just as irony inhabits the present; faith, as Schleifer suggests, combines the two. It is no accident that Kierkegaard's argument here depends on discourse rather than logic as its criterion for meaning because it seeks to represent *and* occasion an act, a choice in time.

Kierkegaard's rhetoric, then, like Derrida's, is a rhetoric of contexts, even if, unlike Derrida's, it pursues choices rather than the impasses of irony. It functions in much the same way the first section of our book functions. This section occasions a critical choice by offering the possibility of reading one discourse against the other. Bové's piece makes the contrast of irony and logic most clear in its analysis of the timeliness and repetition in Kierkegaard's own literary criticism, and the next two articles—Stack's logical analysis of Kierkegaardian concepts and Mackey's rhetorical and ironical analysis of a particular text—embody the choice. Above all, Kierkegaard's insistence on choice is timely, and that timeliness defines the essential discursiveness of criticism.

Here, then, is the most important reason for the appropriateness of a collection of essays such as this one: chief among Kierkegaard's rhetorical procedures is the fact that he wrote pseudonymously. Pseudonymy is a form of irony, but by repeatedly writing pseudonymously throughout his career, Kierkegaard temporalizes the irony of his discourse. Writing under "various hands," Kierkegaard claims in *The Point of View for My Work as an Author* that "the whole work . . . from first to last is dialectical" (*Point of View,* p. 15). Such a procedure entangles Kierkegaard from first to last in literature; he attempts what he calls his "indirect discourse" in order to write, as he says in *My Activity as a Writer,*

10

"without authority" (*Point of View*, p. 151). To write without authority either makes the author disappear or answers author with author in a dialectic of "various hands." Kierkegaard's pseudonymous writing chooses the dialectic. Socrates' dialectic was easy: Socrates, as Plato presents him, has the final word and leaves his adversaries silent. Kierkegaard, however, never gives the authoritative "final word": text answers text (internally, as Mackey shows; externally, as Bové shows) in a repetitious and never-ending movement that precludes "authority." Thus a true dialectic, as Mackey says, "renounces dominion and imperium"; it asks, as Laurie Finke says of *Piers Plowman,* "to be judged not by the meaning it offers, but by the crises it confronts"; it is the "disjunctive" form of drama Markley describes; finally, it alerts readers, as Carole Anne Taylor says, "to the effort of consciousness by undertaking the most rigorous self-interrogations . . . in the form of the literary corrective, a provisional writing which reminds us constantly of the writer's experimental authorship."

Such an "effort of consciousness" is the aim of these essays and of Kierkegaard's writing itself. Consciousness, as Yeats said, is conflict, and what Kierkegaard gives us throughout his "whole authorship"—what these essays attempt to present—is a true dialectic of consciousness: dramatic (that is, defined in opposition and juxtaposition), existing in time (which means, as Bové shows, in particular historical contexts in relation to particular individuals), and confronting (what Kierkegaard calls "noticing") the absolute crises of life. Discussing *Repetition,* Mackey says: "Man is reflection, and woman is reality. But only that reality which is (defined as) alienated by language. Both male and female lie this side of the boundary of immanence. They are conceivable, and only conceivable, together, as the othered and the othering." Only such dialectical, diacritical "conceptions" are possible, and they are, in some essential sense, "literary." This is why we have included in *Kierkegaard and Literature* the literary essays we have. Markley's piece reads the drama as the kind of "drama" Kierkegaard's rhetoric requires, Schleifer and Taylor read pseudobiography and auto-

11

biography in the timely way of Kierkegaard's reading, and Finke reads the religious crisis of *Piers Plowman* in light of the crisis-oriented criticism Kierkegaard teaches.

That is, what we have been calling Kierkegaard's "rhetoric" is a kind of *reading,* in contrast to Derrida's rhetoric, which is a kind of *writing.* "Deconstruction," a recent commentator has noted, "is therefore an activity of reading which remains closely tied to the texts it interrogates, and which can never set up independently as a self-enclosed system of operative concepts."[2] This commentator could have substituted "rewrites" for "interrogates" because the close link between deconstruction's "activity of reading" and the text it examines is created by the rewriting of that text.[3] Kierkegaard, as we have seen, is willing to dispense with his text once the timely and rhetorical situation of choice has been achieved. He offers what literature at its best offers, namely an occasion— what Kierkegaard calls a *"situation"* (*Point of View,* p. 145)—for "upbringing and development" (p. 151). Kierkegaard wrote *My Activity as a Writer* because, as he says in his Journal, "without this little book the whole authorship would be transformed into new doctrine" (*Point of View,* p. 160), whereas the aim of writing "without authority" is more simply "to CALL ATTENTION to religion, to Christianity": "I have regarded myself as a *reader* of the books, not as the *author,*" Kierkegaard said (p. 151).

Such attention is the attention, the "effort," of consciousness

[2]Christopher Norris, *Deconstruction: Theory and Practice* (London: Methuen, 1982), p. 31.

[3]In "The Problem of Textuality: Two Exemplary Positions," *Critical Inquiry* 4 (1978), Edward W. Said persuasively argues that the method of deconstruction in Derrida is above all to realize the *textuality* of discourse: "Every one of Derrida's extraordinarily brilliant readings since and including *De la Grammatologie* therefore build from and around that point in a text around which its own heterodox textuality, distinct from its message or meanings, is organized, the point also *toward* which the text's textuality moves in the shattering dissemination of its unorganizable energy. These points are words that are anticoncepts, bits of the text in which Derrida believes, and where he shows, the texts' irreducible textuality to lie" (p. 694).

directed at itself, seeking to discover its illusions—its *situation* in the illusion of "authority." Consciousness deludes itself with the authority of its "point of view" (not "for" itself as in Kierkegaard's title, but "of" itself); the childhood of Maggie Tulliver in *The Mill on the Floss* is a case in point. The aim of Kierkegaard's authorship is to "call attention" to the dialectic of consciousness deluding itself into imagining its own monolithic authority:

This again, I say, is the dialectical movement, or is essentially dialectics, namely, in one's *action* to *counteract* oneself at the same time, which is what I call reduplication, and it is an example of the heterogeneity which distinguishes every true godly effort from worldly effort. To strive or to work *directly* is to work or to strive in immediate continuity with an actual given condition. The dialectical movement is the exact *opposite* of this, namely, by one's action to counteract one's effort at the same time—a duplication which is "seriousness," like the pressure upon the plough which determines the depth of the furrow, whereas a direct effort is a slurring over, which not only goes more quickly and easily, but is by far a more thankful task, for it is worldliness and homogeneity. [*Point of View,* p. 147 n.]

"Indirect communication," then, assumes the form of reading which is both self-assertion and self-abandonment; it achieves the supreme ambiguity of repetition, always double and consequently nonauthoritative. Instead of the authority of "continuity"—the authority of a logical, linear discourse that compels assent—Kierkegaard's reading offers the "counteraction" to itself, what Yeats calls the "counter-truth" to its own "truth." That is, to write "without authority" is to devise a discourse which doesn't promise "truth" like a kernel to be discovered at the center: fruitfully and fecundly *there,* given and authorized by the author. Rather, it is a discourse that *calls attention,* that presents a crisis, that opens the reader (again) to the drama of possibility. It points, as George Steiner has recently argued,

to a hypostasis of language such as we find, precisely, in the philosophy of Heidegger. It is not so much the poet who speaks, but language itself: *die Spracht spricht.* The authentic, immensely rare, poem is one in which the poet is not a *persona,* a subjectivity "ruling over language," but an "openness to," a supreme listener to, the genius of speech. The result of such openness is not so much a text, but an "act," an eventuation of Being and literal "coming into Being." At a naive level, this image yields the suspect expressionistic tag that "a poem should not mean but be." At the more sophisticated but equally existential level, it generates the poetics of "dissemination," of "de-constructive" and "momentary" reading that we find in Derrida and the current school of semiotics. We do not "read" the poem in the traditional framework of the author's *auctoritas* and of an agreed sense, however gradually and gropingly arrived at. We bear witness to its precarious possibility of existence in an "open" space of collisions, of momentary fusions between word and referent.[4]

Steiner is describing a "momentary," nonauthoritative language of poetry. Kierkegaard, however, wants *discourse,* not lyrics, without authority, and to achieve it he creates the truth and counter-truth of his pseudonymous writings. The philosopher is not a *persona* in Kierkegaard because he is disseminated and "deconstructed" into dialectic, dramatic discourse. Kierkegaard's "space of collisions" is spacious indeed; in fact, as he argues in *My Activity as a Writer,* the division between his aesthetic and religious writing is "roughly equal" in "the quantity of matter presented before and after." More important, however, it is temporal, it is *enduring:* "the time occupied by the authorship before the *Concluding Postscript* and after it is about the same" (*Point of View,* pp. 146-47).

Calling attention is a timely act that, like Kierkegaard's choice, defines temporality beyond the momentary fusions of the aesthetic Steiner describes. Time becomes important—it becomes "interesting" in the double sense Kierkegaard offers, as both valuable and timely—in the fact that his rhetoric seeks not the hypostasis of

[4]George Steiner, *On Difficulty and Other Essays* (New York: Oxford University Press, 1980), p. 46.

"coming into Being" Steiner describes, the wonder before what
is, but ongoing choices that create the "interest," fully in its temporal sense, of life. This points to a central aspect of Kierkegaard
to which Bové ("colliding" with Stack in our volume) calls attention; namely, the importance of "time" in Kierkegaard's texts.
Kierkegaard is attempting nonauthoritative discourse over time,
and to do so, as Bové shows, he has to counteract the "spatialization" of time. He must do so because spatialized time "reduces
the complexity of time to an external series of 'presents,' each
of which is ultimately 'free' from any of the consequences or
claims of the others"; "free," that is, from the kind of dialectic
engagement we have been describing, and therefore self-evidently
authoritative. (In our metaphor of "the authority of logical, *linear*
discourse" we can see that spatialization at work.) It is for this
reason, we suspect, that Stack needs to redefine and relocate
Kierkegaard's concept of the "eternal" within the conflict of consciousness, and that repetition, as Mackey shows, is such a crucial
and "serious" concept for Kierkegaard (as opposed to irony's "play-
fulness"). Repetition, like consciousness, like language itself, is an
(impossible) "unity of immediacy and reflection." Time in its temporality is crucial to literature: "The temporalizing of metaphysics
makes metaphysics interesting." That "interest" is the interest of
literature. It is, in the etymological sense of *inter-esse,* the collision
Stack describes (following Kierkegaard) of "concern" and "knowledge," the collision of time ("in between") and meaning ("passionate interest"; see Bové's "value," "intention," "purpose"). Mackey
calls it a "borderline": "the boundary situation is the scene of this
text and the place at which repetition is (not conceivable, but)
by virtue of the absurd possible."

This is the interest of *discursive* (as opposed to Steiner's lyric)
literature that our essays offer: the impossible coincidence of the
character and the trope, the ethical and the religious, the individual and the type, Hamlet the man and *Hamlet* the play, the
immediate and the reflective. Throughout these essays language
is figured as *irony*—a "concept," as Schleifer suggests, as "im-

possible" as Derrida's "différence"—and discourse as *repetition.* Taken together they offer a Kierkegaardian text which "both is and is not" (*Irony,* p. 161), situated on the borderline, *without authority,* as the individual is, between the real and the ideal. These essays by various hands collide on this issue: Stack takes the "self" as crucial—"the problem of existence is not primarily conceptual . . .; it is a matter of a transformation of the self"— while Mackey and Bové are more "interested" in the tropes of irony and repetition Kierkegaard uses to figure the self.

More than a Kierkegaardian text, however, the collision of these essays offers a Kierkegaardian "reading," the diacritical othered and othering of "the imperfect voice and the divine logos" with which Finke begins our "literary" essays. Thus, the question of imitation Markley describes is centrally interested in this collision: "it is the nature of drama to insist on the disjunctions between its signs—characters, scenery, costumes, and props—and what they are supposed to signify"; the collision of texts and genres Taylor describes in *Walden* participates in this irony and repetition; and the action and counteraction of Maggie's ironic identification of herself against her world and her repetitious identification with it Schleifer examines in *The Mill on the Floss* enact the ironic doubleness, the perpetual discrepancies of language found throughout these essays. This doubleness, finally, ironic and repetitious, is language without authority, an action as much as a discourse, a call for attention. It creates, as Kierkegaard's pseudonymous authorship does, the coincidence of philosophy and literature.

Writing without authority, then, is *ironic* and *repetitious,* but what has it to do with *criticism?* Criticism exists as both possibility and impossibility, as an ideal "recollected forwards" and an actuality that "recollects" a mythic past and discovers that it is its own archetype. Time here is not *of* the essence; it *is* the essence. Criticism is not bound linearly; it is not spatialized. As Bové suggests, it demonstrates finally its own linear incoherence. Criticism exists ironically, seemingly a deconstructive moment: it repeats, in this respect, the paradoxes of artistic existence, the "is and is not" of Kierkegaardian irony that, in one way or another, underlies the essays of this collection. Criticism exists (to borrow Derrida's term) "under erasure"; it is a sign that mediates between the instability of fiction and the instability of an ideologically imagined and imaged reality. To look at criticism as other than parasitic is to expose its fictions of coherence as fictions, as imperfect metaphors. These essays discuss and exemplify, in different ways, the critical act as a dialectical force, mediating between the silence of irony and ideal of repetition. They discuss and exemplify Kierkegaard's rhetoric.

Thus, as Bové says, "Kierkegaard does not author a deconstructive discourse, but a *competing* discourse." Because it relies on extended discourse as well as the words, puns, neologisms, and above all *concepts* (even negatively conceived) encountered in deconstructive texts, Kierkegaard's writing without authority makes reading more clearly a question of choices and commitments in time rather than Heidegger's "destructive" logic. As Taylor says,

A Don Quixote might choose to create his life as though it were a book, or a later Äxel might live life to put into a book, but Thoreau and Kierkegaard make the book secondary to the activities of writing and reading; they take their places as scribes and readers of their own development. Writing a life commits one to choosing a possibility, regarding everyday activity with the intensity and self-consciousness of an author; reading a life implies seeing possibility in the context of other "books," particularly that of the ultimate book that cannot be written.

This sounds more like the later Roland Barthes than Derrida (though clearly they have much in common), and it indicates the central difference between Kierkegaardian and deconstructive readings, the former's *maieutic* function as opposed to the latter's *structural* or *poststructural* function. The Socratic metaphor of *maieutic* work—that is, the work of the midwife—points to the temporal and generational function of understanding, its essential discursiveness, while *deconstruction* contains within itself its own structural metaphor. That is why Bové's essay—strongly emphasizing, in its dependence on Foucault, the historicity of the Kierkegaardian enterprise—is so crucial to our conceiving the possibilities Kierkegaard presents for our criticism:

> The maieutic function of the pseudonymous works is not only to lead the reader through an emotional experience to a point of decision but also to educate him in the skills of decoding the age's major types. As *Repetition* suggests, the Kierkegaardian goal is to find a reader for this reflection of an age so self-alienated that it cannot recognize its own alienation. Those readers adept at decoding the typical characters of their age *can,* for example, tell the difference between the aesthetic monster of immediacy—the Seducer—and Kierkegaard when he abandons Regina.

This "decoding" is an act and a choice that finally—but it is *finally*—reveals some sense of "faithfulness" in time. That faithfulness may be metaphorical or a *chosen* illusion (or, as in Kierkegaard, an almost desperate sense of clinging to the slightest hopeful possibility rather than succumbing to despair), but above all, it is the "faith" in the possibility of *redeemed time.*

Deconstruction, like Steiner, eschews (or "deconstructs") time: Derrida's essay on "Différance," for instance, is "about" an (impossible) *concept;* time itself in Derrida, even *presence,* remains conceptual and not the "lived-time" that Bové and Stack describe; it remains "speculative" in Bové's sense of that metaphor. Thus Edward Said has recently written that the "main ambition" of a reading method like Derrida's "is both to reveal undecidable elements in a text in lieu of some simple reductive message the text is supposed to contain and to shy away from making each reading of a text part of some cumulatively built explicit thesis about the historical persistence of and the agencies for Western metaphysical thought."[5] What deconstruction reveals, Christopher Norris sug-

---

[5] Said, "The Problem of Textuality," p. 701.

gests, "is an ultimate impasse of thought engendered by a rhetoric that always insinuates its own textual workings into the truth claims of philosophy."[6]

On the other hand, Kierkegaard's is the "faith" that time (the immediate) can be meaningful, interesting, and interested and that literature, even if it is ironically conceived, is possible. He attempts an "unauthorized" form of reading that engenders momentary and momentous choices *within* a "cumulatively built" discourse, moments not of impasse but of passage. These moments do not confound time and discourse in what Said calls the "spectacle" of writing in Derrida (which attempts "to work less by chronological sequence, logical order, and linear movement, than by abrupt, extremely difficult to follow lateral and complimentary movement"[7]), but rather, to return to our maieutic metaphor, they attempt to engender meaningful time in a (repetitious) birth. "Irony," writes Kierkegaard, "is the subjective freedom which at every moment has within its power the possibility of a beginning and is not generated from previous conditions. There is something seductive about every beginning because the subject is still free, and this is the satisfaction the ironist longs for. At such moments actuality loses its validity for him; he is free and above it" (*Irony,* p. 270). The ironist seeks a subjective, romantic freedom; but Kierkegaard seeks a sense of redeemed time, redeemed through action and choice that transcends textuality. Thus Kierkegaard finally asserts that "mastered" irony "yields truth, actuality, and content" (*Irony,* p. 338); it yields, in other words, exactly what the immediate experience of irony denies. Criticism, itself an ironic tropology, is the mirror that we need to perceive the essential (as opposed to Markley's "perpetual") discrepancies of art.

That is, criticism always aspires ideally to be the text it discusses; it aspires, in the double sense that Schliefer gives, to identify with and against the authority of its text. That authority is

[6]Norris, *Deconstruction*, p. 49.
[7]Said, "The Problem of Textuality," p. 691.

the *temporalizing* of essence that is also a *temporizing:* it puts off authority as it marks time. The value of Kierkegaard's rhetoric for criticism is that it never lets time escape into speculation, into our more usual sense that significance is somehow timeless, hypostatized, obscured by rhetoric. Rather, it makes the timeliness of rhetoric essential and offers a means to create self-consciously the time of criticism, concerned and in between, that makes its authority a problem. Aspiring both to defer to the text it discusses, yet also to supersede it, the critical act is always a refraction of what it examines: the "primary" text and its own existence. Critics, confronted by the eloquence and silence of the word on the page, must imagine themselves (faithfully, absurdly) as its creator to be able to interpret at all. The critic is a kind of "seducer," violating the immediacy of the text. Yet this "seduction" may be a form of indirection, and the critic perhaps the central fiction, the dominant symbol of post-Renaissance, bourgeois culture: the knight of faith disguised as ironist. On this role are modeled the psychologists, sociologists, anthropologists, and the like, who attempt to read and interpret the secular paradoxes of human nature and social existence, all of whom identify themselves with and against the world. Precisely because criticism *calls attention,* implicitly and explicitly, to fictions as fictions, it is both an action and a contemplation, immediate and reflective, providing at its best upbringing and development.

Underlying Kierkegaard's works is the recognition that language itself is essentially ironic, that its impotence and silence are what create the possibility of faith in time as well as the despair of simply becoming. To read Kierkegaard is to surrender oneself to irony and silence; to write about him is to surrender oneself to a medium that proclaims its inability to do what we insist it must. But each is a surrender which is also a victory, since surrendering to silence is to open oneself to choice. Thus, the critic finds himself trapped—and traps himself—between two possibilities: the meaninglessness of irony (located, as Schleifer argues in one of his "philosophical" notes, in the immediacy of the present, the immediacy of textuality) and the promise of repetition (an ideal that hovers in view only after language has played itself out). The critical act, then, has both the absurdity and the power of its own dialectical rhetoric which joins, as discourse always does, the *action* of its speaker and the *representations* of its language.

Thus criticism is a game played on the shifting grounds of linguistic instability, yet a game that can be quite serious: only a fool, Valéry said in an aphorism that aptly describes Kierkegaard, cannot imagine that one can joke and be serious at the same time. Criticism is both parasitic and re-creative, meekly stating its dependence while boldly declaring its independence and equality. In its very uncertainty, it tries to create its own fictions and appropriates a hermeneutic vocabulary: meaning, stability, coherence, and, of course, interpretation. In a word, it tries to create its own authority. Yet criticism is never "authorized": it is always tripped up by its secondary, refractory nature; it is always temporizing. The critic exists, to borrow Bové's title (itself borrowed from Foucault), in a penitentiary of reflection, a victim of the essential inactivity of criticism. The movement of criticism, in this respect, is forever inwards as it ironically strives to actualize itself as repetition, an absolute re-creation of the experience of the text, at once identical to and different from what it idealizes. Criticism — ironically, absurdly — like literature itself, is a language that tries to transcend language.

Criticism, then, takes its place with *irony* and *repetition;* it takes its place interestingly, in time, between the play of irony and the seriousness of repetition. Such a dialectic is created among the various hands of our essays. It may be difficult to "place" these essays in any context except the ones they themselves create. But certain similarities do show up: the central importance of *The Concept of Irony* in Kierkegaard's aesthetic, the fragility of language itself, the decentering of the self ("a fluid sign," Bové suggests), the analogies, more or less present, to Derrida and other poststructuralist critics. As Kierkegaardian studies are being enriched, they are also (like much contemporary cultural and literary theory) becoming more problematic. Most of the essays in this collection, plausibly enough, pay less attention to Kierkegaard's specifically Christian beliefs and writings than is often the case. "Irony" seems more and more to confuse itself with "faith" as an intriguing element of the dialectic; "indirect communication" becomes more a fascinating subject in its own right than a means to an end. For that matter, the word "existentialism" crops up less frequently than one might have predicted. Such observations will not come as a surprise in a volume subtitled *Irony, Repetition, and Criticism.* But the yoking of the three terms is itself, as we have seen, significant. One gets the sense, perhaps, when reading the writers who are footnoted throughout this collection, notably Derrida and Foucault, that Kierkegaard has been "there" before, illuminating dark corners, dampening candles. If the Christian Kierkegaard lies behind the existentialism of the fifties, possibly a faithfully ironic Kierkegaard lurks in the shadows of post structuralism. Perhaps only now can we see that Kierkegaard can teach us how to reread his texts and discover them to be concerned with and situated between the archetypal light of Christian faith and the half-light of irony and play, interested in the discursive indirection of philosophy, criticism, and literature.

Part One   Kierkegaard and Literature

1. The Penitentiary of Reflection: Sören Kierkegaard and Critical Activity

K IERKEGAARD'S works have been of comparatively small value to contemporary literary critics. With the exception of a series of essays on repetition and irony, contemporary critics seem to find Kierkegaard's theocentrism and attention to the self incompatible with formalist, structuralist, poststructuralist, or neo-Marxian methodologies that in various ways deconstruct or demythologize the ideologies of religion and selfhood. Of course, this was not always the case. Not only existentialist critics but sophisticated rhetorical critics of poetry like W. K. Wimsatt turned at times to Kierkegaard's authorship to explore the important modernist question of the relationship of literature and belief.[1] Postmodern criticism, however, has for the most part different questions and different projects—deconstruction, archaeology, semiotics, Lacanian analysis—to which Kierkegaard speaks indirectly, if at all. I have tried to suggest elsewhere that there is a conjunction between Kierkegaard on irony and the deconstructive interests of Jacques

---

[1] See W. K. Wimsatt, *Hateful Contraries* (Lexington, Ky.: University of Kentucky Press, 1966), pp. 48, 100, 248. It is worth pointing out here that the kind of reconsideration of Kierkegaard I am suggesting does not aim to reestablish either the modernist version of a writer torn between matters of faith and literature nor to reawaken any of the more sentimental and "subjectivist" existential versions of Kierkegaard.

Derrida and Paul de Man.[2] And in different ways William Spanos and Edward Said have treated Kierkegaard's ideas of repetition and authority at some length to relate them to modern and postmodern stylistic and hermeneutic changes.[3]

Despite these few attempts to link Kierkegaard to postmodern thought, most contemporary critics have not tested Kierkegaard's general intellectual project for its value to critical activity. The significance of his intellectual procedures, in fact, the image of the critical intellectual that appears throughout his writings, seems to have no abiding influence inside the critical academy. While we may hope for more and better studies of Kierkegaard's concepts and psychology, we currently need a discussion of his intellectual processes and interests, of his way of being a literary intellectual within his sociocultural context. Such a study would show both the problems he confronted as a religious man and as an intellectual and the methods he adopted to attempt to solve them.

In our own time there is no obvious, generally accepted sense of the literary intellectual's purpose or role, given criticism's current division into deconstruction, semiotics, Marxism, and traditionalist theory. Even more seriously, there is no underlying set of values unifying these various critical practices and approaches. A study of Kierkegaard, in itself, hardly solves our problems. It certainly cannot offer us an adequate model to emulate. But since many of his concerns—alienation, the commodification of language and knowledge, and paralyzing idealism, for example—remain our

[2] "Cleanth Brooks and Modern Irony: A Kierkegaardian Critique," *boundary 2* 4 (1976): 727-60; reprinted in Paul A. Bové, *Destructive Poetics: Heidegger and Modern American Poetry* (New York: Columbia University Press, 1980).

[3] William V. Spanos, "Heidegger, Kierkegaard, and the Hermeneutic Circle: Towards a Postmodern Theory of Interpretation as Disclosure," *boundary 2* 4 (1976): 455-88; Edward W. Said, "Repetition," in Angus Fletcher, ed., *The Literature of Fact* (New York: Columbia University Press, 1976), pp. 135-58; Edward W. Said, *Beginnings: Intention and Method* (New York: Basic Books, 1975), pp. 85ff.

own, albeit differently configured and empowered, studying him helps to explain who we are and how we have come to be. We as critics and theorists both persist in and have forgotten many of the successes and failures of Kierkegaard's practice. No doubt many aspects of late capitalist society have made it difficult to recapture Kierkegaard's insistence upon the mutual reflection of his lived-experience and his work. For example, all too often the professionalization of academic life results in seemingly mechanical research and publication necessary for economic survival. Such work is often good, essential to the institution of criticism, and should be studied in those terms. At the same time, however, it illustrates the alienation of producer and product and the commodification of knowledge that we feel, along with Kierkegaard, to be a major cultural problem. Similarly, again like Kierkegaard, we are perhaps too often pessimistic about the prospects for altering such conditions in our society and "resign" ourselves to our reality and to designing personal and professional tactics to "manage" it and its effects on our lives and work.

Because Kierkegaard anticipates our own intellectual situation we can learn much from him about the nature of the intellectual. Above all he implies, as do Socrates, Montaigne, Emerson, and Nietzsche, that the *value* of intellectual ideas can be judged only by understanding how intellectuals live in their societies. For Kierkegaard, in his age and ours, the primary aim of intellectual work must be to produce meaning at one with the intellectual's pursuit of lived symbolic value. While intellectual work alone may quite sufficiently produce meanings within the semiotic codes culture offers at a given time, symbolic value depends upon the connection of those meanings to the intellectual's shaping of his life and upon their effects on individuals, groups, and institutions within society. In his own work and from his own point of view, Kierkegaard tries to ensure the value of meaning by linking it to, and having it emerge from, his lived-experience as an intellectual who is experiencing problems of communication, isolation, and despair. Put simply, Kierkegaard attempts to minimize in his own lived-intellectual activity the separation of meaning-production-symbol that modern forms of power bring about. His success is, of course, only partial and it is always "guaranteed" by his special relationship to truth, to Divinity. Nevertheless, he experiences and describes the sociocultural forces that reduce intellectual activity to a commodity. His theoretical discussions of these matters arise out of his perception of the inherent contradictions in Danish society, not merely out of self-examination. He reflects the alienation of symbol from meaning in modern culture; his work records a failed struggle against those forces that succeeded largely, as he sees it, in transforming the work of the literary intellectual into a fetishized, often comic commodity.

Mark Taylor's fine book *Kierkegaard's Pseudonymous Authorship* provides a starting point for reconsidering Kierkegaard's figuring of intellectual processes and possibilities.[4] Taylor focuses almost entirely on the "pseudonymous" works from *Either/Or* to *Concluding Unscientific Postscript.* He deliberately sets his study apart from those that have followed the line of biographical-psychological analysis because they too often take the *Journals* and *Papers* as their points of departure and ignore the specific problems of writing implicit in the "authorship"; they fail, too, to locate the essential continuity of Kierkegaard's project. Although influenced by Stephen Crites's important work on Kierkegaard and Hegel, Taylor (rightly, I believe) rejects Crites's historico-comparative method, claiming that despite its virtues, "it frequently forces the writer to abstract Kierkegaard's ideas, or the meaning of his concepts, from the totality of the works. . . . If one is to arrive at an adequate understanding of Kierkegaard, one's inquiry must be conducted in light of the various stages of existence and of the different meanings that terms have at these stages" (*KPA*, p. 33).[5]

Taylor suggests that the historico-comparative approach loses contact with the specificity of the temporal structure of Kierke-

---

[4]Mark Taylor, *Kierkegaard's Pseudonymous Authorship: A Study of Time and the Self* (Princeton, N.J.: Princeton University Press, 1975); hereafter cited as *KPA*.

gaard's writing as it contextually assigns changing meanings and values to seemingly stable figures in his texts. As Taylor demonstrates in great detail, the "meaning" of the various figures of "self," "time," "the eternal," and so forth alter in relation to evolving stages of life and consciousness that Kierkegaard's works represent. The "self," for example, is a fluid sign in Kierkegaard, changing from a designation of an almost fetal sense of immediacy without reflection to the complex double reflection of Christianity. The historico-comparative method takes a global view of the works and systematizes them irresistably; regardless of the commentator's intention, it blurs contextual differences.

To an ever great degree, the descriptive-thematic approach in Kierkegaard studies merges specific differences into a homogeneous image. Paul Sponheim, for example, because he contends that Kierkegaard is "systematic," finds only unity in his work: strands weaving a tapestry. Taylor argues that Sponheim "organizes his study according to what he regards as the most important systematic problems in Kierkegaard's works rather than organizing his analysis according to the writings themselves."[6] Of course, Sponheim's method of close reading is familiar to literary critics. It is a hermeneutic model authorized by the New Critics, Geneva-style phenomenologists, and some structuralists as well. Taylor points to a practical danger in applying this forcefully penetrating procedure to Kierkegaard: "Statements from all of the works are treated in the same manner without regard for the pseudonym through whom they are spoken, and hence without regard for the point of view they represent. This oversight finally proves to be the undoing of Sponheim's analysis" (*KPA*, p. 35). The global approach levels the only distinctions that give meaning to Kierkegaard's fig-

[5]See also Stephen Crites, *In the Twilight of Christendom: Hegel vs. Kierkegaard on Faith and History* (Chambersburg, Pa.: American Academy of Religion, 1971); "Pseudonymous Authorship as Art and as Act," in Josiah Thompson, ed., *Kierkegaard: A Collection of Critical Essays* (New York: Doubleday, 1972), pp. 183-229.

[6]Paul Sponheim, *Kierkegaard on Christ and Christian Coherence* (New York: Harper and Row, 1968).

ures; only the temporal structure of the various pseudonymic stages inscribes his words with dramatic authority. This critical leveling mistakes not only Kierkegaard's sense but also the nature of the process that gives symbolic value to meaning through the dramatic figuring and querying of the various intellectual life-styles represented by the pseudonyms. As Taylor suggests,"Sponheim's 'systematic' analysis cannot comprehend the intention that leads Kierkegaard to employ the pseudonymous method" (*KPA*, p. 36).

Taylor's discussion of "spatialized time" makes clear that Kierkegaard has considered and rejected the global hermeneutic procedure of some of his best critics:

Kierkegaard holds the understanding of time presented in much of the philosophical tradition to be inadequate for explaining human existence. . . . The conception of time of which Kierkegaard is critical can be called spatialized time. The term "spatialized time" is intended to indicate that time so understood refers primarily to *objects*. This is to be distinguished from "life-time," which Kierkegaard thinks is a more appropriate way of conceptualizing time in relation to *subjects* and *selves*.

After insisting that the difference between these two ideas of time does not correspond "to the difference between externality (objective time) and inwardness (subjective time)," Taylor suggests that Kierkegaard conceives of spatial time as a subsuming of time into space.

This spatializing model conceptualizes "before" and "after" as a succession of an infinite number of points, all of which "are homogeneous and equivalent" (*KPA*, p. 83). They are perceived globally, instantaneously. Spatializing time facilities its quantification; it is this quantifying measure that Kierkegaard strongly identifies with reification and commodification. Several consequences follow from this spatializing: it allows for the "placing" of events in spatial relation but does not allow for judgment of their value: intention and purpose are made irrelevant in this objective view because intentionality is always temporal; it reduces the complexity of time to an external series of "presents," each of which is ultimately "free" from any of the consequences or claims of the others; it reduces each particular present to what Kierkegaard calls in *The Concept of Dread* "a silent atomistic abstraction" (p. 75). "Atomism" levels the value of lived moments by disregarding their individual significance and seeing them as meaningful only within a comprehensible pattern. It abstracts the event so completely that its relation to and significance for the individual agent are lost. The event is an element in a pattern perceived after the fact by a reflexive mind that assumes an objective, detached point of view (*KPA,* p. 86). The significance of the event for both the individual and the moment of its occurrence is negated by reflection. Events are denied immediate meaning because meaning is a product of reflection's assembling of data into patterned knowledge. According to Kierkegaard, such ordering connects time to an eternal present forgetful of the past and unconcerned with the future. Time effectively loses all value for a spatializing habit of mind. Kierkegaard hopes to defend or restore time's value by giving priority to "lived-time," an alternative concept of the relation of meaning and event; of past, present, and future. Kierkegaard's metaphor of lived-time reflects his desire to restore value to time as an ideological location for common action, for reestablishing the specific histories of individuals and groups by revealing the coherence of their past, present, and future. This is precisely the coherence spatialized time denies for a more abstract, general "history." For Kierkegaard, spatialization is the self-legitimizing mode of what he sees as the dominant culture of commodities and reflection. "Knowledge" becomes in such a culture the "objectification" of history in space that separates the lived symbolic value of events from their intellectually produced meaning in a reflected image. Hegel and his German and Danish followers are, of course, the worst offenders against lived-time.[7]

---

[7]For an elaboration on the importance of the idea of "spatialized time," see William V. Spanos's seminal essay, "Modern Literary Criticism and the Spatialization of Time," *Journal of Aesthetics and Art Criticism* 29 (1970): 88-104.

Kierkegaard feels that the dominant ideology of his culture is located in "speculative philosophy" and "reflection" and that it expresses the interests of the bourgeois elite in spreading its authority and values throughout every segment of society, especially its intellectual institutions. The reflective mind existing outside of time and seeing the patterns of "general history" is an emblem for Kierkegaard of the transformation of cultural power from theocentrism and sovereign authority to the deployment of abstract reason throughout history and society; reason reconfigures both as legitimations of the dominant cultural elements in whose service they are deployed. This cultural power assumes various forms in Kierkegaard's writings: "spatialization," "reflection," "abstract atomism," "the Idea," "the System," and "speculative philosophy." To understand these figures fully, as well as global perceptions of society, history, and experience and the role of "reflective men," we need to consider them in the context of the disciplinary society that Michel Foucault has so thoroughly studied.[8] It is not an "imposition" of Foucault on Kierkegaard to link their work; the latter's project belongs to the period and problematic that Foucault studies. Moreover, there is adequate textual evidence both to suggest Kierkegaard's concern with matters of power and to insert his work in a genealogy of the struggle against power that Foucault, following Nietzsche, describes.

It is not an accident that the dominance of panopticism, a disciplinary technique of timeless, disembodied surveillance, first appears in Jeremy Bentham's work and public architecture at about the same time as "speculative philosophy" develops. The connection between the two is not limited to the common metaphor of "oversight." Speculative philosophy, especially as Kierkegaard finds it in Hegel, is essentially the philosophy of the bourgeoisie, though perhaps representing also the final attempt to legitimate the ancient regime in its *aeterno modo.* As a cultural instrument, it sug-

[8]Michel Foucault, *Discipline and Punish*, trans. Alan Sheridan (New York: Pantheon, 1977), pp. 195-228.

gests that the end of history corresponds with the coming of bourgeois society, and it effectively turns all intellectual attention away from lived-history to a realm of reflection and ideality that empties "reality" of its materiality. "Meaning" is so rarefied that it becomes disassociated from the symbols of men in everyday life.

His discussion of Kierkegaard's critique of Hegel emphasizes Taylor's analysis of Hegelian alienation:

In speculation, as the etymology of the word suggests, the individual is related to the world in a way similar to a spectator in a drama. The attention of the observer is directed away from himself and towards an object (or objects) that manifests itself to him. The aim of speculation is not self-knowledge, but a clear knowledge of the object being examined. In order to attain this goal, one's idiosyncratic interests must, as far as possible, be overcome. For Kierkegaard, however, such speculation prevents one from coming to terms with one's individual existence. [*KPA,* p. 178]

Kierkegaard's analysis of speculative philosophy takes actual social life as its point of departure. It is not simply the dominant authority of Hegelian metaphysics that obsesses Kierkegaard from 1841 to 1855 but also the nature of social life among the bourgeoisie in Denmark, ideologically represented and legitimated by speculative philosophy.

Yet, because Kierkegaard is concerned with the *social actuality* symbolized by "reflection," "spatialized time," and "speculative philosophy," Taylor's fine thematic study finally misrepresents his work by insisting that the beginning and end of the pseudonymous writings is the integrated, harmonious self in an isolated, private relationship to God. Critics seem to agree that for Kierkegaard the self finds itself in God and that the stages of existence—aesthetic, ethical, "religiousness A," and Christianity—represent *formal* moments in its evolution toward itself and God. And, as Taylor argues convincingly, these stages are psychologically valid for Kierkegaard and can be seen to correspond to developmental phases in Freudian and post-Freudian psychology. One could also argue that to some extent they parallel periods of Kierkegaard's life, and (based on an analogy to Hegel's idea of the evolution of the Spirit in History) they correspond to ages in Western History.

While Taylor demonstrates the formal and thematic coherence of the pseudonymous works quite clearly, his decision to understand these texts solely on the basis of the self's attempt to reintegrate itself in and through individual actions creates some problems. It seems to me that the genesis of Kierkegaard's sense of alienation is not merely a matter of the valorization of the self, but emerges from an understanding of social behavior in the bourgeois intellectual classes. Although Taylor, developing an insight from Crites, establishes the dialogic dimension of Kierkegaard's pseudonyms, he does not seem to have considered fully that each pseudonym's representation of a particular individual and cultural type is meant to reflect accurately a social actuality standing somewhere between individual figures and automatic emblems of the age as well as to lead the reader through an experience of each type or stage. Taylor argues that Kierkegaard views each stage as forms of alienation and despair that are visible as such because of the self's "dis-relationship" to the ideal of a fully integrated and harmonious self immediately present to the Incarnation. Taylor, then, sees the pseudonyms as psychological projections of stages of consciousness as the self moves in time toward the perfect relationship with God. His view, I would suggest, is accurate but incomplete; the "types" also represent actual forms of socially alienated behavior in the intellectual's bourgeois culture.

Taylor very precisely identifies the forms of alienation Kierkegaard dramatizes. The movement from "Religiousness A" or "Infinite Resignation" to Christianity is "the movement of one who recognizes that humanly speaking he has exhausted his possibilities, and who knows that if further possibilities . . . are to be reestablished, it must be through God himself" (*KPA*, p. 317). Indeed, for Kierkegaard, Faith has curious but important social consequences. He stresses repeatedly that the Knight of Faith is unrecognizable, indistinguishable by appearance from his bourgeois neighbors. The inner and the outer are not the same. This cluster of ideas is at the center of Taylor's reservations about Kierkegaard. Because Kierkegaard often claims the priority of inwardness, of states of consciousness, over all other relationships, Taylor concludes ultimately that not only is intention or inwardness more important than action and social relations but also that "one can never be certain that another person's outward actions are congruent with his inward intentions" (*KPA*, p. 305). It is certainly true that Faith is a matter of "inwardness" for Kierkegaard and that his Socratic probings of his age's disease rest on that inwardness; yet there are other elements to be considered here that temper two of Taylor's major reservations about Kierkegaard. Taylor argues that

Kierkegaard's view of faith as inward entails the conviction that there is no definite *outward* distinction among selves at different stages of existence. . . . If faith is inwardness, as Kierkegaard argues, there would seem to be no way for him to know that the lives of the apparent Christians in nineteenth-century Denmark were actually aesthetic. Whether or not one is faithful cannot be discerned by another person, and can be believed only by the faithful individual himself. . . . The result of Kierkegard's argument is the establishment of two fully discrete identities of the individual self—an inward one and an outward one. Furthermore, these identities bear no necessary relationship to one another. One's inner and outer identities can be either consistent or at odds. [*KPA*, pp. 345-48]

While acknowledging that Kierkegaard does arrive at "a sophisticated comprehension of the nature of the self's individuality," Taylor charges, in conclusion, that "he does not proceed to reintegrate the self into the social and natural whole from which it has been distinguished" (*KPA*, p. 354).

To make outwardly clear the nature of inner Faith, however, would be to so validate "objectivity" that it would threaten the man of faith with the loss of mystery and paradox. Kierkegaard has no faith in outwardness. The mystery of faith cannot be adduced directly into an alienated world without sacrilegiously betraying the sublime experience itself. Put differently, one might say that for

Kierkegaard the public symbols of Faith have been taken up by the alienated age of reflection in Christendom; consequently, whenever they are put directly into play in a social context, they have no significance that would legitimately typify the achieved selfhood of the individual or group. In other words, Kierkegaard's rhetorical restriction of Faith to the inner realm of personality is a necessary defensive stance against the hegemony of an abstracted "public" caught in "speculation."

I would disagree with Taylor, however, and suggest that Kierkegaard does *not* abandon the possibilities of communication and association. He attempts to form a "counter-ideology" through his method of indirect communication. Kierkegaard never removes the individual from social actuality. On the contrary, his project is to find a method of signifying the lived-experience of all "stages" in such a way that its symbolic processes can effectively contact "the other." As a good historical thinker, Kierkegaard realizes this cannot be done abstractly; so, in his indirect communications, he adopts the various figures or "symbols" of "Christendom" and "speculative philosophy" current in his age and recontextualizes them. More precisely, he makes explicit in his "existential dialectic," by parody, satire, example, and fable, the actualities present in contemporary modes of self-conception. The problems of interpersonal relations dominate his pseudonymous works, obviously in the aesthetic and ethical stages (in their concern for love and marriage) and indirectly in the religious phases. In the latter, Kierkegaard suggests that individuals, even at their most abstract and individualistic, can achieve intersubjectivity through the mediation of Christ in the same way that the Knight of Faith, though unrecognizable, can indirectly "give witness."

Though Taylor recognizes implicitly that Kierkegaard's use of the "temporal structure" in the pseudonymous works is an attempt to reidentify time as the ideological location for a victory over alienation, his focus on the *subjective* importance of "indirect communication" for the individual obscures Kierkegaard's social intention. Works produced in this "indirect" mode reflect Kierkegaard's sense that certain "truths" cannot be communicated directly because the means of direct communication have been assumed into the "public" sphere of bourgeois reflection. His defensive ironies, however, not only protect his "witness" from those who cannot recognize it but also make it available to those who themselves sense their alienation. In this way the maieutic functions of indirection help, first, to form a *style* in which the impotent are culturally enabled to associate and, second, to form a "counter-ideology" or "counter-practice" to the hegemonic power of the capitalist culture.

In *What Is Literature?* Sartre outlines his thesis that in mid-nineteenth-century France the bourgeois artist turns away from any connection with the values and rhetoric of his class. Saving art means sacrificing society.[9] Edward Said and Eugenio Donato claim that in Flaubert's writing one sees the paradigm of the bourgeois author, alienated from the powerful scientific and empirical discourse of his time, creating a competing, ironic, and deconstructive discourse to disclose the emptiness of the sign-systems of bourgeois representation. Kierkegaard's project is similar—a concern with and a desire to overcome the dominance of the bourgeois intellectual class, an attempt to create an alternative to their self-destructive life-styles and discourse.[10] Perhaps because capitalism is not as advanced in Denmark, Kierkegaard does not author a deconstructive discourse, but a *competing* discourse; its key term is Christ, whom he perceives as the only alternative to the will to power of capitalism's repressive objectification. But if one suspends his Christological concerns, one can still see that his procedure differs from the later critiques of representation in France (even from those of Rousseau) in his willingness to deconstruct the relationship between the subject who writes and the self who lives. Kierkegaard has a strong sense of the cultural power of represen-

[9] Jean-Paul Sartre, *What Is Literature?* trans. Bernard Frechtman (New York: Harper and Row, 1965), pp. 122ff.
[10] See the exchange between Said and Donato in *boundary 2* 8 (1979).

tations to control lived-experience, especially that of intellectuals, and he is particularly adept at discovering the nature of their experience as it is mediated in their writings.

Taylor's objection that there is no way to come to know the inwardness of others seems to minimize the possibilities of indirect association and of discovering such experience. But he does not take into consideration the figures of Abraham in *Fear and Trembling* and the young man in *Repetition.* In both of these texts, Kierkegaard would have us realize the mystery of the Knight of Faith's return to the social world. In *Fear and Trembling,* Johannes de Silentio, the narrator, is a Knight of Infinite Resignation who cannot understand the mystery of Abraham's faith—the paradoxical belief that by killing Isaac he will keep him alive as his son. The Abraham parable indicates how difficult it is to know what Faith is; it shows also how the Knight of Faith always returns to the World. Yet how is the Knight of Faith to be known if he is silent and his inwardness a mystery? The maieutic function of the pseudonymous works is not only to lead the reader through an emotional experience to a point of decision but also to educate him in the skills of decoding the age's major types. As *Repetition* suggests, the Kierkegaardian goal is to find a reader for this reflection of an age so self-alienated that it cannot recognize its own alienation. Those readers adept at decoding the typical characters of their age *can,* for example, tell the difference between the aesthetic monster of immediacy—the Seducer—and Kierkegaard when he abandons Regine. It is true, as his letters to Emil Boesen suggest, that he willfully deceived Regine and their acquaintances so that he would appear "an egotistical and vain man, an ironist in the worst sense" (*Letters,* p. 90). That he confided his complete motives to no one has been the subject of a good deal of psychological speculation and will no doubt continue to be so with the publication in English of his symbolically charged letters to Regine (*Letters,* pp. 61-88). Kierkegaard comes closest to explaining himself to Boesen, his one confidante, when he writes from Berlin, "To allow her to sense my enormously tempestous life and its pains and then to say to her,

'Because of this I leave you,' that would have been to crush her. It would have been contemptible to introduce her to my griefs and then not be willing to help her bear the impact of them" (*Letters*, p. 115).

Yet Kierkegaard is neither the Seducer (the monster of immediacy, the type of the solipsistic aesthete) nor the Young Man of *Repetition* (the poet, the reflective aesthete). In *Two Ages,* for example, Kierkegaard remarks on Mariane's love for Bergland, a love denied passion by being lived in an age of reflection:

Instead of being a source of confident, invincible courage that in matters of love dares to ask anything of actuality, convinced in its inspired ignorance that actuality is the world where love has its home, being in love is for her a source of sadness. The inwardness may be just the same . . . but the difference is essential. Instead of her perceiving her being in love as a vocation tendered by a world that wants to indulge it in everything, she is inwardly accustomed to resigning herself to renunciation: in the split second she falls in love she secretly realizes that this, too, will be forced back into her inward being, will be a secret life others know nothing of, and will simultaneously be improved health and yet, humanly speaking, an infirmity. [*Letters,* p. 50]

The Mariane/Bergland-Regine/Kierkegaard comparison undergoes a series of inversions with Mariane alternately Regine and Kierkegaard himself. Moments of this sort are testimony not only to the truth of Kierkegaard's remark "I serve her" (*Letters*, p. 93) but also to the possibility of decoding actions and writing to distinguish between "faith" and "seduction."

In *Two Ages,* Kierkegaard gives an example of how one "reads" inwardness from external signs. While Taylor may be correct in assuming that for Kierkegaard there is no "necessary" connection between inner and outer, sense and sign, he is perhaps wrong in concluding that one cannot read signs to discover the inwardness of the character reflected in their "meaning." Kierkegaard "reads" the presentation of Mrs. Waller, the housewife of part 2 of *Two Ages,* to discover a correspondence between behavior and character. The novel is "continually illuminating Mrs. Waller's lack of character in the monetary mirror of reflection. . . . The art lies in the repetition of the psychological conception in the presentation itself, and as philandering is the unstable emptiness, so throughout the whole novel Mrs. W. is an unstable flurry of busyness, represented in her transitory relations to the older and younger men" (p. 54). It is axiomatic in *Two Ages* that character must be understood as the type of the age. The age reflects itself in the individual's domesticity; this is, after all, a bourgeois, domestic novel that Kierkegaard is reviewing. The dialectical reading of the character reflected in the age and of the age illuminated by the character's choices produces a critical figure, a "type," located somewhere between the "age" and the "individual"; this "type" offers readers a way of understanding themselves in their social actuality. The characters of the age and of the individual always present themselves to those willing to decode the signs and produce a new set to mediate their critical understanding.

It is precisely in this method of understanding, demanded by Kierkegaard's indirection in the face of an alienating, capitalistic hegemony, that one can see the peculiar nature of his intellectual life. This method requires a willingness to see and understand the connections between life and writing, to see that the works of alienated people are reflections of that alienation and are microscopic tools in its extension. It requires a recognition that the text is never a detached product. While the author may feel detached from the product as commodity, his attachment to the text reflects his alienated, often self-deluded state.

In the introduction to *Two Ages,* Kierkegaard addresses himself to the killing of the father that occurs when each generation establishes its own modernity and "authority." He suggests that this patricide reflects an impatience, egotism, and lack of care that prohibit education:

Zealousness to learn from life is seldom found, but all the more frequently a desire, inclination, and reciprocal haste to be deceived by life. Undaunted, people do not seem to have a Socratic fear of being deceived. . . . Even less do people seem to have above all a Socratic fear of being deceived by themselves, do not seem to be the least aware that if the self-deceived are the most miserable of all, then among these, again, the most miserable are those who are presumptuously deceived by themselves in contrast to those who are piously deceived. [P. 10]

In the moment of self-definition, the cultural parricide relegates the past to the junk heap of history and thus furthers his own demise. Youth's violence destroys its innocence and inserts it in history. The loss of innocence is the loss of "the happy days of youth when we ourselves were the demand of the times" (p. 10). As Taylor suggests in his discussion of atonement and as this passage indicates, Kierkegaard always warns of consequences: the results of birth in a certain family and time, the effects of past actions, the inescapability of "character" formed by one's environment and decisions (see *KPA,* pp. 307ff). Even forgiving sins is, for Kierkegaard, remembering consequences. The act of parricide is endlessly repeated and generates the eternal drama of children becoming their "father" and then being killed.

This pattern not only constitutes one example of the way in which classes and individuals are self-deluded but provides the paradigm of such self-delusion because it contains the essential images of "original" alienation, ignorance, and self-destruction. It marks also the historical rebellion of the bourgeoisie against sovereign authority and suggests that the origin of this revolution contains the seed of its own self-destruction. As Marx indicates in *The Eighteenth Brumaire,*[11] this seed matures when capital sacrifices bourgeois civil liberties to Louis Bonaparte and, in late capitalism, when capital sacrifices the family and other staples of bourgeois culture to isolate and repress the workers. "Faithlessness," says Kierkegaard, "is the mutual likeness of the antagonists" (*Two*

[11]Karl Marx, *The Eighteenth Brumaire* (New York: International Publishers, 1963), pp. 114-15.

Ages, p. 11). In opposition to this form of self-delusion, Kierkegaard offers his own practice as a counter-example. In his *Journals
and Papers*(5:5891) he writes: "Given the conditions in the world
as it is, to be an author should be the extraordinary employment
in life. . . . Therefore not only should the author's production be
a testimony to the idea, but the author's life ought to correspond
to the idea" (*Two Ages,* p. 141).

Two Ages is, of course, Kierkegaard's most political text. The third
part, particularly "Conclusions from a Consideration of the Two
Ages," gathers many of his important themes and gives them authoritative formulation. There are three parts to *Two Ages* (after
the introduction discussed above). In the first, "Survey of Con-
tents," Kierkegaard provides a plot summary and a general sketch
of the characters outlined against the background of the "two ages":
the "age of revolution," the French Revolution; and the "present
age," Denmark in its period of transition to a constitutional mon-
archy with an elected assembly. The second section, "An Esthetic
Interpretation," examines Gyllembourg's novel as an attempt to
reflect the particularity of each age. But Kierkegaard does not look
to the novel merely to discover the immediate "realistic" presentation of the age and its individuals; on the contrary, his idea of
art's "reflection" of social order and psychological structure depends on one's recognizing the mediating processes of the novel's
art:

The novel has as its premise the distinctive totality of each age, and
the production is the reflexion of this in domestic life; the mind turns
from the production back again to the totality of the age that has been
so clearly revealed in this reflexion. But . . . the author did not in-
tend to describe the age itself; his novel lies somewhere between the
pre-supposed distinctive character of the age and the age in reflexion
as illustrated by this work. [P. 32]

As critic, Kierkegaard is not interested in the question of the uniqueness of characterization—is Claudine or Mariane "believable" and "possible"? "No, the critic's question is: may a girl like Claudine appear as *typical* in this particular age" (p. 33).

Kierkegaard continues his discussion in the second section with a detailed psychological analysis of the central characters in both parts of the novel. His aim is not merely to understand each figure but to suggest how each is a "reflexion" of the age. Kierkegaard's hermeneutics involve moving into the text and his specific analyses with a "presupposition" about the external age and its "effects" and then back out again from the characters to the age. He tries always to understand one in terms of the other because, in his mind, it is impossible to understand either by itself. His interest lies in decoding the signs Gyllembourg's novel has inscribed to mediate between the domestic level of representation, plot and character, and the general nature of history and society that the novel "reflexes" and from which it self-consciously emerges.

Kierkegaard's fullest statement on the "double-vision" of his technique stresses both its correspondence to the technique of the "author" and its efficacy in accounting historically for psychological forms of action:

The critic is obliged to assume the double approach by which the story has made its task so difficult. The author does not dare to present the age as having automatic consequences in the individuals, for then he would transgress his task as novelist and merely describe the age and *illustrate it by examples,* instead of viewing the reflexion in domestic life and through it illuminating the age. Action must always occur through the psychological middle term of the individual. . . . The relation between the age and an individual's action must be psychologically motivated, and only then can there be any mention of the special character of the age as influencing or permitting this manifestation.[P. 41]

Kierkegaard's analyses in the rest of section two provide the terms in which his discussion of the present age develops in the third section.

Kierkegaard concludes the second section with a disclaimer that although the "superficial reader" might mistakenly believe that he has found more in the novel than is "really" there, he has only been exposing what lies beneath the "unpretentious" surface of the text. "Yet I cannot accept a compliment from the reader but must convey it to the proper person, the author, who, even if I did understand all of it, is, after all, first the creator and is also the one who had the art to conceal the fact and, finally, perhaps knows and puts into the novel much that I have not been able to discover" (p. 58). Here Kierkegaard addresses the central problem of indirect communication. In a typically offhand and parenthetical way, he represents the precise hermeneutic situation that forms an association of individuals who recognize the essential connection between subject and society. The "superficial reader" who consumes texts and reviews not only will mistake the novel's complex reflection of the entanglement of the intellectual and bourgeoisie with their age but "will be startled" (p. 58) by the revelations of Kierkegaard's review. It is characteristic of Kierkegaard to keep the cycle of writer-reader-critic-reader in view. Hermeneutic activity exists in every relationship among these figures. The "superficial reader" is not merely the careless reader but (seen in the context of Kierkegaard's later discussions of the "public") the typical reader, who, in the age of reflection, is so alienated from his own intellectual and emotional processes that he does not have available to him directly and immediately the interpretive techniques necessary to realign symbol and meaning. Symbolically, Kierkegaard's figure here represents the reading public's divorce from the conscious process of associating the inwardness of the character or author with the outwardness of the age. In fact, we see clearly that the age produces readers unable to mediate between the subject and history; the age herds the self-deceived intellectual bourgeoisie into a public, which, under the guise of "association," so abstracts interpersonal relations that individually and as a group they are unaware of their own alienation.

Yet, at the same time, Kierkegaard's figure in this passage does not represent merely an abstract counter-possibility. It offers instead a true association among himself, Gyllembourg, and their understanding readers. Even the superficial reader, shocked by the results of Kierkegaard's hermeneutic action, is momentarily drawn up into the counter-discourse of indirection, even as he attempts to deny it. The novel itself is indirect because its simplicity masks the social and psychological complexity that Kierkegaard excavates. And Kierkegaard's own task is indirect; while his review seems merely an interpretation of the novel's "meaning"—its reduplication in name and strategy—it gives witness to the efficacy of the indirect method in preserving unified symbolic processes from abstraction and in reinforcing the association of those trying to develop a counter-discourse to capitalism's "reflective public." "To give witness" is to attempt to extend this counter-discourse subversively throughout the intellectual classes. In this respect, both Kierkegaard and Gyllembourg prefigure the later nineteenth century's alienation of literature from the bourgeoisie and those displaced bourgeois authors' attempts to establish a "religion of the word" as an alternative to the social world of capitalism.

In part three, "Conclusion," the longest part of the review, Kierkegaard emphasizes the difference between the type of association he advocates and that which his age enforces through a variety of "leveling" processes. Towards the opening of this section, in a lyrical, but satiric, passage, he casts three different social orders into musical images. His topic is "the measure of essential culture" (p. 61). Romantically, he suggests that an uneducated maidservant, passionately in love, is "essentially cultured." He goes on to suggest that "there is only affection, the pretense of form, in the external piecemeal training correlative with an interior emptiness, the flamboyant colors of swaggering weeds in contrast to the humble bowing of the blessed grain, the mechanical counting of the beat correlative with the lacklustre of the dance, the painstaking decoration of the bookbinding correlative with the deficiency of the book" (p. 62). The temptation is to dismiss this comparison as obvious, Rousseauistic, and naïve. But what Kierkegaard reflects here are the very processes of self-alienation resulting from a social order that *trains* individuals in various disciplines; these are concerned with success ("flamboyant colors of swaggering weeds"), order ("the mechanical counting of the beat"), and the consumption of products answering to no lived need ("the painstaking decoration of the bookbinding"). In *Discipline and Punish*, Foucault suggests how, during the nineteenth century, the expansion of highly detailed mechanical processes for extending power throughout society led both to the formation of the "self" and its "human sciences" and to apparatuses that internalized the need for social uniformity in "individuals." Kierkegaard's concern with the hegemonic extension of power, resulting in the leveling of individuals, seems to anticipate Foucault's discussion.[12] In fact, Kierkegaard's remarks on training, education, and the homogenizing effects of the press and schools gain considerably in resonance when considered in the context of Foucault's discussion of disciplinary machinery. I will return to this idea later.

Kierkegaard goes on to offer a utopian image, again in musical terms, of the ideal order he envisions:

When individuals (each one individually) are essentially and passionately related to an idea and together are essentially related to the same idea the relation is optimal and normative. Individually the relation separates them (each one has himself for himself), and ideally it unites them. Where there is essential inwardness, there is a decent modesty between man and man that prevents crude aggressiveness. . . . Thus the individuals never come too close to each other in the herd sense, simply because they are united on the basis of ideal distance. The unanimity of separation is indeed fully orchestrated music. . . . The harmony of the spheres is the unity of each planet relating to itself and to the whole. Take away the relations, and there will be chaos. [Pp. 62-63]

This is the fullest representation of Kierkegaard's vision of a society united "indirectly," seemingly the only mode of association available to the antagonists of disciplinary unanimity. His description

[12]Foucault, *Discipline and Punish*, pp. 170-94.

of the world that fails to sustain this harmony is meant to represent the "present age":

Remove the relation to oneself, and we have the tumultuous self-relating of the mass to an idea; but remove this as well, and we have crudeness. Then people shove and press and rub against each other in pointless externality, for there is no deep inward decency that decorously distances the one from the other; thus there is turmoil and commotion that ends in nothing. No one has anything for himself, and united they possess nothing, either: so they become troublesome and wrangle. Then it is not even the gay and lively songs of conviviality that unite friends; then it is not the dithyrambic songs of revolt that collect the crowds; then it is not the sublime rhythms of religious fervor that under divine supervision muster the countless generations to review before the heavenly hosts. No, then gossip and rumor and specious importance and apathetic envy become a surrogate for each and all. Individuals do not in inwardness turn away from each other, do not turn outward in unanimity for an idea, but mutually turn to each other in a frustrating and suspicious, aggressive, leveling reciprocity. [P. 63]

Kierkegaard's dialectic arrives at the conclusion that the age of reflection, objectivity, discipline, and training, produces individuals united as the public and leveled in competition and envy—individuals who are absolutely alone and apart precisely because this mode of social ordering denies them any "conviviality" or "contemporaneity" (p. 91). The individuals, even among the bourgeois intellectual classes who think of their products as their own, are only marking the "mechanical counting of the beat." The failure to examine their own relation to society, to try to understand what makes possible their success and individuality, indicates how the social order of the bourgeoisie has co-opted them, produced them, and denied them a role in the process of challenging the society that they sometimes undoubtedly call into question. They think they dance either to their own tune or that of an oppositional group when they are marionettes jerking to the rhythms of the metronome hidden from them in their modernity and power.

How has the individual lost his ability to act as a part of a true association that forms a counter-discourse to capitalism's disciplinary hegemony? For Kierkegaard, the answer lies in the idea of "reflection." As he points out repeatedly, the age of revolution is a passionate age, capable of action, of defining itself by movement and choice. It "has *not nullified the principle of contradiction*" (p. 66). In other words, it has not yet entered the period of domination that marks the end of history and finds in Hegel's insistence on speculation the perfect emblem of its endurance. History is formed by action and its consequences are inescapable. The age of reflection makes no choices because its will has been suspended to maintain the status quo. Its actions are calculated to extend itself. It has negated negation. Kierkegaard comments repeatedly on the expansionary powers of "reflection" (see p. 97, for example). The intellectual cannot understand his life because it cannot be a life or assume a shape if he cannot act; his life degenerates into "gossip." "The coherence of his life becomes a garrulous continuation or a continued garrulity, a participial or infinitive phrase in which the subject must be understood or, more correctly, cannot be located at all because, as the grammarians say, the meaning does not make it clear for the simple reason that it lacks meaning" (p. 67).

The loss of the subject that Kierkegaard identifies in the intellectual discourse of the bourgeoisie produces *anonymity*. Instead of speaking, the intellectual chatters:

The comments become so objective, their range so all-encompassing, that eventually it makes no difference at all who says them. . . . And eventually human speech will become just like the public: pure abstraction—there will no longer be someone who speaks, but an objective reflection will gradually deposit a kind of atmosphere, an abstract noise that will render human speech superfluous, just as machines make workers superfluous. [P. 104]

The final term of this figure is not accidental but part of an entire network of images drawn from the mechanical and financial world of capitalism. Kierkegaard has perhaps not been given enough

credit for recognizing the economic causes of the cultural alienation he describes. While his analysis is hardly systematic or pro-
longed, it is recurrent and intertwined with his exposure of the
leveling of society's products to commodities through the disciplinary practices of capitalism. For example, he immediately juxtaposes the following figure of the disciplinary apparatus to the
previous quotation:

> In Germany [had he known he could have added "and England"]
> there are even handbooks for lovers; so it will probably end with lovers
> being able to sit and speak anonymously to each other. There are hand-
> books on everything, and generally speaking education soon will consist
> of knowing letter-perfect a larger or smaller compendium of obser-
> vations from such handbooks, and one will excel in proportion to his
> skill in pulling out the particular one, just as the typesetter picks
> out letters. [P. 104]

This is not merely an objection to the false learning codes that
stifles individual "authentic" expression. Kierkegaard is pointing
also to the proliferation in his culture of the various "conduct
books" and other media that created ideologically acceptable representations of social behavior. The final part of this image, with
its allusion to mass circulation of ideas and images, its echo of
the previous image of empty but decorated books, its suggestion
of the automatic, self-perpetuating, neutral commodification of
"culture," is only one of many figures in the text aligned with
the metaphor of writing. Consistently, allusions to typesetting,
written grammar, and sentence structure point to the absence of
the subject from any adequate means of social symbolization—
they point, in other words, to anonymity. The direct writing of
commodities, by which authors become successful in their anonymity, is merely a form of chatter and garrulity, of self-interest
and self-deception. Chatter is not just what we know in everyday
life as "gossip" but the commodification of discourse, the reification of knowledge in positive forms, and the means of usurping
what Kierkegaard sees as the crucial element in the formation of

a counter-culture to preserve the self against instrumental reason: language in history as a means of association.

The power of capitalism's systems of representation leads, for Kierkegaard, to the fetishization of money. Everything is sacrificed to its gain. The present age is an age without passion. "But an age without passion possesses no assets; everything becomes . . . transactions in *paper money*. Certain phrases and observations circulate among the people . . . but there is no person to vouch for their validity by having primitively experienced them." But it is clear that Kierkegaard is not, like some antiquarian, calling nostalgically for a return to species, hard currencies. "Just as in our business transactions we long to hear the ring of real coins after the whisper of paper money, so we today long for a little primitivity." So awesome is the expansionary power of the network of capitalist society's systems of representation that even wit, which Kierkegaard claims is more primitive than Spring itself, is transformed into a commodity. His satire ironically sums up his vision of this expansion. "Suppose that wit were changed to its most trite and hackneyed opposite, a trifling necessity of life, so that it would become a profitable industry to fabricate and make up and renovate and buy up in bulk old and new witticisms: what a frightful epigram on a witty age!" (pp. 74-75). Nostalgic prose is a production of a "need" created by the alienation of the present. But the nostalgic grasping for origins, the primitive species, is incapable of escaping from the context that engenders it. Such antiquarian turning backward to better times diverts the intellectual from the confrontation with the present. And how disturbingly like the modern critical academy Kierkegaard's "wit industry" seems to be.

Kierkegaard is remarkably alert to the ways in which the age of reflection deludes its intellectuals into believing that they are, in fact, establishing a willful opposition to the hegemony of industry and finance. It is not necessary here to point out how important action is for Kierkegaard in the formation of self and society. What is important, though, are his insights into the mechanisms hegemonic culture applies to divert its opponents from passionate action against it. These mechanisms exist on the level of discursive representation and on the level of social structure. Kierkegaard represents all of these under the rubric "reflection." He describes the effects of reflection on both levels:

A passionate, tumultuous age wants to *overthrow everything, set aside everything.* An age that is revolutionary but also reflecting and devoid of passion changes the expression of power into a *dialectical tour de force: it lets everything remain but subtly drains the meaning out of it; rather than culminating in an uprising, it exhausts the inner actuality of relations in a tension of reflection that lets everything remain and yet has transformed the whole of existence into an equivocation that in its facticity is—while entirely privately a dialectical fraud interpolates a secret way of reading—that it is not.* [P.77]

Kierkegaard's success in using the figure of "reflection" as the sign of the present age stems from its resonance as a representation of both the states of inwardness he is analyzing and the outward or social reality he is describing. Inwardly, "reflection" indicates the age's fascination with the endless play of the dialectic that Kierkegaard credits to Hegel and especially his Danish followers. Outwardly, or socially, "reflection" represents the mechanisms for ensuring the hegemony of its own cultural reproduction.

The individual, then, cannot act because reflection neutralizes the will. It valorizes cunning, shrewdness, and "understanding"— the calculating intelligence—at the expense of the will and thus makes decision, change, resistance, and self-definition impossible. Change becomes simple "flux, a blend of a little resolution and a little situation, a little prudence and a little courage, a little probability and a little faith, a little action and a little incident" (p. 67). Indolence results from reflection's enervation of passion.

How can this enervation be enforced? How is the habit of mind created and maintained? The individual cannot "tear himself out of the web of reflection and seductive ambiguity of reflection" (p. 690). Reflection displaces one from historical reality into an

51

erotic relation with the infinite ambiguities of endless beginnings. Consequences apparently never exist for the reflective individual; there is always the possibility of creating another, sometimes purely personal, myth for escape. Energy is exhausted in the act of loving one's own self-projection. But this death-dealing enervation is internalized by the external, social modes of organization that in the name of "common sense"—ideologically approved patterns of behavior in which the public is well disciplined—transform "actuality into a theater" (p. 72). Everywhere in society the effects of "reflection" are legitimized in signs that have replaced symbols and, while obscuring other perceptions, mirror its authority.

The machinery for establishing and maintaining the hegemony of capital in culture can be described, in Foucault's phrase, as the "micro-physics" of power.[13] As Kierkegaard says, reflection turns power into a "dialectical tour de force." The paradigm of the disciplinary apparatus, for Foucault, is Bentham's panopticon, the ultimate penitentiary; because the observing authority in the panopticon is himself never seen by the observed, they internalize the responsibility for regulation. The prisoners guard themselves, so to speak. Disciplining the body extends to training the mind to guard against rebellion. Kierkegaard extends the social equivalent of the panopticon's internalizing regulation and authority as the means by which his reflective age extends itself.

This fact is evident not only in Kierkegaard's adopting the penitentiary as a metaphor to describe the entrapment of the individual who hopes to rebel against the forces of alienation and oppression but also in his recourse to visual metaphors in suggesting how society regulates itself and homogenizes its misfits. Analyzed on the social level, reflection becomes envy, the metaphor for the leveling process that acts as a barrier against any escape from reflection. "Envy becomes the *negatively unifying principle* in a passionless and very reflective age" (p. 81). Envy is part of the central process for deluding intellectuals in their rebellions. "The environ-

[13]Ibid., p. 149.

52

ment, the contemporary age, has neither events nor integrated passion but in a negative unity creates a reflective opposition that toys for the moment with the unreal prospect" (p. 69). Envy, the "negative unity," has the power of "tyrants and secret police" to level all distinctions and to maintain itself by thwarting all perception of its actions, a thwarting made possible by the universality, the ubiquity of its insinuating powers. "Negative unity" is the parodic inversion of association in which subjects, history, and their products can be united; leveling takes the form of the illusion of "equality," "the negative unity of the negative mutual reciprocity of individuals" (p. 84). Under the ideologically acceptable guise of equality the disciplinary machinery takes effect. "The *participants* [in a world-historical event] would shrewdly transform themselves into a crowd of *spectators*" (p. 73). Kierkegaard's statement not only suggests how the *visual* becomes the all-absorbing sign of the disciplinary hegemony but also points that the power of the disciplining process is so subtly discrete that the people who are exploited, dehumanized, and oppressed are made to *transform themselves* into distanced, alienated abstractions furthering the expansion of capitalist power.

Equality produces peers who live only in the *form* of relationships learned piecemeal. The forms of these relationships have been kept; in fact, they are only recently being abandoned by capitalist society. But they were maintained as an essential part of the disciplining of the culture. Kierkegaard suggests that if the relation is "impeccable," it has still "become a problem in which the parties like rivals *watch* each other instead of relating to each other, and count, as it is said, each other's verbal avowals of relation as a substitute for resolute mutual giving in the relation" (p. 79; my emphasis).

Kierkegaard's analysis of the age returns to the principle of indirection to invalidate the will of individuals associated within culture. For the nature of this culture is such that no direct representation of an alternative can escape being co-opted. "Leveling is not the action of one individual but a reflection-game in the hand of an abstract power" (p. 86). Power is not simply held or exercised by a group or individual. Kierkegaard anticipates Foucault's suggestion that property metaphors may not adequately characterize the operations of power. He concludes that abstract "microphysical" power is self-reproducing and, when challenged directly, *always* emerges victorious. "The individual who levels others is himself carried along, and so on. . . . No assemblage will be able to halt the abstraction of leveling, for in the context of reflection the assemblage itself is in the service of leveling" (pp. 86, 87). Of course, Kierkegaard opts for a religious answer to this dilemma. He insists that the only idea capable of motivating the relation of one self to an idea, and through that idea a relationship to other selves, is the belief in God. Yet even if one does not accept the theocentric dimensions of Kierkegaard's argument, his insight and analysis remain substantively useful. Capitalist, disciplinary society has appeared to many to be nearly omnivorous. "It has cunningly bought up every possible outlook on life," Kierkegaard suggests (p. 89), and at times Foucault and the Frankfurt School seem to agree. But from Kierkegaard's point of view this is because capitalism's ideological opponents have acted "willfully" to gain recognition as alternative, representative figures within and from a public structured to dehumanize value. And in doing so they have succumbed to the process of commodification.

Kierkegaard suggests as an alternative a strategy of indirection, of pseudonymity. His "counter-example" is an "unrecognizability" that attempts to redeem history and the will from the abstraction of leveling by renouncing the direct public pursuit of power, by refusing to offer oneself as representative, as hero or leader. He offers not a social revolution as a response to alienation but an association of those who have renounced the appeal to and pursuit of authority, an association of those who value their suffering as witness to the possibility of maintaining a consciousness of full human association. In a passage near the end of *Two Ages*, Kierkegaard returns us to the position that Taylor describes as quietism; but it is placed now in a social context that allows us to understand what he is suggesting and why:

54

The unrecognizables recognize the servants of leveling but dare not use power or authority against them, for then there would be a regression, because it would instantly be obvious to a third party that the unrecognizable one was an authority. . . . Only through a *suffering* act will the unrecognizable one dare to contribute to leveling and by the same suffering act will pass judgement on the instrument. He does not dare to defeat leveling outright—he would be dismissed for that, since it would be acting with authority—but in suffering he will defeat it and thereby experience in turn the law of his existence, which is not to rule, to guide, to lead, but in suffering to serve, to help indirectly. [P. 109]

Three figures lie behind this conception: Christ, Socrates, and Kierkegaard himself. The ubiquity of power drives the witness to a nonalienated life underground. It makes him despair of the possibility of ever existing within the social world; in this sense, it succeeds in alienating even so sensitive an analyst of alienation as Kierkegaard from the *idea* of a social order not spontaneously and inevitably oppressive in its use of power. Faith is indeed the only option remaining for renewing human possibilities if one believes, as Kierkegaard does, that society inevitably alienates man from himself. In this respect, his analysis of "the present age" seems to have fallen short. He has replicated liberalism's trust in the individual and gets caught up in its contradictions. By not wondering himself what role the oppressive forces he so brilliantly analyzes might have played in helping lead him to his conclusion in favor of unrecognizability, he makes us ask if *he* has not been marking— on a very sophisticated level, indeed—"the mechanical counting of the beat correlative with the lacklustre of the dance." He seems not to have realized that the final hegemonic effect of social alienation is the alienation of the individual from the idea of society's regenerative possibilities.

Yet, as we have seen, Kierkegaard often does attend to, and his works do emerge out of, his social context. He does not, however, conclude from the possibility of hermeneutic association between Gyllembourg, himself, and their understanding readers— those attentive to indirection—that reforming society could put an end to the need for this sort of association to be underground. Instead, he falls victim to one version of the myth of the end of history. He decides that the disciplinary society of the bourgeoisie is not only expansive but permanent. One must tend to one's garden.

The bourgeois intellectual's pessimism about society leads, even in Kierkegaard's case, to a position that reinforces the entrenched social order it so dislikes. This pessimism contributes to the mythology of capital's invincibility and permanence, to its mystique of inevitability. To offset this pessimism, critical intellectuals must practice negation in theory and history to prevent the reification of reason in reflection. Most important, criticism must negate its own assumptions and query its own genealogy to understand its relation to the conditions of its own social being, the extent of its own inevitable participation in maintaining and changing society's institutions—particularly the university. Although Kierkegaard's own negation stops at the intersection of the self and God, his theory and practice suggest that this sort of critique can begin only when the critic no longer sees himself or herself as a transmitter of knowledge to the public or as an author of elegant studies that disregard their own origins and effects in lived-history and experience. If criticism is to be more than a "wit industry," it must risk its own (minimal) stability to enter the mainstream of cultural understanding. It must abandon its fascination with the belletristic, with bourgeois conceptions of textuality that neglect the subject (but do produce sophisticated "readings") and confront the crisis of its own history, role, and future.[14] Finally, it must question even

---

[14]See Geoffrey Hartman, *Criticism in the Wilderness* (New Haven, Conn.: Yale University Press, 1980), p. 301. Hartman concludes by insisting that "it is a mistake to think of the humanist as spiritualizing anything: on the contrary, he materializes us; he makes us aware of the material culture (including texts) in which everyone has always lived." Hartman, however, goes on to say in a somewhat different spirit: "Only the passage of time spiritualizes us, that is, volatizes and deracinates." His unwillingess or inability to see history as the medium of material existence rather than its antithesis is

its own anti-instrumental defense of negation to refocus its energies on how we have come to be what we are, how we might
realistically imagine alternate ways to be, and how we might re-
shape production and rediscover modes of cultural interaction to
overcome the dehumanized social life that Kierkegaard has helped
us understand.

typical of contemporary criticism and reflects the same sort of pessimism we
have seen in Kierkegaard. This attitude allows Hartman to describe life as
"a feast of mortuary riddles and jokes."

2. Kierkegaard: The Self in Truth

ONE of the most often misunderstood notions in Kierke-gaard's thought is his view that an individual can exist in truth, can manifest truth in finite existence. It is misunderstood, in part, because it is not seen how radical the idea of truth in subjectivity actually is. Certainly the claim that "subjectivity is truth" does not mean something like Protagoras's principle of homo mensura, that each individual is the "measure" of what is true or false, real or unreal. The belief that Kierkegaard is de-fending anything like an epistemological relativism is absurd. His standpoint is far more radical than that.

What concerned Kierkegaard was a "truth" for which one could live and die, a "truth" that would give meaning to an existence permeated by a bewildering plurality of finite goals or ends. Al-though he was quite willing to admit that all of us are more or less "subjective" in a psychological sense, he believed that only in an ethical or a religious existence do we attain an accentuated existence or, as he called it (before Heidegger), an "authentic existence." Finding ourselves in being, confronted by a multitude of possibilities, we discover no objective guideposts for life. Or rather we discover too many guideposts, too many alternative paths. It is a sceptical self-consciousness, as Hegel called it, that awakens us to the ambiguous nature of our being in the world.

58

If there is no objective truth other than a theoretical possibility, a metaphysical postulate, then it may be that there is only existential truth. Perhaps the intrinsic value of our existence is not a matter of "knowledge." Conceptualization always brings us into the realm of "possibility," insofar as cognition gives us only the hypothetical. Kierkegaard agreed with Kant that we cannot proceed from conception to existence in the strict sense because at the level of conceptualization per se there is no distinction between the concept of x as possible and the concept of x as actual. The problem of existence is not primarily conceptual, even though thought is necessary for authentic existence; it is a matter of a transformation of the self. Truth in subjective actuality pertains to *how* a person exists, to the qualitative dimension of life, to the intensification of self-existence. It will be my intention here to try to elucidate what Kierkegaard means by this "lived" truth and why he was led to propose it.

The use of the word "truth" in relation to the subjective actuality of the self is deliberately provocative and paradoxical. Having been exposed to Hegelian philosophy throughout his education, Kierkegaard had heard a great deal about objective knowledge (*Wissenschaft*) and was quite familiar with the notion that thought and being are identical. He had learned that the full exercise of reason (*Vernunft*) is the way to truth. In this philosophical context, the claim that there is such a thing as "subjective truth" would be considered absurd or as a contradictio in adjecto. And, of course, Kierkegaard's idea of subjective truth would be disdained by those who believe that "truth" is found in the propositions of the empirical sciences, in tautologies, or in analytic propositions.

What Kierkegaard is concerned with is the conception of an individual existing in truth, in a state of being in which truth is manifested in the actual existence of a person. Existential truth is a telos, a goal that one "strives" to realize in life. He contends that only in an ethical or a religious existence is there a sincere attempt to actualize truth in the actuality of the self. The emphasis in Kierkegaard is always on the "striving" (*Straeben*) and not on the attainment of an "ideal." In his journals he remarks that if "the ideal" were actually attained, then it would no longer be ideal. Both in ethical and religious existence he stresses the "movement" of the psychospiritual individual toward a goal, toward an ideal possibility. In this sense, it is not the case that living in "a state of truth" means that the "actual condition" of the individual "corresponds to his essential nature."[1] What makes the goal of authentic subjectivity so difficult, in Kierkegaard's terms, is that it cannot in any strict sense be completely attained. Ethical subjectivity and religious subjectivity are paradoxical because there is always a distance between the "ought" and the "is," between the ideal of living truth and the "imperfect actuality" of the self. It is for this reason that Kierkegaard often says that "existence is striving."

That Kierkegaard is quite aware of what he is doing in his critique of objective knowledge is shown in the compressed arguments he presents in *Concluding Unscientific Postscript.* If truth is construed as a "conformity" between thought and being, then it is either a desideratum or a tautology. If the "being" to which thought conforms is understood as "empirical being," then truth is a desideratum insofar as the empirical phenomenon is "unfinished" or is in process, and the "existing cognitive subject" is also in a process of "becoming." Anticipating twentieth-century conceptions of empirical knowledge, Kierkegaard suggests that empirical truth is a matter of "approximation" or probability. There can be no apodictic empirical knowledge because the object of such knowledge is subject to change, process, "becoming," and the empirical observer is in the same condition. To hold that thought and being are identical may mean that this concept of being is but an "abstract reflection" of a putative empirical *being.* What Kierkegaard suggests here is that being may be considered as an abstraction from an empirical order that is falsely construed as an order of

---

[1]Richard Schacht, "Kierkegaard on 'Truth is Subjectivity' and 'The Leap of Faith,'" *Canadian Journal of Philosophy* 2 (1972): 300.

being rather than of becoming. In this case, the relation between being and thought is, at best, an "abstract self-identity" that expresses a tautology (*Postscript*, p. 170). The objectivity of objective knowledge is, then, either (1) a metaphysical postulate assuming a tautological relationship between thought and a mode of being abstracted from the empirical order or (2) the assumption of an approximate correspondence between thought and empirical actuality. In *Johannes Climacus*, Kierkegaard suggests that there may be objective knowledge in logic or in metaphysics. Objective knowledge or truth is possible in logic because it deals with logical being or the realm of "essences." In metaphysics there may be objective knowledge or truth in the sense of the internal coherence of the metaphysical system. In neither discipline, however, is there any direct concern with empirical actuality or concrete existence.

Having given the devil his due, Kierkegaard is free to explore the possibility of another modality of truth that is revealed in the individual self. He found the model for existential truth (in an ethical sense) in Socrates and the model for the religious expression of truth in existence in Christ. In order to understand the development of the idea of subjective truth, we must turn to his phenomenology of Socrates' existence in *The Concept of Irony.*

In his struggle to find his way out of the Hegelian labyrinth, Kierkegaard searched for the Ariadne's thread that would lead him to an exit. He found it in the thought and existence of Socrates. What he calls the "Socratic wisdom" is that subjectivity and inwardness are the truth, that "the knower is an existing individual" (*Postscript*, p. 183). In *The Concept of Irony* he is concerned not so much with the "concept" of irony as with the meaning of Socrates' existence. This remarkable master's thesis is an ironic work that has the appearance of being a Hegelian study, but is actually a demolition of Hegelian rationalism. The method used in this demolition is itself Hegelian—a phenomenological description of Socratic irony. Kierkegaard shows that the concept of irony could only be understood in terms of the subjective *existence* of Socrates. This reverses the Hegelian procedure because it suggests that the "idea" of irony can only be comprehended by seeking to penetrate the meaning of Socrates' "ironic standpoint." Before Marx, Kierkegaard, in his own way, tries to turn Hegel's thought "right side up." Ironically, he follows Hegel's lead in this regard, because it was Hegel who pointed out that the notion of the centrality of subjectivity entered Western thought in Socrates' reflections.

In his existential phenomenology of the being of Socrates, Kierkegaard seeks to illuminate the meaning of subjectivity. He argues that irony is the essential determination of subjectivity (*Irony*, p. 279). The negative function of irony is, on one hand, to undermine presumptions to knowledge in oneself and others and, on the other, to put in question conventionally accepted values by suggesting an ideal or an "ideality" that is not being realized in the world. In its negative expression, irony accepts no "holding-for-true" and, in Sartre's term, "nihilates" the realm of actuality. It is for this reason designated the "nihilistic standpoint." The critical, destructive use of irony is a *via negativa* that opens up new existential possibilities for man. In the expression of "negative freedom" the "ironic subject" affirms his individuality.

As Hegel states, the Socratic ironist practices a "subjective form of dialectic."[2] This subjective dialectic is described by Kierkegaard as a process in which commonly accepted claims to truth are questioned and the individual testifies only to his ignorance. Socrates seems always to suggest an ideal reality that is shrouded in obscurity. Repeatedly questioning the thoughts, values, and actions of others, Socrates appears as a chronic negator. In Kierkegaard's interpretation of Socrates, the negativistic employment of irony implies that there is no distinction between "essence" and "phenomenon," no apparent, knowable essence to which phenomena can be contrasted. What Kierkegaard emphasizes is that throughout his interrogations, his ironic negations, Socrates continues to exist and expresses self-confidence. He seems to exist precisely by virtue of a negative freedom. The unstated motto of his life seems to be *negito, ergo sum*: "I negate, therefore I am."

[2]G. W. F. Hegel, *Geschichte der Philosophie*, 18:60. Cited in *Irony*, p. 283.

Extrapolating from *The Concept of Irony*, we may say that the first psychospiritual "movement" in the "dialectic of life" is to encounter and to live through "the nihilistic standpoint." The admittedly one-sided portrait of Socrates that the young Kierkegaard creates seems to suggest, by characteristic "indirection," that there is a nihilistic stage of existence that each of us may have to live through.[3] Socrates is pictured as playing with alternative theoretical possibilities, as expressing vertiginous reflections in the face of death. He relishes the "*aut-aut*" ("either/or") of the high noon of promise or the darkness of an eternal night (*Irony*, p. 117). Socrates seems to thrive on what crushes most of us — uncertainty. He seems to have found a center in himself, a self-control and confidence that testify to a positive value, a positive meaning. The critical, negative use of irony is not an end in itself; rather, the aim and purpose of irony is the "actuality of subjectivity" (p. 228). The movement toward ethical consciousness entails a contrast between the "ideal self" (as it is called in *Either/Or*) and the "imperfect actuality" of the self. By turning irony back upon himself, the individual discloses a capacity, an "oughtness-capability" (*Journals*, 1:307) that initiates ethical self-consciousness. This capacity is, of course, an ideality, a possibility that may or may not be realized. Self-reflexive irony lies at the heart of ethical existence, because what Kierkegaard called the "ethical faith" involves a sense of the paradoxical relationship between the moral ideal and the imperfection of the actual self. By being ironic toward himself, Socrates manifests what Kierkegaard calls a "mastered irony."

Yet ironic reflection is a double-edged sword, and irony can become an "abnormal growth" that kills the individual. An irony directed outward toward man and his culture can easily become, as we see in the case of Nietzsche, a deadly, consuming passion,

[3]Cf. George J. Stack, "Kierkegaard's Ironic Stage of Existence," *Laval Théologique et philosophique* 25 (1969): 192-207; and G. J. Stack, *Kierkegaard's Existential Ethics* (University, Ala.: University of Alabama Press, 1977), chap 1.

a self-consuming one at that. However, if irony is mastered and controlled, if it "limits, renders finite, defines, and thereby yields truth, actuality, and content," it can impart "stability, character, and consistency" (*Irony*, pp. 338-39). The "cleansing baptism of irony" disciplines the self and enables "the personal life to acquire . . . truth" because of its emphasis upon actuality. The subjective actuality of the self, Kierkegaard suggests, acquires its validity through action. Because mastered, self-directed irony signifies the emergence of a truly personal existence, Kierkegaard remarks that "no authentic human life is possible without irony" (p. 338).

Socrates, then, is pictured as the paradigmatic existential thinker who is sceptical about objective truth, who "leaps" back into himself, who lives an examined life that entails the pursuit of self-knowledge. In the language of Hegel, he has negated the negation of irony, has revealed in his existence the "truth of irony," and has attained "reflective individuality." The idea that an individual can exist in truth is put forward for the first time in Kierkegaard's imaginative reconstruction of the life of the prototype of the "ethically existing subject."

Certainly one of Kierkegaard's central notions is that of inwardness. Inwardness, "close reserve," or "introspection" is a basic requirement for the task of becoming subjective, a process in which there is an "intensification to realize the truth" (*Postscript*, p. 175). Although the idea of inwardness has sometimes been characterized as vague, Kierkegaard is quite explicit about what it means. It is particularly related to "subjective reflection" and to "passion." In subjective reflection one reflects back upon oneself in such a way that truth becomes a matter of appropriation and subjectivity. Since passion is the highest expression of subjectivity, it is the state of the highest intensity of inwardness. This passion is not, of course, any simple deep feeling or desire. Rather, it is a pathos imbued with subjective concern, either an "infinite" longing for a goal or a "passion of the infinite." Existential pathos is directed towards a telos that gives meaning, direction, and purpose to a life. When Kierkegaard refers to the "passion of the infinite," he is sometimes led to express himself obscurely. Thus, in speaking about Socratic "uncertainty," he remarks that Socrates' nescience is embraced with the "passion of his inwardness," an expression of the principle that "the eternal truth is related to an existing individual, and that this truth must . . . be a paradox for him as long as he exists" (*Postscript*, p. 180). What is obscure here is the meaning of this "eternal truth."

In the interpretation of Socrates' life we find that the "eternal truth" to which an individual is related is not to be taken for God or the "absolute telos." Kierkegaard suggests that Socratic ignorance or uncertainty pertains to ignorance of "the reason underlying all things, the eternal, the divine." Socrates knew that there was "the eternal," but he did not claim to know what it was (*Irony*, p. 195). Socrates, then, is pictured as one who is directed toward the possibility of the eternal (or eternal truth) as an ideality but not as a reality. The "infinite negativity" of irony leaves open the theoretical possibility of the eternal but precludes any claim to positive knowledge of it. Although he sometimes tries to view Socrates as a proto-Christian, Kierkegaard's considered view is that Socrates was skeptical about the nature of the eternal.

The discussion of Socrates' intensification of existence generates two distinct modalities of inwardness. Unfortunately, Kierkegaard tends to join these two and separate them at various points in his writings. This confusing proclivity does not serve any obvious dialectical purpose and is probably the result of Kierkegaard's vacillation on the question of whether ethical existence is integrated with the religious sphere of existence or whether it is separated from it. One can find evidence for both standpoints in his pseudonymous writings. However, the logic of his analysis of subjective, ethical inwardness leads to its separation from religious faith.

It is clear that one conception of inwardness pertains to the "objective uncertainty" that is nevertheless the "eternal essential truth." Kierkegaard characterizes the nature of a subjective relationship to an objective uncertainty as "passionate inwardness." The act of relating an eternal truth as possibility or ideality to a specific, individual person is fundamentally paradoxical. However, the Socratic version of this process involves a passionate relationship to an objective uncertainty that has no definite content. The inwardness displayed in Socrates' existence is an "analogue of faith," but it is not religious faith. For "Socrates was in truth by virtue of his ignorance" (p. 182). This is an experience of subjective inwardness that is a lived truth or one that expresses truth existentially. When an individual holds fast to an objective uncertainty, one conceives of the possibility of eternal truth or eternal reality that is the "thought-content" of this state of being. This becomes clear when we consider the use of "truth" in this context. Truth is construed as paradoxical *because* it is objectively uncertain. However, the passionate inwardness of the individual who seeks to relate himself to "truth" as an objective uncertainty becomes the truth—that is, the subjective truth. We must distinguish here between "Truth" (the eternal or the essential) as an objectively uncertain possibility and truth as manifested in the passionate inwardness of the existing individual. It is the latter notion that is paradigmatic of authentic existence and central to the conception of the ethical reality of the self. Kierkegaard pictures the existential tension in Socrates' life as brought about by his attempt to relate himself to the "Truth" as objectively uncertain, while at the same time remaining ironic toward the actuality of the world and the self. The central telos of Socratic existence is ethical subjectivity.

In *The Concept of Irony* Kierkegaard suggests that instead of leaping up to the eternal or making the religious "leap of faith," Socrates leaps back into himself. As the prototype of the ethically existing individual, he has an immanent goal. In his journals Kierkegaard makes quite clear what ethical (Socratic) inwardness means. He remarks that "The ethical man is turned inward, but the development of inwardness is self-affirmation . . . . he strives with himself . . . because he has fortified himself in a possibility by which he conquers himself" (*Journals*, 2:462). In the next breath he makes very clear the demarcation between Socratic inwardness and religious inwardness. For in "the inwardness of religiousness" there "is a crushing of the self before God" (*Journals*, 2:462). In what is sometimes called "ethical faith" there is a subjective concern with the telos of becoming the "ideal self." The inwardness of this mode of existence is twofold: it is generated by the dialectical opposition between, first, the notion of the possibility of the eternal and the passion for this unknown infinite in the individual and, second, the contrast between the ideal self one knows one ought to become and the flawed actuality of the self. Thus, ethical inwardness is distinguishable from religious inwardness.

The "Socratic principle" involves the belief that there is an ultimate, metaphysical ideality, even though its nature is unknown or objectively uncertain. This is the affirmation that there is "Truth," even though we do not know what it is. So far, we are only at the level of conceptual possibility insofar as Socrates is considering a possible object of objective reflection. Faith enters in when an individual has an "infinite passion" or a passion for the infinite that is directed toward this objectively uncertain possibility. In general, "Faith is essentially this—to hold fast to possibility" (*Journals*, 2:13). Faith is neither the subjective passion itself nor the objectively uncertain, possible reality. It is the experienced contradiction between the passionate inwardness of the self and the "objective uncertainty" (*Postscript*, p. 182).[4]

The inwardness characteristic of religious existence is distinguishable from the inwardness of ethical self-existence. Kierkegaard insists often enough that religious faith entails an absolute relationship between a finite person or subject and an absolute telos, an "absolute Subject," or God, who is construed as objectively un-

---

[4]"Faith is precisely the contradiction between the infinite passion of the individual's inwardness and the objective uncertainty." It may be noted that in an antecedent passage "truth" had been defined in virtually the same terms as "*an objective uncertainty held fast in an appropriation-process of the most passionate inwardness*" (p. 182).

certain from the standpoint of reason. Religious inwardness, then, is generated by virtue of the paradoxical tension between the subjective, infinite passion of the self and an objectively uncertain, transcendental "I," or God. Ethical inwardness, on the other hand, results from the dialectical contrast between the passionate striving to become a self, to realize the essentially human in one's existence and the imperfect, flawed nature of the actual self. In addition, as we have seen, Socratic or ethical inwardness is exacerbated by the contrast between a perfect, ideal "Truth" that is possible but uncertain, and the passionate longing for such an absolute "Truth." The process of seeking to attain an ethically determined inwardness is by its nature paradoxical. It is paradoxical in the sense that true or authentic existence combines thinking with existence. But thought, of course, pertains to the universal or is concerned with ideality or conceptual-linguistic ideals. The paradox of ethical existence is found in the attempt to relate conceptual-linguistic ideals to one's own concrete actuality by appropriating such ideals in one's existence. The ethical individual

cannot conform his temporal existence to the eternal ideal, but he can make his intellectual and imaginative vision of the idea constitutive for his existence . . . he can appropriate it, literally *tilegne*: make it his *own*. Not once and for all and *simpliciter*, but through a lifetime of striving and rededication he can live the idea by causing the idea to live in him.[5]

The aim of ethical existence is self-realization, an immanent striving to actualize the ideal in existence that entails considering the ideal, ethical self as absolute. Naturally, throughout a lifetime this is a repetitious process, a process in which the individual strives "to seek again" (*repetere*) to realize his potentiality for becoming a true self.

In religious inwardness there is a passionate striving to attain

[5]Louis Mackey, *Kierkegaard: A Kind of Poet* (Philadelphia: University of Pennsylvania Press, 1971), p. 181.

a relationship to an absolute being conceived of as transcendent, as the "unconditioned." The paradox here is that a finite, subjective individual seeks an absolute relationship to an absolute "I" or an eternal being. Given the distinctions between ethical subjectivity and religious existence, it is misleading to assume that a person can be "in the truth" only when he or she is in "the state of faith."[6] Yet such an interpretation of Kierkegaard is certainly understandable given the way in which he sometimes conflates ethical and religious existence. This occurs even in his early work, *The Concept of Irony.*

Kierkegaard agrees with Hegel that the standpoint of Socrates is subjectivity or "the inwardness of the subject, which knows and decides in itself."[7] But he refuses to allow Hegel to dismiss ironic negativity or subjective inwardness as a mere moment (*Momente*) in a rational dialectical process. The subjective inwardness of Socrates is a turning in upon himself in the face of objective, metaphysical uncertainty. Socrates' ethical individuality is described in terms that Kierkegaard later uses to characterize the ethically existing subject. For example, he maintains that "it is certainly true that subjectivity in its fullness, inwardness with its infinite richness, may also be designated by the words 'know thyself'" (*Irony*, p. 202). In *Either/or*, the motto "Know thyself" is related to an "absolute choice" of oneself or the acceptance of the factors that have shaped the self up to the point of self-reflection. There is a direct relationship between the portrayal of Socratic inwardness in *The Concept of Irony* and the later elucidations of the way in which a person may seek, by opening himself to possibilities and by choosing individuating states of being or actions, to express the truth of the "essentially human" in temporality (*Timelighed*) or to live "in truth." Certainly, the "intensified subjective consciousness" attributed to Socrates is central to realizing truth in subjectivity.

[6] Schacht, "Kierkegaard on 'Truth is Subjectivity,'" p. 306.
[7] Hegel, *Geschichte*, p. 95. Cited in *Irony*, p.191.

69

The intensification of the self individuates it, while at the same time expressing the "paradigmatic man" (*Either/Or*) or revealing "the essentially human" (*Concluding Unscientific Postscript*). Before Dilthey, Kierkegaard sought to delineate the "categories of life" (*Lebenskategorien*) or the "existential categories" that would expose the universal traits of man insofar as he is true to "what he was meant to be."

The clearest exposition of a central existential category that deepens the selfhood of the individual is found in *Johannes Climacus*. In this essay Kierkegaard develops a phenomenology (à la Hegel) of the emergence of consciousness to demonstrate the "pain of becoming."[8] Using Hegelian terminology, he emphasizes the distinction between immediacy (or the indefiniteness of unreflective actuality) and ideality (or the thought-world of concepts and language). He seeks to show how concerned consciousness arises in the individual and what its effects or signs are. Anticipating some passages in *Concluding Unscientific Postscript*, he remarks that the question of truth arises "through untruth." By inquiring about truth, consciousness (*Bevisthed*) is brought into relation to "something else." It is "untruth'" that makes this relationship possible. It is discovered in contradiction. Immediate reality cannot be expressed in speech because we must use ideality (language) in order to express it. This is a contradiction or untruth (*Climacus*, p. 147). Consciousness is construed as this particular relational activity by which conceptual-linguistic ideality is related to actuality. Through this relational process *possibility* emerges for consciousness.

Kierkegaard distinguishes the intentional act by which the ideal is brought into relation to the actual from "reflection," that mode of thought involving a disinterested activity of the mind. Reflection or objective reflection is characteristic of logic, mathematical thinking, and metaphysical speculation; consciousness in its pri-

---

[8] *Johannes Climacus*, p. 150. What the "pain of becoming" seems to refer to is the initial stage of reflective self-consciousness, the emergence of a sense of responsibility, subjective concern, and the necessity of authentic choice.

mary sense involves the process of relating an ideal to one's own actuality. The self in such a mode of consciousness lies "in between" (*interesse*) ideality and actuality. The act of relating an ideal (say, being resolute in one's life) to one's own actuality generates concerned subjectivity, since decisiveness is necessary in order to bring to fruition what is posited as an ideal possibility. In effect, what Kierkegaard suggests is that the resolution of the contradiction between the ideal and the actual can be attained only through choice, decision, and action. And choice, decision, and action in regard to matters of concern intensify subjectivity or inwardness in existence. The subjective concern that is the basis for existential choice is a means by which a person attains subjective inwardness.

The act of concernful consciousness by which we relate an ideal possibility to our subjective actuality is paradoxical insofar as "there is already, in the very nature of things, an opposition between reality and ideality. The former gives us the particular example set in time and space. The latter gives us the universal" (*Papirer*, IV (B) 10, 7). The realization of existential possibilities (e.g., choice, resolve, willed repetition, concern, mastered irony, subjective teleology, etc.) that are all idealities intensifies the inward self. The individual realizes truth in existence, as far as possible, by appropriating them and actualizing them in his existence.

The conception of the distinction between the posited, conceptual-linguistic realm of ideals and concrete actuality is the key to the repeated references to the eternal in man. In most of Kierkegaard's writings, the words *infinite* and *eternal* are used in misleading ways. Sometimes the term *eternal* is used to refer to a transcendental realm in which there is neither movement nor change. At other times it is used as a synonym for ideality. In this regard, Croxall has correctly noted that "Eternity and Time, or in other words Ideality and Reality, . . . are in contact with each other . . . in . . . consciousness."[9] This insightful observa-

9T. H. Croxall, An Assessment, in *Johannes Climacus*, p. 85.

tion clarifies some otherwise obscure passages in *Concluding Unscientific Postscript*. For, at one point in a discussion of the distinction between God and man, Kierkegaard states that the individual is eternal. This claim is at odds with the description of man as immersed in becoming (*Vorden*), movement, and temporality. Furthermore, because movement, in the sense of psychospiritual transitions from possibility to actuality in the pursuit of a posited telos, is possible only in time; the existing individual who strives to become a genuine self cannot be eternal here and now. If the individual were eternal in time, then he would be the same, would not be subject to change and becoming, and would have no possibilities that he would seek to realize. If man were an eternal being, then his essence, in the language of medieval thought, would be identical with his existence. But existence requires striving precisely because of what Sartre calls a "lack" (or possibility) in our being, a negativity that can be vitiated only through choice and self-becoming. On this point Kierkegaard explicitly contradicts himself when he asserts that "an existing individual is . . . in process of becoming . . . for as long as he is in existence he will never become eternal" (*Postscript*, p. 368).

Even though an individual can seek a subjective and absolute relationship to an eternal being (God) or can apprehend the eternal in thought, in the sense that "all thought is eternal," he cannot legitimately be said to be eternal in existence. The fact that thought pertains to the universal or the eternal presents a difficulty for the reflective individual because "existence itself combines thinking with existing" (*Postscript*, p. 274). The point, however, is that it is false to assume that subjective existence "in truth" means that the person exists, in some way, in the eternal and is "in truth" by virtue of a participation in "eternal truth." Even though the aspirations of the man of faith may be toward the "eternal," he nonetheless exists in time and becoming and is thoroughly finite. This, of course, is not to say that he may not believe in or have faith in the possibility of immortality or "eternal life." That is quite a different matter.

72

Against the above remarks it may be argued that, in point of fact, Kierkegaard does join an anticipation of the eternal to genuine ethical existence and is, therefore, putting forward a consistent ethico-religious idea of existence "in truth." This objection, though, can be overcome by pointing to what appears to be Kierkegaard's most fundamental conception of the meaning of "eternal." Although Kierkegaard often refers to the traditional notion of the eternal as a realm without beginning or end, as that which always is, in particular instances he defends a more unusual notion. In *Concluding Unscientific Postscript*, for example, he raises a curious and revealing question. He asks, "Is it not the case that eternity is for an existing individual not eternity, but the future, and that eternity is eternity only for the Eternal, who is not in process of becoming?" (p. 273). For a finite being immersed in time and becoming, the eternal may be construed as a possible future, a possible "future life." By relating eternity as futurity to the individual who exists in process of becoming, we are able to comprehend "coming into being and futurity" (p. 273). In *The Concept of Dread*, Kierkegaard presents a similar conception of eternity. Contrasting time (as indefinite succession) with the eternal, Kierkegaard avers that

the eternal means first of all the future (which preserves past and present), or that the future is the incognito in which the eternal, as incommensurable for time, would nevertheless maintain its relation with time. . . . we sometimes speak of the future as identical with eternity: the future life—eternal life. [P. 80]

Such an interpretation of the meaning of the eternal is central to the idea of existence in truth as it is manifested in inwardness. Kierkegaard suggests that inwardness or subjectivity is the seriousness of the person and is "the determination of the eternal" in the individual (*Dread*, p. 134). In a clarification of the notion of inwardness, he equates it with seriousness concerning one's self; with concrete consciousness as a "deed"; and, of course, with subjectivity. Inwardness is understood as an expression of concrete freedom in actuality. This freedom is experienced in relation to possibility, not only in the temporal future but in the subjective anticipation of "the eternal" as an unknown future. In a religious mode of being, it is the subjective, passionate anticipation of a future eternity that establishes the eternal validity of subjective existence. However, in ethical existence it is the endeavor to relate an ideality (the universal, the eternal) to subjective actuality that signifies that the individual is striving to realize truth, as the eternal, the essential, in concrete existence. In both cases, the individual approximates authentic human existence and the truth comes to being in time.

The paradox of an ethical existence is analogous to the central paradox of Christian faith in its assumption that an eternal being (God) came into being in time in the form of the God-man. This is only an analogy, however, because as long as man lives in the world, he exists in time and becoming. *Existence* involves a repetitious movement towards the realization of an ideal possibility that entails repeated transitions from possibility to actuality in time. For the Christian man of faith, the "absolute paradox" is actually realized: the eternal comes into existence fully in time. The existential goals of ethics or religion are repeatedly sought by a finite individual who never achieves a perfect fusion of the eternal and the temporal in actuality. This is central to the paradoxical tension of human existence.

The reality of the ethically existing individual is an "intermediary state," an *interesse* ("to be between," "to be concerned") in which the person is the point of intersection between the universal and the particular, the ideal and the actual. Ethical knowledge is self-knowledge, a form of knowledge that is not objective, but may be understood as "subjective knowledge" (*Journals*, 1:289). A reflective individual is the only being to whom one can have something other than a cognitive relation. That is, the existential thinker engages in a subjective reflection upon his own existence that is unique in the sense that every other mode of reflection, including thought about another or the states of being of another, involves objectification or reflection in the form of possibility. Here Kierkegaard anticipates Sartre's view that we have no cognitive access to the "interiority" of the other, even though we are free to speculate about the *possible* subjective states of the other. The point, at any rate, is that in ethical subjectivity the individual relates thought (construed as "the eternal") to existence in his own concrete actuality. The subjective thinker engages in an "active interpenetration" of himself by means of a reflection upon his own existence that is shot through with subjective concern and passionate interest. In this "interested knowledge" or in this search for "concernful knowledge," the object of the interest or concern determines whether we are considering the ethical or the religious sphere of existence. This crucial distinction between ethical inwardness and religious inwardness is not artificially imposed upon Kierkegaard's thought. It is stated clearly in his journals and especially in a passage in *Concluding Unscientific Postscript*. Through the persona of Johannes Climacus, Kierkegaard says that

to ask with infinite interest about a reality which is not one's own, is faith, and this constitutes a paradoxical relationship to the paradoxical. . . . the sole ethical interest is the interest in one's own reality. . . . the believer differs from the ethicist in being infinitely interested in the reality of another (in the fact, for example, that God has existed in time). [P. 288]

Despite this difference between the ethicist and the man of faith (*Troen*), there is one thing they have in common. Both are directed towards an "intensive deepening of the intensive" or an inward intensity that "is the truth" (*Journals*, 2:457). In religious faith there is a paradoxical relationship between a finite self and an infinite being, a "God-relationship" that is a source of both consolation and suffering. By holding fast to the possibility of God and the possibility of the God-relationship, the religious person intensifies his existence, his inwardness, and his individuation. In this intensified state of faith the individual exists in truth. In "ethical passion," however, there is a mode of inwardness that "infinitely ac-

75

centuates the private self" (*Journals*, 2:267). In both ethical and religious subjective inwardness the intrinsic value of the person is manifested in the form of an approximation of subjective truth.

For Kierkegaard, inwardness involves a synthesis of concrete understanding and pathos. The difficulty for one who would become a true individual is to bring the existential categories into relationship to one another in the concreteness characteristic of "inwardness in existing as a human being" (*Postscript*, p. 320). Existing in truth is achieved by opening oneself to individuating states of being and by striving to realize a telos that consolidates the energies of the individual. The psychospiritual movements of the self require repetitious resoluteness. The goal of "movement" in life ought to be the attainment of selfhood or the actualization of our primitive potentiality for self-existence. As we saw earlier, the intentional act of consciousness by which an ideal is related to the actuality of the self generates subjective concern as well as possibility. The basic problem in trying to live the existential categories is relating "ideal being" (*ideel Vaeren*) to "actual being" (*actuelle Vaeren*). By striving to live in accordance with an ideal telos (e.g., becoming an ethical individual or becoming a "knight of faith"), we intensify subjectivity. The goal of becoming subjective, however, must undergo a dialectical transformation; the individual must become "objective" toward his own subjectivity. This endeavor to become objective toward our own subjective existence is a "reduplication" that serves as a "corrective." Such a "reduplication of subjectivity" is characterized by the fact that no one can attain a perfect objectivity toward himself, nor can he become so subjective as to fulfil completely what he has projected for himself in objective understanding (*Last Years*, pp. 235-36). Of course, Kierkegaard assumes that this attempt to become objective toward one's subjectivity only contributes further to the intensification of existence and thereby to the living of truth. When the question of truth is raised in regard to life, we are concerned either with a form of objective reflection in which some objective, hypothetical possibility is entertained in thought or with a form of subjective reflection in which "truth becomes a matter of appropriation." In the latter case, thought must probe more deeply into the subject and his subjective existence (*Postscript*, p. 171). By bringing thought as close as possible to the pathos of existence, the individual intensifies the paradoxical, dialectical tension of existence, or, in effect, realizes truth in existence, as far as this is possible.

Insofar as the person is able to attain existence in truth, the self is accentuated, intensified, and deepened. "Truth is subjectivity" in the sense that the truth of an authentic existence is lived or is expressed in hidden inwardness. The self of the individual in a state of truth is neither a perfect, concrete actuality nor a perfectly ideal entity that is completely fulfilled. Rather, the self that strives to exist in truth is "in between" thought and concrete actuality, is the oscillating, dynamic center that is intermediary between the two. A thought-world pertains to the eternal in the sense that the universal and concrete actuality pertain to immediacy. The existential truth of the self is found in neither, but is the intersection of both; it is the dialectical center of the ideal universal and the concrete particular. What is called the "reality-significance" (*Realitets Betydning*) of subjective existence is manifested in what Kierkegaard calls the "reality of the self." He is very careful in his language in this regard; he specifies that the reality of the truly existing person lies at the point of intersection of "ideality" and immediate "actuality." Man, and probably man alone, is the only being capable of realizing his reality in existence. If God is, then God is a perfect actuality that *is* an absolute, unconditioned "Truth." By implication, Kierkegaard suggests that nonhuman beings cannot conceive of truth and are, therefore, immersed in immediate actuality. It is precisely the paradoxical condition of man that makes possible the attempt to realize truth in existence. The paradoxical, not to say contradictory, nature of man is such because of the tension between reason and passion. Human reason can only posit or postulate truth as possible or can posit ideals that may or may not be realized. It is passion (*Lidenskab*) that is the motivational basis of action, the motivational basis of the quest to appropriate truth in existence. Objective claims to truth are always only theoretical or hypothetical possibilities. Even from the standpoint of reason, God or, more accurately, the "God-idea" is considered as a "postulate." That there is "Truth" in the sense of eternal, unchanging "Truth" is, for Kierkegaard, only logically possible from the rational point of view. It is for this reason, among others, that he insists upon the notion of truth manifested in existence. If the actuality of God is accepted in subjective faith, then in "ethical faith" there is a similar belief in the value and meaning of striving to attain the ideal of becoming subjective. Against all forms of rationalistic ethics, Kierkegaard maintains that the postulation of universal moral principles entails no moral commitment or, put in another way, rationality in ethics commands no existential assent. Pathos is essential to ethical as well as religious existence and so, too, is "faith."

No doubt Kierkegaard acquires from Christianity the insight that truth has historical significance. In the person of Christ, he believes, truth came into existence in time and becoming. This means to him that if truth in its most significant form is to be attained, it has to be attained in this world of time, process, and development. The conception of existential truth is obviously modeled upon the centerpiece of Christian faith: the eternal came into being in time. This emphasis upon the historical meaning of truth is not original but a variation on a Hegelian theme. Hegel sees the appearance of the God-man as a symbol of the meaning of world-history, as an indication that the Absolute is fulfilling itself in human history. Kierkegaard agrees with this general observation, but applies it to the historical becoming of the individual. He boldly declares that just as truth came into existence in time in the being of Christ, so, too, may truth in an analogous fashion come into existence in the becoming of the human self. Christian existence requires an "imitation" of Christ, a heterogeneity to the secular world, a renunciation of finite goals or aims. But by living out this existence, as far as this is possible, the man of faith realizes a form of subjective truth in his life by relating the eternal to his own temporal actuality. In an ethical existence, on the other hand, the individual is passionately interested in his own self-realization and is guided by the telos of realizing the ideal self in time. In another sense, this also involves an attempt to relate the eternal (in the sense of the ideal universal) to the finite actuality of the self. In both ways of existing, Kierkegaard believes, truth can be manifested in temporal actuality.

Kierkegaard does not put forward existential truth as "eternal truth," because it is restricted to *finite* existence or to what Nietzsche calls "the innocence of becoming." Subjective truth is never a permanent possession, but rather a goal that must be repeatedly pursued in transitions from possibility to actuality. It is a goal well worth striving for, Kierkegaard suggests, because it is the only modality of truth that can be lived, a value that heightens and enhances individuality. In its strictest sense, as we have seen, the eternal pertains to the future, to what may lie beyond this world of time and becoming. Kierkegaard, of course, hopes that there would be *in futuro* a reconciliation of the contradictions and injustices of existence or, expressed in other words, he has faith in the eternal as a transcendental future. Here and now, however, the aim of life ought to be to realize, as far as possible, truth in human existence. The self ought to strive to exist in truth because it knows that it can do so. In the case of Kierkegaard, it is clear that it is precisely his scepticism concerning the possibility of attaining truth by means of objective knowledge or a speculative use of reason that intensifies the importance of striving to attain subjective truth in existence. The most universal form of his faith is found in his belief that it is possible for the self to exist *in* truth.

3. Once More with Feeling: Kierkegaard's *Repetition*

> *There is only one real tragedy in a woman's life.*
> *The fact that her past is always her lover, and*
> *her future invariably her husband.*
>
> —Oscar Wilde

THE title of this book is *Repetition*. But his subject will be . . . woman. *Repetition*? About woman? Yes, in the only way it can be. By being about everything else under the sun. Woman is reality. This is not under the sun.

The book describes itself as "an essay in experimental psychology" (*Repetition*, p. 29). In his epistle to the reader the author reveals that the subject of his experiment is a fiction and his adventure is a fabrication. The narrative metonymies of the text dissimulate a metaphoric identity of truth and fiction. Unsuccessfully. This too is not in the world.

The first part of the text, not entitled, is uninterrupted narration. Its typographical continuity suppresses an intricate scheme of divisions and relations. Brought to the surface, the scheme is as in the figure on the facing page.

A)1. In the philosophical parenthesis that opens the book, Constantine Constantius reflects: recollection glances off the present moment into an idealized past, while hope turns away from the present toward an idealized future. The point would be to recuperate every present moment for the ideal and to install the ideal in every present moment, so that the actual becomes the repetition (re-presentation) of the ideal and the ideal becomes the repetition (the meaning and truth) of the actual. In this way repetition would redeem what is lost in hope and recollection alike.

The Structure of Kierkegaard's *Repetition,* Part 1

A)
B)
C)

1. An opening philosophical parenthesis, pp. 33-35.
2. The story of the young man, pp. 35-50.
3. Transition: on "the interesting," pp. 50-52.
4. A second philosophical parenthesis, pp. 52-54.
5. Constantine Constantius' trip to Berlin, pp. 54-80. [In this account is the digression on the farce, pp. 58-73, which falls outside the story.]
6. Conclusion: the apostrophe to transience and the invocation of death, pp. 80-81.

In another sense recollection and repetition are the same movement turned in opposite directions. What is recollected is repeated backwards; what is repeated is recollected forwards. Retreating from the present that is, recollection is unhappy; advancing to meet the present that comes, repetition is happy. It has "the blessed certainty of the instant" (p. 34), which is the power of endurance. Repetition is "reality . . . and the seriousness of life" (p. 35). Without it one would be a tablet on which time writes at every instant a new inscription, or a mere memorial of the past: the present irrecoverably past or perpetually passing.

Recollection is to repetition as the ancient (that is, pagan) view of life is to the modern (the Christian). On the ancient view time is without direction and without order, so that one can only "escape backwards" (upwards?) into eternity; one tries "to find a pretext for stealing out of life, alleging . . . that he has forgotten something" (p. 33). An umbrella, perhaps? On the Christian view time is ordered and directed; eternity, to which one moves through time, lies ahead at the end of history. The ancient and the modern views of life offer alternative soteriologies. The former recommends redemption from time. The latter proposes to redeem time itself: fruits, not flowers. Repetition is incarnation and resurrection.

A)4.   The discussion of repetition with which the book begins prefaces the story of the young man's unhappy love. In the brief passage that introduces his own failed attempt at repetition Constantine says that modern philosophy has not yet developed the category of repetition, but must do so: "Repetition is the new category which has to be brought to light. . . . The dialectic of repetition is easy; for what is repeated has been, otherwise it could not be repeated, but precisely the fact that it has been gives repetition the character of novelty" (p. 52). The novel is such only in relation to a past and a constant of change, else it were opaquely unique. Radical novelty is radically unintelligible and cannot even be comprehended under the rubric "novel":

When the Greeks said that all knowledge is recollection they affirmed that all that is has been; when one says that life is a repetition one affirms that existence which has been now becomes. When one does not possess the categories of recollection or of repetition, the whole of life is resolved into a void and empty noise. [Pp. 52-53]

Temporality is intelligible only in relation to the eternal. Apart from recollection or repetition, which are the possible forms of this relation, existence in time is sound and fury, signifying nothing. "Repetition is the *interest* of metaphysics, and at the same time the interest upon which metaphysics founders" (p. 53). One asks, Who am I? in the sense of, Where did I come from? in order to know, What shall I do? The temporalizing of essence makes metaphysics interesting. But since metaphysics is properly disinterested it is also the rock on which metaphysics goes aground. Therefore "repetition is the solution contained in every ethical view" (p. 53). Everything merely temporal is discretely and unrepeatably "this now." Only the continuity provided by the eternal allows for the repetition necessary to moral decision and the development of character. But the eternal alone is also an uniterated "now," and only its distribution along the course of time yields repetition. Without the possibility of repetition the moral ideal remains a bondage from which there is no release, a problem without a solution. Repetition is, finally, "a *conditio sine qua non* of every dogmatic problem" (p. 53). On the other side of faith, "repetition will have the meaning of atonement."[1] From the standpoint of Christian doctrine, repetition means the restoration of fallen human nature to the image of God.

Apart from faith, "a religious movement by virtue of the absurd,"[2] "the finite spirit falls into despair" (*Dread*, p. 17n.).[3] The first part of *Repetition*—at least the first part—is the despair of the finite spirit.

B)2. A young man falls in love. He represents immediacy. Constantine Constantius tells his story. Constantine is reflection. Or language, which is the actuality of reflection. Falling in love is an immediate passion. But no sooner has he fallen than the young man begins to recollect his love as a thing past. His recollection takes the form of language. As falling in love is to the recollection

---

[1] Sören Kierkegaard, *Sören Kierkegaards Papirer* (Copenhagen: Gyldendal, 1909-), IV B 120, p. 309; hereafter cited as *Papirer.*

[2] Ibid.

[3] The whole of the long note on pp. 16-17 of this work is relevant to Kierkegaard's concerns in *Repetition.* Cf. also Sören Kierkegaard, "Johannes Climacuor de omnibus dubitandum est," pp. 146-255. *Papirer,* IV B 97-124, deals with *Repetition* and with J. L. Heiberg's review of the work. Some of these materials are quoted in Lowrie's introduction to his translation of *Repetition,* pp. 7-28.

of love, so the young man is to Constantine Constantius.

In the letter to the reader with which he concludes his book, however, Constantine confesses that he has imagined the young man. And Constantine himself is a pseudonym of Sören Kierkegaard. The plot(s) thicken(s). Constantine's immediacy is his concern to know whether repetition is possible. He creates the young man and his story as a "psychological experiment" to try the possibility of repetition. But there is also Sören Kierkegaard's immediacy, which impels him to inscribe this fiction and ascribe it to a figment. Kierkegaard's immediacy is his unhappy relationship to Regine Olsen. The book is, in its multiply indirect way, Kierkegaard's attempt to scout the possibility of repetition with Regine. The faulted repetition of the young man is, across all the intervening distances of reflection, Kierkegaard's own.

Like Kierkegaard himself, the young man cannot marry the girl. And so, saved not by the grace of God but by the magnanimity of woman, he becomes (take that word in the strongest possible sense) . . . a poet. The actuality of Sören Kierkegaard is his texts. He is a discourse. Everything—Kierkegaard, his fictions, and his fictions' fictions—is language.

In the first part of *Repetition* there is no repetition. No recuperation of immediacy on the other side of reflection. In the book as a whole (we shall have to ask if it is a whole) there are none but faulted repetitions. Unless we count Job. But we shall have to ask: in what sense is Job (*Job?*) in this book?

The young man's recollection of his love distances the girl. It also breaches his identity with himself. He is in love with the girl. Call that relation 1:

$$YM\text{----}\overset{R1}{\text{----}}\text{----}G.$$

He recollects his love for the girl. Call that relation 2:

$$(YM\text{----}\overset{R1}{\text{----}}\text{----}G)\text{----}\overset{R2}{\text{----}}\text{----}[YM].$$

He recalls his love by repeating again and again a stanza of Poul Möller's *The Aged Lover*. Call that anticipation of senility relation 3:

$$(YM\text{------}\overset{R1}{\text{------}}G)\text{------}\overset{R2}{\text{------}}[YM]\text{------}\overset{R3}{\text{------}}(YM\ old).$$

Reflection preserves the virginity of the girl by effecting the impotence of her lover.

The young man's recollection of his love for the girl, a recollection that follows directly upon his first falling in love, effaces his presence to her by thrusting it into the past. Being in love is transformed by reflection into the preterite having been in love. The same recollection thrusts the young man into the future and effaces his presence to himself. By reflection he becomes an old man who has lived his life and can recollect it only in the same impuissance of absolute seniority. The agent of this double effect is language: poetry.

In the event there is no presence at all. The young man and the girl are absent from each other and from their original relationship. The young man is distanced from himself. Only the girl abides intact in the self-presence of her immediacy; an immediate self-presence, however, which as such must remain a fruitless *an sich.* In the absence of a unity of immediacy and reflection there is no hope of repetition. The young man has lost his immediacy, the girl has not attained to reflection (she does not speak in this book), and their love can never enter upon the repetition of marriage.

The condition of woman's virginity is the impotence of her lover. Woman is reality, a reality not enlightened by the sun of reflection. Existence remains pristine because reflection is powerless to invade it. Being is forever too young; reflection is always already too old. Reality not illumined by consciousness remains in the dark. In the glare of reflection it cannot be seen. In the day as in the night all cows are invisible. There is neither marrying nor giving in marriage.

(This story, which is at first presented as a case history, is at the end re-presented as Constantine's recollection of his own creation. Constantine's visit to Berlin both repeats an earlier visit and parodies the young man's dilemma. Yet Constantine has imagined the young man, and all that he says and does is calculated to "throw light upon him.")

When the girl finally marries someone else (the young man reads about it in the paper), her loss of innocence restores the young man's potency . . . as a poet, not a husband. His repetition, which only doubles his reflective self-awareness, is not perfected. A Job would have married the girl, *quia absurdum*, but the young man can do nothing. Constantine says:

He was in love, deeply and sincerely in love; that was evident, and yet at once, on one of the first days of his engagement, he was capable of recollecting his love. Substantially he was through with the whole relationship. Before he begins he has taken such a terrible stride that he has leapt over the whole of life. . . . Recollection has the great advantage that it begins with the loss, hence it is secure, for it has nothing to lose. . . . His mistake was incurable, and his mistake was this, that he stood at the end instead of at the beginning. But such a mistake is certainly a man's undoing.

And yet I maintain the correctness of his mood as an erotic mood, and the man who in his experience of love has not experienced it thus precisely at the beginning, has never loved. Only he must have another mood alongside of this. . . . It must be true that one's life is over at the first instant, but there must be vitality enough to kill this death and transform it into life. [Pp. 38-40]

Yet there is no vitality at all. The lover can only recollect his love and spout poetry. The girl can never become a woman. She is merely the occasion that awakens his poetic gift. By making him a poet, turning him into language, she signs her own death warrant. She is remanded to perpetual virginity, and he is committed to a guilt he cannot expiate.

Of course, he has options. He could go ahead and marry the girl anyway. But that would be a lie, since they are essentially unmarriageable. He could tell her the truth; that she is only a semblance of the ideal, a figure of something more important than herself. But that would mortify her, and his pride will not allow him that. Or he might arrange to make himself despicable in her eyes. Following Constantine's plan, he might cause her to believe that he is living in sin with a loose woman. Believing that, she would surely break off the relationship herself. Thus retaining her own integrity, she would restore his freedom. But he lacks strength for this option.

He remains, therefore, the melancholy knight of recollection. A Job would have married the girl.

B)5.   Although it is prophesied on the first page of his book, Constantine Constantius's second trip to Berlin parodies the sad story of his young friend. Having once experienced (i.e., recollecting) a half day of absolute contentment, certain that he will never enjoy the same experience again, Constantine nonetheless becomes interested in the possibility of such a repetition. As an experiment to test this possibility, he undertakes to repeat an earlier sojourn in Berlin, of which he has the most pleasant memories. Hoping to match his recollections of the first visit, he settles in the same apartment, frequents the same cafes, attends the same theaters. But all the particulars have altered, Berlin is not the same, and the experiment fails.

That is the parody. Or part of it. In the young man's case repetition would have to occur at the level of spirit through the agency of freedom. For him repetition would have meant the recovery by an alienated spirit of its lost immediacy. But Constantine expects immediacy to confirm his recollections. And that expectation spoils the whole thing. Constantine himself is clear about this—more or less:

I discovered that there is no such thing as repetition, and I had convinced myself of this by trying in every possible way to get it repeated. . . . Time and again I conceived the idea of repetition and grew enthusiastic about it—thereby becoming again a victim of my zeal for principles. For I am thoroughly convinced that, if I had not taken that journey for the express purpose of assuring myself of the possibility of repetition, I should have diverted myself immensely on finding everything the same. What a pity that I cannot keep to the ordinary paths, that I will have principles, that I cannot go clad like other men, that I will walk in stiff boots! . . . How . . . can one get so foolish an idea as that of repetition, and, still more foolishly, erect it into a principle? [Pp. 76, 79-80]

Constantine's parody, like any other worthy the name, exposes the weaknesses, the lines of stress, and the concealed hiatuses in the structure it "copies backwards" (*Fragments*, p. 63).[4] To make a principle of repetition, to try for it, is exactly what makes it impossible. Repetition must occur in the realm of the spirit: it is the recovery of nature by and for freedom. It does not just happen. But it may not be contrived. Shrewdness is of no use. The recovery of immediacy by and for reflection is not another immediacy (though it may be a *new* immediacy); neither is it a further reflection. Immediacy is gone as soon as it is there, and reflection is incurable.

Job might say: It takes a thunderstorm. But Constantine Constantius does not believe in thunderstorms.

And yet. Although Constantine's experience is a travesty, it is still a repetition. A parodic repetition. And it does incorporate several repetitions. Constantine's failure to achieve a repetition is repeated so often in Berlin that he finally becomes weary of repetition (p. 76). But these *are* parodies, repetitions in reverse, in which life takes again (*tager igjen*) what it gives without giving a repetition (*Gjentagelse*) (p. 77).

Constantine's serious preoccupation is something he calls "the interesting." In principle unrepeatable, the interesting is a token of transience, which is a portent of death. Figures on the ground of nothingness.

---

[4]"Parody" in this passage renders *bagvendt copierer*, "to copy backward."

C)3. The interesting "does not lend itself to repetition" (p. 30). "A girl who does not crave the interesting believes in repetition. Honor to her who is such by nature [immediacy], honor to her who became such in time [by repetition]." But "a girl who craves the interesting becomes the trap in which she herself is caught" (p. 52). The interesting is something from which a wise girl can save a man, something that a foolish girl might elicit from him. The interesting is not defined, but Constantine's metaphor is sexual. And a metaphor, while it may be no argument, is no accident either. It is the metaphor of accident. What is it that women (the wrong kind) desire in a man, from which other women (the right kind) would redeem him? Seduction, from which a man (!) is saved by marriage. By the magnanimity of woman.

It is not accidental that the metaphor of accident dominates this transitional episode in the text. The interesting is the confinium between the actual and the ideal, conceived aesthetically as the occasion of surprise. A threshold. The same threshold, ethically conceived, is opportunity: the opportunity, earnestly desired by the resolute will, to actualize the moral ideal. Marriage, for example. For sure. Interest, as opposed to the interesting. Repetition is reality and the seriousness of life, the interest on which metaphysics founders, and the solvent of ethics. The interesting, a thing of no essential interest, is the interruption of the ideal by the anomalous actual. From which, once you succumb to it, there is no salvation but repetition: the sine qua non of dogmatics. For example?

Seduction cannot be repeated. The seducing male requires novelty and variety: a constant supply of original sexual occasions. He is obliged to run wild. For the feminine victim seduction is, simpliciter, the loss of innocence, *einmalig* and irreparable. A trap. Virtue is something that men must acquire but women can only lose. There is no repetition in seduction. You can only (be) seduce(d) once. Marriage is the renunciation of seduction. Seduction is either an interminable pursuit or a dead end. For the male, transience; for the female, death. The two are indistinct.

The feminist phalanx will advance on this argument. But it is only a metaphor. It is interesting (is it an accident?) that Constantine fills this interval of his story with the account of an occasion on which he refused a chance at seduction. He does that more than once.

C)6. Transience and death. The first part of *Repetition* ends with that. Constantine apostrophizes the post horn ("that is my instrument"), which is a symbol of transience and the impossibility of repetition. On this instrument you can never play the same note twice. Or, what is worse, you can not be sure of it (p. 80).

Temporality is the rhetoric of death. Life, neither comic nor tragic, is interesting. But life does not captivate like death. Death has the superior eloquence: *peisithanatos*. By the transience of life it persuades all things to mortality. A conclusion of sorts. Of this, no repetition. This is the despair, and the hope, of the finite spirit.

Hors-texte

The first half of *Repetition* ends with Constantine Constantius (and, we may presume, the young man) giving up on repetition. The whole of part one is calculated to enforce this defeat. But there is a part of the first part that falls outside its structure: at once outside and inside the trinity of binaries that organizes this region of the text. We have:

A)1 and A)4: Recollection versus repetition
B)2 and B)5: The stories of the young man and Constantine Constantinus.
C)3 and C)6: Repetition (in the sense: redemption from "the interesting") versus the triumph of transience and death

Embedded in B)5, in the structural center of the text, is the digression on the theater occasioned by Constantine's visit to the Königstäter in Berlin. This is no accident.

Concerning the theater in general Constantine writes:

> Surely there is no young man with any imagination who has not at
> one time been captivated by the enchantment of the theater, and de-
> sired himself to be carried away into the midst of that fictitious
> [*kunstige*] reality in order to see and hear himself as an *alter ego*
> [*Doppeltgaenger*], to disperse himself among the innumerable possibil-
> ities which diverge from himself [*i sin al-mulige Forskjellighed fra
> sig selv*], and yet in such a way that every diversity is in turn a single
> self. Of course it is only at a very early age such a desire can express
> itself. Only the imagination is awake to its dream of personality, all
> the other faculties are still sound asleep. In such a dream of imagina-
> tion the individual is not a real figure but a shadow, or rather the
> real figure is invisibly present and therefore is not content with casting
> one shadow, but the individual has a multiplicity of shadows, all of
> which resemble him and for the moment have an equal claim to be
> accounted himself. [p. 58]

Through the agency of that fictitious reality (the theater), the
youth, all of whose egos are alter, is enabled to disperse himself
among numberless possibilities. All these selves are imaginary,
mere shadows; and equivalently, since his other powers are dor-
mant, each of them is himself. Or would be, were it not for that
invisible presence:

> Every possibility of the individual is therefore a sounding shadow. The
> cryptic individual no more believes in the great noisy feelings than he
> does in the crafty whisper of malice, no more in the blissful exalta-
> tion of joy than in the infinite sigh of sorrow; the individual only
> wants to hear and see with pathos, but, be it observed, to hear and
> see himself. However it is not really himself he wants to hear. That
> is not practicable. At that instant the cock crows, and the figures of
> the twilight flee away, the voices of the night fall silent. If they con-
> tinue, then we are in an entirely different domain, where all this goes
> on under the alarming observation of moral responsibility, then we
> are at the demoniacal. In order not to get an impression of his real
> self, the cryptic individual requires that the environment be as light
> and ephemeral as the figures, as the frothy effervescence of the words

which sound without echo. Such an environment is the stage, which for this reason precisely is appropriate to the shadow-play of the cryptic individual. [Pp. 59-60]

The play provides a show of possibilities for the *cryptic* one: the person who is still hidden within himself, buried in the crypt of his immediacy. Until the cock crows (for the third time?), announcing the dawn of moral responsibility, such a man can only imagine his being, still secreted from himself, as a procession of evanescent passions. Because he requires an ephemeral environment, figures of foam, and words without resonance, a man like this desires the serious theater: it is all the reality he has; the stage is "not merely for pleasure" (p. 67).

But the mature person turns to farce:

Although in the individual life this moment vanishes, yet it is reproduced in a riper age when the soul has seriously collected itself. Yes, although art is perhaps not serious enough for the individual then, he may perhaps have pleasure in turning back occasionally to that first state and rehearsing it [repeating it, not practicing it] in sentiment. [Once more with feeling: *i en Stemning.*] He wishes now to be affected comically, and to be himself in a comically productive relation to the theatrical performance. Therefore, though neither tragedy nor comedy can please him, precisely because of their perfection, he turns to the farce. [P. 61]

Second time as farce. All the characters and situations of farce are types: abstract generalities represented in fortuitously concrete particulars. (Constantine is having a bit of fun at Schiller's expense. Naïve is to sentimental as serious theater is to farce. Naïveté diffuses its reality in the imaginary; or rather, since it has no reality as yet, it *is* the imaginary. Sentimentality recovers the reality it has never lost, farcically, in the instantiation of the imaginary by the accidental.)

After the ideal comes in the very next place the accidental. A wit has said that one might divide mankind into officers, serving-maids, and chimney-sweeps. To my mind this remark is not only witty but

92

profound, and it would require a great speculative talent to devise a better classification. When a classification does not ideally exhaust its object, a haphazard classification is altogether preferable, because it sets imagination in motion. A tolerably true classification is not able to satisfy the understanding, it is nothing for the imagination, and hence it is to be totally rejected, even though for everyday use it enjoys much honor for the reason that people are in part very stupid and in part have very little imagination. When at the theatre one would have a representation of a man, one must either require a concrete form corresponding absolutely to the ideal, or else the fortuitous. . . . In the case of farce, the subordinate actors produce their effect by means of that abstract category "in general" and attain this by a fortuitous concretion. With this one has got no further than to reality. Nor should one seek to go further; but the spectator is reconciled comically by seeing this fortuitous concretion claiming to be the ideal, which it does by treading into the fictitious world [*Kunst-Verden*] of the stage. [Pp. 66-67]

The superiority of the farce (for mature persons) consists in this: in the farce the accidental secures reality, or the effect of reality, for the essential. Comically, the ideal generality achieves fortuitous concretion. Like Beckmann's ability to "come walking" (literally *at komme gaaende* (p. 68), "to come going"), by which he creates an environment for himself.

Farce therefore is the comical repetition. You do not even have to follow it closely and carefully; you can watch it as casually as it presents itself. In the farce the ideal and the actual are reconciled in laughter, a laughter produced as much by the capricious attention of the observer as by the wholly gratuitous events on the stage.

Of course: this farcical repetition has its serious side. The girl in the box opposite Constantine's, maybe also the lady at the inn, surely the farm girl whose idyllic ambience concludes the digression on the theater; all of them are women whom Constantine scrupulously refuses to seduce. The tender gravity of these scenes is a necessary supplement of (is it also finally superior to?) the raucous laughter of the Königstäter's gallery. The farcical repetition,"blissful" as it is (p. 71), is an experience of exuberance, but is for that reason unsettling. It needs to be put to rest (p. 71) by the reality (or is it the dream?) of innocence (p. 72) and by the promise (or is it the illusion?) of true love. "Happy girl! If ever a man should win your love, would that you might make him as happy by doing everything for him as you have made me by doing nothing for me" (p. 73).

The digression on the farce tells what the first part of *Repetition* shows. As in the farce, so in the first part of this book, the only viable meaning of repetition (is it unsettling or pacifying?) is the chance conjunction of the abstract ideal and the unmotivated actual. Freedom and nature accidentally made one. An uncertain and unstable recuperation that begs, sentimentally, for the reality it comically dissimulates.

Like life itself, the farce is neither tragic nor comic but ambiguously shuttles back and forth in the space between. Interesting. It may even be of interest.

A whore-text? Maybe a pretext. . . .

The first part of *Repetition* is untitled. Part two, repeating the title of the book, calls itself "Repetition." A repetition within the work of the work as a whole. (What does that do to its integrity?) And the accomplishment at last of that project which in the first part was abandoned in despair. Now it begins in earnest. Again. (What does that do to the accomplishment?)

The architecture of part one was intricate and insidiously concealed. By contrast, the divisions of part two are simple, symmetrical, and plainly marked:

A) Constantine Constantius: introductory essay, pp. 82-91.
B) The young man: letters to Constantine Constantius (August 15-February 17), pp. 92-120. (These letters include the discourse on *Job*.)
C) Constantine Constantius: second essay, pp. 121-24.

D) The young man: letter to Constantine Constantius (May 31), pp. 125-27.

E) Constantine Constantius: letter to "N. N., this book's real reader," dated at Copenhagen, August 1843, pp. 129-37.

A) Constantine's introductory essay, written some time after his return from Berlin, assesses the young man's condition in the wake of his unfortunate engagement. "There is nothing left for him," Constantine says, "but to make a religious movement" (p. 87). The realization of his love being impossible—it "cannot be declined in accordance with the case forms of the regular declensions" (p. 87)—it can come about, if at all, only "by virtue of the absurd" (p. 88). He is melancholy by nature (pp. 83, 87-88, 91). And his nature is androgynous (pp. 84, 87).

In the first part of this book Constantine Constantius is the androgyne. He is moved to feminine devotion by the melancholy beauty and the passionate intensity of his young friend. But he is masculine-manipulative at the same time, in relation to the youth and all the other subjects of his psychological experimentation. Part two of *Repetition* (the "repetition") begins with a reversal of roles.

Like a woman the young man requires positive assurance of the legitimacy of his confidante: some token of trustworthiness. But like a man he wants a negative guarantee: he would as soon unburden himself to a madman or a tree (p. 86). The sexual ambiguity of the young man puts Constantine in an equally ambiguous position. He is both being and nonbeing, at the whim of his friend (pp. 83-84). Constantine, whom formerly he regarded as queer, he now describes (Constantine alludes proleptically to the young man's letter of August 15) as mentally deranged. Constantine does not resent this attribution. It almost flatters him. As he says, "Now he knows my most intimate secret" (pp. 83, 86, 87). Eventually, Constantine conjectures, the young man will kill him with his confidence. The position of an observer is dangerous.

The girl, when her fiancé disappears, is at first unaffected and only gradually slumbers "gently into a dreamy obscurity as to what has occurred and what it might mean" (p. 84). Another ambiguity. Both physically and spiritually the young man has vanished to a place unknown, leaving behind him a girl adrift, a confidant in a contradictory situation bordering on madness and death, and . . . uncertainty. A story that begins abruptly, ends indecisively, and bears ambiguous meanings, or none at all.

The youth himself is in a state of ambivalence. Really, but he imagines himself still in love with the girl, an imagining thrown up by his melancholy and his androgynous sympathy. He is, more than all else, captivated by the regret that he may have done the girl a terrible wrong. May have. This too is not certain. Is his guilt real or, like his love, only imagined?

At the outset of part two the positions of the personae are perfectly indeterminate, and the future of the narrative is obscure. Three undecided people in an undecidable relationship. Equivocation on all hands has settled into indifference. But: a troubled indifference. It may be the quiet just before the storm.

The young man wants to "come back." His problem has narrowed itself to a point:

Indubitably it is not possession in the strictest sense which concerns him, or the content which develops from this situation; what concerns him is return, conceived in a purely formal sense. Though she were to die the day after, it would not any more disturb him, he would not feel the loss, for his nature would be at rest. The discord into which he has been thrown by contact with her would be resolved [*forsonet*] by the fact that he had actually returned to her. So again the girl is not a reality but a reflection of the movements within him and their exciting cause. The girl has a prodigious meaning, he actually will never be able to forget her, but what gives her meaning is not herself but her relation to him. She is as it were the boundary of his being. But such a relation is not erotic. Religiously speaking, one might say that it was as if God himself employed the girl to capture him; and yet the girl herself is not a reality but is like the artificial flies one sleaves upon hooks. [Pp. 88-89]

What concerns the young man is return in a purely formal sense. The girl is not the obscure object of desire but only a reflection of the movements within himself. And their efficient cause. She has momentous significance, not erotically but as the limit of his being. She is, like the characters and situations in a farce, the fortuitous intrusion of transcendence into the circuit of reflection. But her effect is not comic. Her reality slants the indifference and disturbs the ambiguity of the dialectic. Something stirring in the depths that ever so slightly ruffles the surface.

She is like the bait on a fishhook with which God proposes to capture the young man for himself. The cross of Christ is a fishhook and Christ himself the bait with which God catches the devil.

What baffles the young man is neither more nor less than repetition: return in the purely formal sense (p. 90). And repetition is always transcendence: the eruption of the other into the circuit of the same. No other way to the reconciliation of the alienated. Therefore the young man gets no help from Constantine Constantius or from the philosophers ancient or modern. Immanence (here: reflection) is of no use. His problem is religious, and no man can solve it. So he turns to Job.

Job too was bait. The stake, ostensibly, in a wager between God and Satan. But in fact: the bait with which God caught his unruly son.

Constantine will not deny the reality of repetition. How could he? But he cannot manage a religious movement. And his desire—that he might induce the girl to persuade the young man that she is married so as to disengage him from his melancholy conviction that he loves her—is offset (ambivalence again) by his misgiving—that the bait might be tempted to play God, that the girl might decide to capture the youth for herself by appealing to his melancholy (pp. 90-91). In that case, Constantine fears, the matter will come to a bad end—for the girl. The young man's revenge on existence, for making him guilty when he was innocent, would become the revenge of existence on the girl, for wanting to exploit his guilt (pp. 89, 91).

Suppose that Job, or Christ, had decided to catch the Devil himself.

Constantine's assessment of the situation ends as part two begins, uneasily poised between the absurd possibility of repetition and the dreadful possibility of irrecoverable loss.

B) *August 15.* We have already had, in Constantine Constantius's opening essay, a review of this letter. The original first appears as the revisitation of a revision. It repeats, from the young man's point of view, what has already been repeated from Constantine's perspective. The indeterminateness and ambiguity of the situation, reported dispassionately in Constantine's essay, are here pathetically suffered. Constantine's madness, which concerns himself only analytically, is here confronted with fervent horror. The repetition of the repetition is the origin of the beginning.

The young man (he has never been named) has lost his own name and acquired a false name. He desires no name. Not his own, which (still unnamed) belongs to the girl (whose name he never utters), and not a glorious name if it is not his own (p. 99). Throughout this correspondence he signs himself "your devoted nameless friend," "your nameless friend," "devotedly yours," and sometimes "   " (pp. 100, 103, 108, 111, 116, 118, 120, 127).

In his self-imposed exile (he is in Stockholm but gives no address) the young man exhausts himself in aimless and fruitless activities. "The man who believes in existence," he says, is as well insured as the man who, to hide his feelings when he prays, holds before his face a hat without a crown (p. 100). But life evokes no feelings and existence is void of meaning: it smells of nothing (p. 104). The nihilism is bleak and total: Constantine, the girl, and the young man, are all brought to nothing, like clouds that tumble down into the womb of earth and there make their grave (p. 100).

That, depressingly enough, is the state of affairs at the beginning of the second part of the story. The decisive event reported in the letter of August 15 is the young man's loss of his name. The loss of his name, a name that he has never had, expands to become the loss of name-in-general: the loss of the function of the name.

Identities evaporate on every hand: impending madness, inexponible grief, the distraction of unaccountable guilt. Impotently ambivalent, language collapses in the confusion of tongues. Words, words, words.

The Job Letters

Beginning with the letter of *September 19*, a new language and a new text are woven into the language of this text: a text and a language called *Job*. A different discourse altogether. Job contends with God and makes his complaint before Him. A loud complaint that echoes in heaven and evokes, in response, the voice of the thunderstorm. The language of Job breaks through the bounds of immanence and forces a word from beyond. As Job is to his comforters, so the young man is to the "miserable shrewdness" (p. 102) of Constantine Constantius. As Job is to God, so the young man is to . . . ? The movement of transgression begins. Transcendence hangs in the air like the calm before a storm.

In the letter of *October 11* the speech of Job is contrasted with human language, a wretched invention that says one thing and means another, the miserable jargon of a clique, a collection of poems, proverbs, and pithy sayings gleaned from the classics and from *Balle's Lesson Book*. Human language has no words for the young man; it cannot without contradicting itself tell the truth about his condition. At this moment, however, the young man is already beginning to speak of himself in the language of *Job* (p. 104). Even as he complains of the inadequacy of human speech, he inscribes his predicament in this new and (from a human point of view) paradoxical system of signs. The canonical text, breaking into the discourse of man, restructures and rewrites it. But to describe himself in the language of Job is not to make himself intelligible to men. The young man and his problem remain (from a human point of view) nameless.

The transcendent, which here takes the form of the sacred

Scripture, bursts irrationally into the normal and (from the human point of view) normative conversation of the world. Where did Job come from? He appears abruptly and without explanation at the beginning of the letter of September 19: "Job! Job! O! Job!" (p. 101). His eruption into the correspondence at this point has the effect of deforming all its words and deranging all its significations, from henceforth.

"Existence," the young man writes, "is surely a debate" (p. 104). Between God and man? Man is rationality is language. The other than man is the irrational, the language man cannot speak. God?

In the letter of *November 15* the young man says that he sleeps (not with the girl but) with the words of Job under his pillow. He makes transcripts of them in characters of all sorts on sheets of all sizes. But he will not (though in these letters he repeatedly does) quote them. That would be to appropriate them. Even as he makes them his own, the young man knows they do not apply. Except as therapy. The words of Job, transcribed, are a divine poultice, laid like the healing hand of God upon his sick heart.

Job is stationed at the confines of poetry (p. 110). In the same breath: he stands at the limits of faith (p. 115).

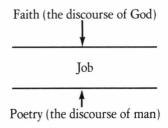

As the language of God, Job cannot be quoted. His speech is inappropriate and may not be appropriated. But if Job is "a poetical figure, if there never was any man who talked like this, then I make his words mine and assume the responsibility" (p. 110). The real Job may not be represented in the discourse of man. Job as *figura dictionis* goes without remainder into the letters of the young man, himself at most a poet and at last a poetic figure.

Between faith and poetry there is only silence. A silence broken broken by Job's anguished cries. "This I understand, these words I make my own. The same instant I sense the contradiction, and then I smile at myself as one smiles at a little child who has put on his father's clothes" (p. 111). Were anyone but Job to say what he says, the effect would be humorous. And still the mere reading of these words produces dread.

Job and the girl are beginning to converge. She too is a boundary of the young man's being, as if dropped there by God to captivate him. Nothing in herself, she is, like a fishing lure, artifice to the angler and reality to the fish. At the limit that divides being from nonbeing (p. 89). The boundary situation is the scene of this text and the place at which repetition is (not conceivable, but) by virtue of the absurd possible.

The interesting is also at the borderline. The confinium between life and death. Repetition is the interest of metaphysics, but where the possibility of repetition beckons, the threat of seduction looms. There is more than one way to be surprised.

The next three letters are preoccupied with categories of the boundary. *December 14.* Job is in the right. But his rectitude transgresses the limits of human jurisprudence. Every interpretation of his case misunderstands it. He and God understand one another, but this understanding cannot be rendered in human language. The passion of freedom within him "is not stifled or tranquilized by a false expression" (p. 112). Beyond the jurisdiction of man, he takes leave of his friends, certain that God can explain everything, if only one can get Him to speak.

Job is subjected to a trial of probation. But this is a thing unspeakable, a phenomenon that escapes every science. Job is made the exception, in whom ethical and religious categories (the human and the divine) collide. Both sacrifice and phoenix, he burns and blooms in the fire of purification. "The border conflicts incident to faith are fought out in him." He is "the whole weighty plea presented on man's behalf in the great suit between God and man."

Therefore "probation" is not expressed in the discourse of immanence. "Neither aesthetic, nor ethical, nor dogmatic, it is entirely transcendent" (p. 115). To be on trial as Job is on trial is to stand in contradiction to the divine: Job is the plea of man spoken against the judgment of God. Of a single man. Job's trial is *his* thing. It exceeds explanation "at second hand." Not the sublation of time into eternity, which would "erase . . . reality as a whole" (p. 116), Job's probation is the confrontation and reconciliation of time and eternity in time. A repetition. Dealt into this game by the wager in heaven, advised by an expert to "curse God and die," the chosen one plays out his hand. He cannot win. Barring a change in the weather.

January 13. Job gets his repetition. At the precise moment when it is perfectly clear that all is lost, the storm breaks:

Job is blessed and has received everything *double*. This is what is called a *repetition*. How much good a thunderstorm does after all! How blessed it must be after all to be reproved of God! . . . Who could have conceived this conclusion? And yet no other conclusion is conceivable—and neither is this. When everything has come to a standstill, when thought is brought to a halt, when speech becomes mute, when explanation turns homeward in despair—then there must be a thunderstorm. Who can understand this? And yet who can discover anything else?

Did Job lose his case? Yes, eternally; for he can appeal to no higher court than that which judged him. Did Job win his case? Yes, eternally, because he lost his case *before God.*

So then there is a repetition. When does it make its appearance? That is not easy to say in any human language. When did it appear for Job? When all conceivable human certainty and likelihood had found it impossible. [P. 117]

And so (*February 17*) the young man awaits *his* thunderstorm: the repetition that will restore his potency and make him a husband.

Job is acquitted . . . by the *Donnerwort* that condemns him. Had he won his case against God, he would have demonstrated conclusively that life cannot be endured. The swift logic of a woman. It is a parlous thing (the education of Eve) to win your case against God. Happily Job loses and so, absurdly, wins.

When human language has exhausted its powers and broken against the boundary of transcendence, then God may speak. When the discourse of man has talked itself out, then the voice from the whirlwind may ask its devastating and redeeming questions.

C) Constantine is not impressed. He thinks the young man badly confused. Against all logic he expects a thunderstorm to make him a husband. But, although he thinks himself fortunate that he did not "follow your admirable clever plan" (p. 118), he would still be well advised to get rid of the girl. That is the way of a man with a maid, or the way of reflection confronted with an awkward and inconvenient reality. The youth suffers from an "untimely melancholy magnanimity" (p. 121) that only a poet's brain could nurture. Let him take a religious view of his predicament and misread nervous apoplexy as divine intervention. He would have done better to exhaust his human shrewdness. Or Constantine's, since the young man himself seems to have none.

As usual, Constantine is right, in his way. Human shrewdness must be carried at least to the breaking point, and the young man may, too, previously have cast himself as an erotic Job. How does one know when he has reached the limit?

The young man is a disappointment to his mentor (his poet). He has not respected the ideal possibilities inherent in his situation. No help may be expected from the girl. Women (so Constantine) are incapable of the ideal, though they routinely use it as a ruse with which to dupe poets. The unhappy lover has not employed the idea as a regulative principle in the conduct of this affair. Even he admits that his flight to Stockholm, a particularity infinitely remote from the ideal, was a bungling and mediocre move. In these circumstances there is little chance of a thunderstorm.

Into the young man's overheated and long-winded pathos, his frantic invocation of Job, and his fascination with thunderstorms, Constantine's Olympian detachment, his algebraic summary of the ideal options, and his curt dismissal of the whole performance as a mass of confusion and misprision come like a blast of cold analytic air. The place needed airing. Repetition is possible, by virtue of the absurd, only after the exhaustion of human possibility. But to use up the humanly possible means not only to carry oneself in passion to the point at which, all passion spent and all the discourse of passion voided, one is exposed to the whirlwind. It also requires the dialectical reduction of this passionate evacuation to ludicrous misconception and bungling malfeasance. The romantic agony is incomplete without the ironic deflation.

Both Constantine and the young man are textual fictions produced by Constantine Constantius (it is not as clear about Job).

D)   Reality (not Sören Kierkegaard) surprises both of them. Without consulting her lover or his confidant or (presumably) the ideal possibilities, the girl finds a husband:

She is married—to whom I do not know, for when I read it in the paper it was as though I had a stroke of apoplexy, and I lost the notice and have not had patience to make a closer inspection. I am again myself, here I have the repetition, I understand everything, and existence seems to me more beautiful than ever. It came as a thunderstorm, too, though I owe it to her magnanimity that it happened. [p. 125]

When his beloved marries someone else, the young man loses no time in fulfilling Constantine's predictions. He calls it a thunderstorm, though he admits it felt a bit like apoplexy (cf. p. 121). And he attributes his release to feminine magnanimity (cf. pp. 46, 48, 123).

But he gets his repetition. "I am again myself. . . . The discord in my nature is resolved, I am again unified. . . . Did I not get myself again, precisely in such a way that I must doubly feel its

significance? . . . The magic spell which bewitched me so that I
could not return to myself has now been broken. . . . I am born
to myself" (pp. 125, 126).

"I belong to the idea" (p. 126). The self to which he is restored
is not his immediacy. *That* he could only have recovered in marriage by virtue of the absurd. A religious movement. He is instead
restored by virtue of the magnanimity of woman, to the idea. He is
(re)born as a poet—to "the flight of thought, . . . the service of
the idea" (p. 127)—when the girl (woman is reality) takes herself
out of the way. Ilithia unfolds her hands (!), and a man is born
again. But he returns not to his primal state, that first fine
rapture of first love, but to his subsequent recollection of love.
A recollection that has made him happy at last by making him
miserable at first. He is released not to the sobriety of the actual
but to the inebriation of the ideal.

His repetition, therefore, is ever so slightly faulted, his return
ever so slightly abbreviated, and his rebirth ever so slightly aborted.
It is difficult not to sense an undertone of cynicism, ever so slight,
in his panegyric to the magnanimity of woman.

Like the letter of *November 15,* which wonders whether Job is
a real man or a poetical figure, this one has no closure. Like all
of them, it bears no signature.

E) Constantine Constantius's concluding letter is addressed to
"Mr. N. N., this book's real reader" (p. 129). The real reader of
this book is masculine. He is also "a fictitious figure [*en poetisk
Person*]" (p. 131). N. N., who is "not a plurality but only one"
(p. 131), is something of an ideal reader, who reads the book, as
opposed to the host of unreal readers (carefully listed and identified by Constantine) who read in(to) the book only their own
anxieties, prejudices, desires, professional psychoses, and privileged
doctrines.

Constantine writes like Clement of Alexandria, so that the here-
tics will not be able to understand him. But the real reader will
perceive, through the "inverted development" (p. 132) of the

thought, what the book is about: the dialectical struggle whereby the exception breaks with the universal and is justified not by getting around it but by going through it. Like Jacob/Israel wrestling with the angel. Like Job contending with God. Like the one sinner who repents, over against the ninety and nine just persons who need no repentance. Or like the poet emerging victorious from his conflict with existence.

The poet, as a justified exception to the universal, is a stage on the way to that superior exception, the religious man. The universal, that which is required of every man (the word *Almene* also means, "common, general, public"), is a coherence of freedom and nature confected by duty. Marriage, for example. And in principle: the marriage of Kant's practical freedom and Hegel's ethical substance. Constantine's young man is justified when existence itself (reality is woman) absolves him from his guilt: that he has defaulted his obligation to being by recollecting it rather than wedding it. In the nick of time the girl withdraws her accusing presence and releases the poet into his exceptional absence. The debt is canceled, and the account is cleared.

His liberation ab extra is quasi-religious. But only "as if." He is never more than latently religious. For the young man repetition is not "reality and . . . the seriousness of life" (p. 35). It is just "his own consciousness raised to the second power" (p. 135). To make him a religious exception, the shock would have to come from higher up. From God, who can do what no ordinary woman, no matter how self-effacing her magnanimity, can even aspire to. Man is reflection, and woman is reality. But only that reality which is (defined as) alienated by language. Both male and female lie this side of the boundary of immanence. They are conceivable, and only conceivable, together, as the othered and the othering. Within this domain the Hegelian logic plays its nasty little game in never-ending closure. God is reality in an altogether different sense: the transcendent, the wholly Other, which language can neither distance nor appropriate, because He is always already infinitely far off and infinitesimally proximate.

The young man's problem is solved and his repetition achieved within the circuit of the same. As the shifting sexual identities in this story indicate, the difference between male and female structures an immanent dialectic, of which man and woman are the terms always posited and ever again sublated. The ideal and the actual are two mirrors reflecting each other to infinity.

Job, however, is addressed by the Other. His transgression is precipitated and his protest silenced by the divine prerogative, which neuters the dialectic of man and woman as it moots the argument between Job and his comforters. The unspeakable transcendent takes Job through the universal and beyond it: the universal (marriage), from which the poet is conveniently exempted by the amiable dispensation of existence, becomes in the religious instance the universal (justice), from which Job is terribly redeemed by the connivance of God and Satan.

There remains the difference of infinity between religion and a poetry which has the presentiment of religion. This text, which is poetry of a sort, can incorporate the religious only by excluding it. The sacred gloss, appropriated by the young man to describe his own perplexity, is written in the margins of *Repetition*. Intruding ambiguously into Constantine's fiction, *Job* proposes an unaskable question.

Constantine's fiction. Who is Constantine Constantius? A ventriloquist's dummy. A psychologically necessary presupposition. A serviceable spirit who serves by repeatedly becoming someone else. His name is a mockery . . . of the name. Who is the real author of this book? Who concludes by offering his real reader (who?) the barest hint of a possibility of reconciliation (a repetition?) after all the bewildering transformations through which the book has led him (p. 137)? Whose name goes in the blank marked "N. N."? The blank marked "C. C."? There is a blank marked "Sören Kierkegaard." There is also . . . a mark.

But this is serious business. In part two of *Repetition*, called "Repetition," the repetition vainly sought in part one is finally achieved. After a fashion. The story of the young man repeats, in its own way, the story of Job, which repeat, in its own way, the story of the young man. At the end of it all the "real reader" is offered a chance at his own repetition. (*Forsoning.* In theological terms, atonement.) He is invited to "be reconciled" to the text that has brought him to this pass.

A young man in Stockholm (no address given) is failing to contact a girl in Copenhagen who has recently changed her name. He's lost his own. Job on his ash heap is shouting at the wind. His words are blown back in his throat. Someone has just finished reading an illegible script. A repetition of sorts. This is getting us nowhere. Where were we?

Some birds can be taken only from the rear. Here is a little salt for the tail:

The idea of the book is the idea of a totality, finite or infinite, of the signifier; this totality of the signifier cannot be a totality, unless a totality constituted by the signified preexists it, supervises its inscriptions and its signs, and is independent of it in its ideality. The idea of the book, which always refers to a natural totality, is profoundly alien to the sense of writing. . . . If I distinguish the text from the book, I shall say that the destruction of the book . . . denudes the surface of the text. That necessary violence responds to a violence that was no less necessary.[5]

Bound securely between its covers, *Repetition* appears to be a book. A finite totality of signifiers, organized by a superintendent meaning that assigns to beginning, middle, and end their rightful places in a system closed upon–within itself. We expect it to contain, or be contained by, all it expresses.

Yet it begins with a digression remarking the contrast between the Eleatics' absurd denial of motion and Diogenes' equally absurd denial of that denial. It ends with an open letter to the reader,

[5] Jacques Derrida, *Of Grammatology* (Baltimore, Md.: Johns Hopkins University Press, 1976), p. 18.

Mr. N. N., that asks him to be reconciled to the errant ways of the narrative. To continue (for how long?) the dialectic of repetition which the book begins to enact. Or perhaps to achieve for himself (how?) the repetition which Constantine's experimental psychology has shown to be impossible. An invitation to an indefinitely postponed atonement. The middle of the book is a blank: a silence and a silent passage of time between the death with which part one concludes and the "repetition" with which part two begins.

The putative totality of the signifiers called *Repetition* is exceeded by the digression on the farce. It is breached and invaded by the canonical discourse of *Job.* It is the work of a protean author, a shape-shifter ironically named "constant," and it is addressed to a real-ideal reader who is only a blank without a name. If *Repetition* is a book, it is a book of which there is no definitive edition. A book that does violence to itself as book.

There is reason to think that this "book" is (in the technical sense and *avant la lettre*) a text: writing in which the violence done to writing by the book is countered by the violence inherent in the nature of writing itself. A necessary violence. The book attempts a conquest of being through the consolidation of meaning. But if the guardian of the integrity of being is the impotence of language, then it is expedient that *Repetition* (which says as much) perform the solicitation of this conquest and the dissemination of this meaning. A repetition. Of sorts.

In the body of the narrative there are two proper names, both of which stand (in) for absences. Somewhere in Stockholm the young man takes refuge from the scene of his engagement. Poul Martin Möller, deceased for five years when *Repetition* was published, provides a (pre)text for recollection. Remotions in time and space. The letter to the reader is situated and dated, but in the course of the letter Constantine's identity is dissolved at last and for good. "Copenhagen, August 1843" (p. 137) marks the place and the moment at which *Repetition* was finished by its "real" author, whose absence from his text is absolute.

It is only where the text transgresses the story, Constantine's *aparté* on the farce, that it is suddenly punctuated by names that function as indices of presence: the Royal Theater in Copenhagen ("not merely for pleasure," p. 67), the Königstäter in Berlin, the actors Beckmann and Grobecker. Reality enters the text only at that place where the text is beyond itself: being is always the excess of the text. And perhaps at that place where the text is interrupted *ab extra*. The *Job* letters. Perhaps. For who knows whether Job is a human being or a trope? Job? or *Job*? That is only, but always, a maybe. We might check up on the Königstäter and its troupe. There is no way to verify Job. The being that is the excess of the text might be pursued. The being that invades the text—for that we would require a thunderstorm. Whose voice would we hear? And how would we know?

In the hierarchy of life-styles by Johannes Climacus, humor is the proximate *confinium* of faith. In the Aristotelian sense, its place.

One of the excesses of this text (his name appeared on the Stationer's Register) was a subject of Christian VIII named Sören Kierkegaard. A writer on religious subjects. Through the pseudonym Johannes Climacus he professes an interest in Christianity, proclaimed throughout history as the incarnation, in history, of the Word of God, and demanding a decision, also in history, for or against the miraculous Presence. So historical is the reality of Christianity that history itself, since the Incarnation, has had no reality but Christianity. Yet Climacus, for all his concern with the concrete historical actuality of Christianity, is exclusively preoccupied with the abstract dialectic of rationality and radical alterity: not the historical reality but the absurd historicity of Christianity is the sole *topos* of his meditations. He even goes so far as to suggest that we could dispense with the New Testament and the whole of Christian history if only the contemporaries of Jesus had left "this little advertisement, this *nota bene* on a page of universal history": "'We have believed that in such and such a year God appeared among us in the humble figure of a servant, that he lived and taught in our community, and finally died'" (*Fragments*, p. 130). Those few words, alleging the bare fact of incarnation, would have been enough to provide the opportunity for faith and the occasion of offense.

This is a contradiction only if we forget that the historical incarnation, the Christ who is also Jesus, is, like the characters and situations in farce, a fortuitous concretion. On the one hand, history is beside the point. What matters are the "dialectic movements." But on the other hand, to be a Christian is to be contemporary with the historical Christ and to appropriate the history of Christianity. The Christian is not one who has correctly worked out the logic of incarnation. He is one who lives a perfectly determinate kind of life: *imitatio Christi.* Although the concretion is fortuitous (how could it be otherwise when the category to be incarnated is the Absolutely Other?), yet it *is the* concretion of the Absolutely Other and therefore the Absolutely Other itself. This particular actor, who just happens to work at the Königstäter, *is* the miles gloriosus. Likewise the gratuitousness of the incarnation of the Word in the man Jesus, like the second birth of every new Christian, is no accident. Although it is an absolute surprise.

Is it an accident that in *Repetition* the young man and the girl are never made concrete, not even fortuitously? He is described, but description is abstraction,[6] and he remains for all of it a category: the young man. The girl is not even described. She is never more but never less than the alienated term of an allusion *ins Ferne.*

Reality is, in relation to every movement of reason, the unmotivated. An other which the dialectic can never generate and so never consume. The irrational. Woman is reality. Like the Christ absurdly incarnate in Jesus, that impossible possibility whose reality we call the God-man, woman can save us all. From the interesting. From ourselves. We are all men. The women too. All of us bear, inside out or outside in, the signifier of our lack.[7] This is not under the sun.

[6]Kierkegaard, *Papirer*, VIII¹ A 622.
[7]Cf. Samuel R. Delany, *Tales of Nevèrÿon* (New York: Bantam Books, 1979), pp. 87-101. See also Jacques Lacan, *Écrits* (New York: Norton, 1977), pp. 281-91.

111

This is absurd. Of course. Nevertheless, in *The Point of View for My Work as an Author*, Kierkegaard says that his life has been a love affair with God, who is metonymically identified with Regine, the rejected bride, and Michael Pederson, the dead father. God, his true lover, is also the mother he never had, replacing and effacing the biological mother, whom his father had possessed without right, to his lifelong despair. This too is absurd. But the sexual identities in his life, as in his texts, will not respect the limits of gender. In the possibility opened by the death of the father, God gives himself as mother and bride to the prodigal who returns from harlotry to his true home. A repetition of sorts ("he came to himself"),[8] in which Kierkegaard returns to that origin from which he never departed. How far is the grace of God from the magnanimity of woman?

In the book, as the forced containment of the irregularity of writing, phallogocentrism asserts its possession of the signifier and essays the appropriation of being. (Anne Lund, so rudely forced.) But if the book is an attempted rape of reality, then the original violence of writing responds to the violence of the book with a gesture of castration that liberates the transcendent. In *Repetition* the signs neuter themselves. The verses of Paul Möller, by which the young man quotes himself into senility. His copybook, containing citations from the classics and the catechism, and his transcripts of the biblical text; his removal from Copenhagen to Stockholm; and his letters themselves, addressed to "my silent confidant" and left unsigned: signifiers of something missing. Occupying the place of an absence and exposing its impotence, *Repetition* renounces dominion and imperium. The mastery of being by the book is unmasked as sterile self-manipulation; the hymen remains intact.

From Philostratus the Elder, Kierkegaard took a motto for *Repetition*: "On wild trees the flowers are fragrant, on cultivated trees wild the fruits" (p. 31). The conjunctions (wild-flowers, cultivated

---

[8]Luke 15:17. Cf. Kierkegaard, *Point of View*, pp. 19-20, 64-65, 76-84 (where the relationship with Regine is characterized as a "*factum*").

fruits) are paradoxical. These words, Kierkegaard remarks, could stand as an epigram over the relationship between paganism and Christianity.[9] Paganism, in all its declensions a religion that centers in fertility and procreation, only flowers. Christianity, which has decentered sexuality to the point of glorifying perpetual chastity . . . bears fruit. Untamed nature expends itself in show. Artifice gives birth. (A virgin birth?)[10] In both cases it is a question of fragrance, and therefore of perception at a distance.

It is paradoxical, and beyond paradox surprising, to be told that Christian fruits smell like pagan flowers. But Christianity repeats paganism as the fruit repeats the flower. And a repetition is always something of a surprise. To be taken again (*gjentages*) is to be overtaken (surprised): taken over, without warning, perhaps unawares. Seized or captured by that which is always there before you because it runs faster (*overraske, überrasche*). Faster even than irony, of which surprise is in a sense the opposite. Irony knows everything, and more than everything. It has used up reality and explored possibility and found them wanting. Irony is beyond surprising. Insofar as every text takes itself out of the race by turning on itself in a cipher of emasculation, every text is ultimately troped as irony. Therefore repetition is never inscribed in the text. Especially a text entitled with a double irony, *Repetition.*

And yet: irony is a necessary condition of repetition. Only the unsurprisable is absolutely surprised. The ash heap comes before the thunderstorm. "No authentic human life is possible without irony," and every authentic human life is a function of repetition, "a history wherein consciousness successively outlives itself, though in such a way that happiness consists not in forgetting all this but becomes present in it" (*Irony*, pp. 338, 341). Repetition cannot be written. *Repetition* is a way of writing this.

The Crucifixion was an event in history, as the Creed testifies.

---

[9]*Papirer*, IV A 27. Cf. Galatians 5:16-23. For the previous paragraph, cf. Galatians 3:28.

[10]Cf. Kierkegaard, *Irony*, p. 47, and, by contrast, p. 262. The virgin birth issues in an incarnation at p. 259.

He was crucified under Pontius Pilate: a time and a place and an undistinguished agent of the imperial Roman government (now forever marked with a distinction he might have wished to decline, from which his wife tried to save him). After 1900 years the human race managed, in Nietzsche, to comprehend the Crucifixion. This is in the world. But the Resurrection took place in accordance with the Scriptures. An event beyond history, of which history knows nothing but an empty tomb. The signifier of absence. Tolkien has said that Christianity is the fairy tale that came true.[11] The man-god, the historical Jesus who died and the eternal Christ who was reborn in him, is the metonymy that became metaphor. This is not in the world, though the Resurrection (of which the Crucifixion is the impossible possibility) is the repetition that contains the world. Creates it anew and for the first time by restoring to it that beginning from which it never departed.

But the Crucifixion comes first. Being cannot be forced by the signifier. Like truth, she keeps her legs crossed. The violence of language turns on itself. The catachrestic seizure of being by the sign yields only the indefinite deferral of presence and the dispersal of the sign itself in sterile dissemination. Alluring fruit and miserable pittance, which do not satisfy (p. 34). Fragrant flowers of evil.

Maybe. These may be dragonseed. It is necessary to pass by the dragon. The impotence of language preserves inviolate the alterity of being. And thereby—perhaps—opens the way for repetition. But the hook must be baited. Irony is the penance of language, by which it acknowledges its original fault: the incapacity to let be. And a kind of reparation. A refusal to foreclose the possibility that reality may, in the extremity of language, bestow itself. The manna that satisfies with benediction (p. 34). Beyond irony there is the possibility—*just* the possibility, which can neither be activated nor shut off, but only allowed to remain in its absolute dehors—that being may, gratuitously, give itself. Being is inconceivably conceivable as

[11]"On Fairy-Stories," in C. S. Lewis, ed., *Essays Presented to Charles Williams* (Grand Rapids, Mich.: William B. Eerdmans Publishing Co., 1974).

gift. A graceful and gracious self-giving of which the restoration of Job is a singularly thunderous instance. Of which the magnanimity of woman (the self-withholding of being) is an ironic inversion.

Or is it? In the first draft of *Repetition* the young man kills himself in febrile imitation of Werther. When Kierkegaard learned that Regine had married Fritz (from whom she had been temporarily distracted by Sören), he rewrote the ending. The magnanimity of woman saved, among other things, this text. Among other things, Sören Kierkegaard? Perhaps: a fortuitous concretion of the young man, Sören in *Repetition* repeats his love affair, and his faulted self-recovery, with feeling. Not quite autobiography, since the life follows and repeats the fiction. The end of the story and the beginning of the history were written by Regine. Regine is the grace of *Repetition*. What saved Regine?

Pogo says, very sensibly, that bait never wins.[12] But the girl achieved a repetition. She found another man and began a new life. Who was he and what did she do for him? "She is married— to whom I do not know. . . . I read it in the paper. . . . I lost the notice and have not had the patience to make a closer inspection" (p. 125). His signifier is effaced in the very mention. But he got the girl. The unsurpassable is surpassed. The "movement" by which the girl finds a man and enters upon her marriage is made by virtue of the absurd; it is unmotivated by her "ideal" relationship to the young man. This bait died and was resurrected: she had the vitality to kill her death and transform it into life (p. 40). What was for her lover a matter of life of death became for her a matter of life and death. The past her lover, the future her husband. Is that a tragedy? Perhaps it is a farce. More than interesting, it is the interest of this text.

Being, which can never be taken at the origin but only repeated, is grace. The beloved and fruitful wife of whom one never tires. In Hebrew she is the maternal grandmother of our Savior.

[12] Walt Kelly, *Ten Ever-Lovin' Blue-Eyed Years with Pogo* (New York: Simon and Schuster, 1972), p. 19.

Part Two Literary Studies

4. Dowel and the Crisis of Faith and Irony in *Piers Plowman*

NO one who has read *Piers Plowman* would deny that it is a difficult work, but, like Kierkegaard's *The Concept of Irony*, its difficulties are in some respects what the text is about. Many of these difficulties inhere in Langland's paradoxical attitudes toward language—his compulsion to verbalize set against a deep mistrust of easy equivalences between signifiers and signifieds, phenomenon and essence. This ambivalence toward language is essentially Christian and Augustinian, reflecting the paradox of the imperfect voice and the divine logos:

Have we spoken or announced anything worthy of God? Rather I feel that I have done nothing but wish to speak: if I have spoken, I have not said what I wished to say. Whence do I know this, except because God is ineffable? . . . For God, although nothing worthy may be spoken of Him, has accepted the tribute of the human voice and wished us to take joy in praising Him with our words.[1]

In this sense *Piers Plowman* is truly Christian. As the question of language problematicizes the poem, it also enacts the archetypal crisis of faith, the attempt to confront the discrepancies between

---

[1] Augustine, *On Christian Doctrine*, trans. D. W. Robertson, Jr. (Indianapolis, Ind.: Bobbs-Merrill, 1958), pp. 10-11.

the world and the Word. Yet the questions raised in the poem are also, perhaps, ultimately ironic—if its paradoxes are typically medieval, they are also timeless, Kierkegaardian. The paradoxes of faith and irony, language and silence that animate the poem also structure and problematicize our response. They call into question what George Steiner has called "the contract of ultimate or preponderant meaning between poet and reader, text and meaning."[2] Like Kierkegaard both Christian and ironic, *Piers Plowman* asks to be judged not by the meaning it offers but by the crises it confronts.

Kierkegaard's exploration of the Socratic dialogue—the importance of questioning and the relationship between question and answer—provides a significant link between the philosopher's comic conception of the "infinitely correcting moment" (*Irony*, p. 63) and the impenetrability of *Piers Plowman*. In *The Concept of Irony*, Kierkegaard characterizes Socrates' activity in relation to humanity: "He approached each man individually, deprived him of everything, and sent him away empty-handed" (p. 199):

> . . . the purpose of asking a question may be twofold. One may ask a question for the purpose of obtaining an answer containing the desired content, so that the more one questions, the deeper and more meaningful becomes the answer; or one may ask a question, not in the interest of obtaining an answer, but to suck out the apparent content with a question and leave only an emptiness remaining. The first method naturally presupposes a content, the second an emptiness; the first is speculative, the second is ironic. [P. 73]

This method of sucking out all content with a question describes metaphorically the operation of *Piers Plowman* as it questions and undermines its own premises—the rhetorical and metaphysical assumptions of medieval civilization. The poem is "ironic" rather than "speculative"; it celebrates, finally, its emptiness. Its move-

---

[2]George Steiner, "On Difficulty," *On Difficulty and Other Essays* (New York: Oxford University Press, 1978), p. 40.

ment is toward silence, the void behind language. It "confront[s] us with blank questions about the nature of human speech, about the status of significance, about the necessity and purpose of the construct which we have, with more or less rough and ready consensus, come to perceive as a poem."[3]

Piers Plowman opens with a question: How may I save my soul? Presumably, the text, in its three versions, represents an answer, the "desired content." When we reach the last passus, however, the dreamer is still asking the same question and getting the same answers, none of which he finds satisfactory. The dreamer's inquiries about salvation are never fully answered because they cannot be. Rather, the poet's first metaphysical question is quickly transmuted into an ethical one. The central inquiry of *Piers Plowman* (as its critics suggest)[4] becomes the question the dreamer asks each of his guides in the *Vita de Dowel*: What is dowel? That the answers he receives are less than satisfactory seems clear from the uncertainty of the poem's critics about dowel's meaning and purpose. The narrator seems to create the threefold division of dowel, dobet, and dobest at the beginning of the *Vita* to give shape to the shifting and elusive experience of his dreams, his "pilgrimage to the center." As a structural device to distinguish three movements in the B and C continuations, this "plan" is arbitrary, itself a fiction. It collapses again and again under the circularities, the

---

[3]Ibid., p. 41.

[4]For standard interpretations of "dowel," "dobet," and "dobest," see Henry Wells, "The Construction of *Piers Plowman*," *PMLA* 44 (1929): 123-40; Neville Coghill, "The Character of Piers Plowman from the B text," *Medium Ævum* 2 (1933): 108-35; R. W. Chambers, *Man's Unconquerable Mind* (Philadelphia: Albert Saifer, 1953), pp. 149ff.; T. P. Dunning, "The Structure of the B Text of *Piers Plowman*," *RES*, n.s., 7 (1956): 225-27; D. W. Robertson and Bernard Huppé, *Piers Plowman and the Scriptural Tradition* (Princeton, N.J.: Princeton University Press, 1951), pp. 234-48; Howard Meroney, "The Life and Death of Long Wille," *ELH* 17 (1950): 13; E. Talbot Donaldson, *Piers Plowman: The C Text and Its Poet* (New Haven, Conn.: Yale University Press, 1949), pp. 196-97.

repetitions, contradictions, and tentative discoveries of the poet-narrator's quest. The difficulties of narrative structure in the poem seem closely tied to the many explanations of dowel (and dobet and dobest) given throughout the *Vita de Dowel*. The variety of these partial answers offers the reader two alternatives: either the explanations of the terms correspond to the themes of the sections bearing their names or they do not. Yet, rather than elucidating this problem, the poem celebrates the impossibility of choosing between the alternatives. The misunderstandings that the dreamer's questions engender empty them of all meaning, creating a void that the critics in their frustration (and the reader in his) attempt to fill with their triads (Active, Contemplative, and Mixed Lives, or Purgative, Illuminative, and Unitive states of the soul). But such frustrations are what constitute the experience of the poem. The response to the ineffable, to the problem of faith and salvation, becomes a repetition of what Kierkegaard calls Socrates' "infinite silence" (*Irony*, p. 64). This inability to speak, to articulate, is the basis of Langland's ironic metaphysic.

Dowel seems to be introduced abruptly into the poem at the end of the *Visio* with the words of Truth's pardon: "But do wel and haue wel, and god shal haue ϸi soule, / And do yuel and haue yuel, and hope ϸow noon ooϸer / That after ϸi deeϸ day ϸe deuel shal haue ϸi soule." (7. 115-17).[5] In fact, the concept of doing well is defined throughout the *Visio* as an ideal of ethical behavior against which the vices and follies of the world (embodied in the seven deadly sins of passus 5) may be judged. Holi Chirche first introduces this standard in her discussion of truth (1, 88-91); Conscience reiterates it in passus 4, adopting as the basis for the proper understanding of meed the distinction between those who do well and those who misdo. Throughout the *Visio*, the dreamer's questions about salvation are answered by the refrain "do well."

[5] All references to *Piers Plowman* are from *Piers Plowman: The B Version*, ed. George Kane and E. Talbot Donaldson (London: Athlone Press, 1975).

The words of the Fourteenth Psalm "Domine, quis habitabit in tabernaculo tuo?" quoted at length by Conscience in the debate with Lady Meed (3. 234-45), echoed in the description of Truth's pardon (7. 40-43, 52-53), and implicit in most of the *Visio's* action, offer a transparent gloss on dowel. Those who "enformeþ pouere peple and pursueþ truþe" and

> . . . helpen þe Innocent and holded wiþþe riȝtfulle,
> Wiþouten Mede doþ hem good and þe truþe helpe,
> Swiche manere men, my lord, shul haue þis first Mede
> Of god at gret nede whan þei gon hennes.
>
> [3. 241-45]

The satire of the *Visio*, then, offers both dreamer and reader a commentary on the vices and virtues of the age, as well as convenient exempla in the conventional symbols of estates satire and in Piers, the virtuous laborer. If one reads only the first six passus of the *Visio*, the poem seems to answer the dreamer's questions about salvation speculatively in the familiar rhetoric of alliterative satire and contemporary preaching manuals and sermons, but one single moment in passus 7, the tearing of the pardon, calls into question, "deconstructs" in a single stroke, all that precedes it, forcing the poem to begin over again. Piers's tearing of the pardon and his subsequent rejection of dowel, the life of virtuous labor, undermine the *Visio's* definition of dowel, with its emphasis on the essentially economic virtues that dominate and eventually corrupt first the society of the fair field, then the neutral concept of meed, and finally the society of the "half acre." The scene defies causality by halting the progressively linear impulse of normative satire; it subverts its orthodox Christian grounding and undermines the very contract that makes human speech possible at all. It problematicizes faith itself. (That Langland, or someone else, left the scene out of the C text altogether suggests that it was apparently as enigmatic to its original audience as it is to modern ones.)

Truth's pardon, one imagines, should dramatize the central paradox of faith: the necessary relationship between grace and good works, God and man. This relationship, Kierkegaard notes, cannot be one of knowledge because "the paradox in Christian truth is invariably due to the fact that it is truth as it exists for God. The standard of measure and the end is superhuman; and there is only one relationship possible: faith" (*Journals*, 1:210). A pardon metaphorically embodies this faith, recognizing that because men often fail to "do well" they require God's indulgence. As a signifier, however, "pardon" creates all sorts of difficulties. By the fourteenth century the theological significance of the word had been largely diluted by satires directed against pardoners. The corruption that surrounded the buying and selling of indulgences is the butt of satiric set pieces throughout the *Visio*, beginning with the description in the Prologue of the pardoner hawking his indulgences to "lewed men." The language that describes Truth's pardon only emphasizes its ambiguity as a signifier. "Purchaced" (7.2), although it may have the morally neutral meaning of "obtain," suggests both Christ's "purchase" of man's salvation on Calvary and the mercenary trafficking in papal indulgences. The phrase "a pena & a culpa" (line 3) increases our wariness. It is often associated with false indulgences since, strictly speaking, no indulgence could remit the guilt of sin, only its temporal punishment (*poena sed non culpa*). Equally disturbing is the legal formula "for hym and for his heires" (line 4), since no pardon could presume to extend its benefits to a man's heires.[6] Yet, within the poem this cannot be a false pardon because it comes from Truth. Each signifier—true pardon, false pardon—refers to the other endlessly. Each plays off against the other contradictory expectations about a pardon—as satiric image, as theological symbol. Signifiers and signifieds become relentlessly ironic in Langland's fallen world.

[6]For a discussion of the linguistic difficulties in the description of the pardon see *Piers Plowman: The Prologue and Passus I-VII of the B Text as Found in Bodleian MS Laud 581*, ed. J. A. W. Bennett (Oxford: Clarendon Press, 1972), pp. 216-17.

The words of the pardon, when read by the priest, reveal the essentially ironic nature of the scene. The pardon "is and is not," to borrow Kierkegaard's description of irony (*Irony*, p. 161). The stern warning from the Athanasian Creed, "Et qui bona egerunt ibunt in vitam eternam: / Qui vero mala in ignem eternum" ("And they who have done good shall go into eternal life; / And truly they who have done evil shall go into eternal fire"), reveals that the pardon is not a pardon at all. Far from offering the forgiveness that a pardon implies, these words promise only justice untempered by mercy. This apocalyptic note introduced so abruptly into a scene of forgiveness colors the rest of the action in ways that are more easily understood ironically than as logical effects of clearly recognizable causes. The scene's language becomes increasingly self-referential, while the *Visio*'s key concepts, dowel in particular, become empty shells. The pardon finally means nothing.

The question remains, however, why Piers destroys the pardon, since the only indication of his motives is the phrase "for pure tene." If Piers tears the pardon out of anger (the usual interpretation of "tene"), the context does not specify its object, whether the priest, the folk, the pardon, or Piers himself. If, however, Piers reacts out of shock or distress, a harder reading but one supported both by other instances of the word in the poem and other Middle English texts, his motivation seems clearer.[7] Piers tears the pardon, rejecting the life of virtuous labor that he and it represent, because he perceives that the words of the Athanasian Creed demand a perfection that imperfect man cannot hope to achieve. In this respect Piers's anxiety resembles that of the dreamer

[7]The *OED* offers a wide variety of meanings for the word, ranging from "anger and vexation," to "grief and distress." Elsewhere in *Piers Plowman* (3.348-50; 6.115-17), Langland uses the word in apocalyptic contexts to emphasize the shock and horror of damnation. Chaucer uses the word in a variety of contexts as well, but at least once, in *Troilus and Criseyde*, the word means something very close to fear or distress. In the first amorous encounter between the two lovers, the narrator describes Criseyde overcoming her natural "daunger": "Creiseyde, al quyt from ever drede and tene" (3.1226).

who, after hearing Scripture preach on the parable of the feast, doubts whether he "were chosen or noȝt chosen" (10. 117). The difference between the two—Piers's virtue against the dreamer's forty-five years of dissipation—cannot obscure the real fear that lies behind Piers's rejection of the pardon, a fear that the dreamer defines with scholastic precision: "Seuene sipes, seip þe book, synneþ þe rightefulle; / . . . dowel and do yuele mowe noȝt dwelle togideres" (8.22, 24). Reading the scholastic method against itself, the dreamer logically concludes that, since this is an imperfect world, all are guilty. Piers must dread the implacable justice that damns even the most virtuous.

Yet clarifying Piers's motives reveals the more complex ontological difficulties at the heart of the scene. Piers realizes that such a fear of divine justice is grounded in the experience of this world. Once again the temporal world of sense misrepresents the atemporal and invisible. Piers's tearing of the pardon implicitly underscores his recognition of how inadequate human language is to comprehend the divine Logos. As he rejects the terms of perfection offered by the *Visio* and the pardon, he transforms the *Visio*'s language to propose a very different notion of perfection. He rejects the largely economic definition of virtue (do well), suggested by the image of plowing, by divorcing the sign from its signified. The plow itself he transforms into the spiritual activities of prayer and penance—"Of preieres and of penaunce my plouȝ shall ben heafter" (7.122)—the tangible product, "whete breed," into tears (*lacrime*). The plowman who up until now has occupied himself solely with the physical needs of the folk ceases to concern himself with such necessities as food and turns to asceticism, identifying himself with God's holy hermits. Like them he abandons the world, placing his trust in a power his experiences cannot confirm. By way of authority he cites Luke's parable of the birds who are fed in winter though they neither sow nor reap. The parable's command, "ne soliciti sitis" ("be not solicitous"), replaces dowel as the poem's definition of spiritual perfection. For Piers dowel gives way to dobet when he turns his back on the world and sets out on a journey whose goal he perceives but obscurely.

Piers's blind "leap of faith," however, wins for him the world's scorn rather than its understanding. The folk do not understand the nature of his conversion because it is cast in a language that does more to obscure meaning than to reveal it. Piers deliberately describes his transformation in a parable, the narrative form Christ frequently used. Since a parable is primarily a "similitude," usually between the physical and spiritual realm, it requires an act of interpretation to distinguish the "carnal sense" from the spiritual, hidden sense. As with Kierkegaard's discussion of Socrates, the ability to discover the latent and more significant meaning that the external narrative both proclaims and obscures will separate the insiders from the outsiders: "He becomes visible for those with eyes to see, audible for those with ears to hear" (*Irony*, p. 234).

That the *Vita de Dowel* begins once again from the beginning suggests the poet's awareness that the *Visio* has not arrived at a result.[8] Piers's conversion cannot answer Wille's questions about faith and salvation. The uninitiated dreamer, lacking the grace necessary to comprehend the nature of Piers's transformation, must content himself with acting on the carnal sense of his dream, the homiletic command to "do well." Herein lies the significance of the dreamer's repeated question: What is dowel? As the dreamer asks this question of each of his guides, the inadequacy of the answers compel the reader to question the act of questioning itself. If the poem asks again and again "What is dowel?" the bewildering number of different and contradictory answers "suck out the apparent content . . . and leave only an emptiness remaining" (*Irony*, p. 73). *Dowel* asks, "How can I understand such answers?"

Long Wille's journey educates him in this process of indirect

[8]Langland suggests that the poem is beginning all over again when he repeats the poem's opening lines at the beginning of *Dowel*: "Thus, yrobed in russett, I romed aboute / Al a somer seson for to seke dowel" (8.1-2). Compare with the opening lines of the poem: "In a somer seson whan softe was þe sonne / I shoop me into a shroud as I a sheep weere; / In habite as an heremite, vnholy of werkes, / Went wide in þis world wondres to here."

communication, in the negativity of irony,[9] but if it divests him of knowledge and certainty, it must be concerned essentially with the cognitive processes by which man comes to know or not to know the divine. This section of the poem examines the usefulness of both rational and nonrational thought in discovering faith, employing the tools of both speculative discourse and irony. Yet such an epistemological search cannot proceed without examining how language functions both to reveal and conceal the divine. For Langland, as for Augustine, Kierkegaard, and virtually every writer on the metaphysics of language from Plato to Hegel, human speech is an imperfect replica of a divine and perfect language, the logos.[10] For Langland, the logos predates creation (in fact is the vehicle for creation) and coexists with God: "For poruȝ þe word þat he warp woxen forþ besstes, / And all at his wil was wrouȝt wiþ a speche, / *Dixit & facta sunt*" (9.32-33). Many of the biblical stories recounted in *Dowel* characterize this divine logos as the vehicle for God's presence throughout sacred history. In passus 12, Imaginatyf recounts the story of the woman taken in adultery. The first two lines of the passage (12.72-82) call to mind another instance of the divine

[9]Lee M. Capel, "Historical Introduction," *Irony*, p. 7, discusses Kierkegaard's concept of indirect communication.

[10]Jaques Derrida describes the history of logocentrism (the metaphysic of presence) in *Of Grammatology*: "All the metaphysical determinations of truth and even the one beyond metaphysical ontotheology that Heidegger reminds us of, are more or less immediately inseparable from the instance of the logos, or of a reason thought within the lineage of the logos, in whatever sense it is understood: in the pre-Socratic or the philosophic sense, in the sense of God's infinite understanding or in the anthropological sense, in the pre-Hegelian or the post-Hegelian sense. . . . All signifiers, and first and foremost the written signifier, are derivative with regard to what would wed the voice indissolubly to the mind or to the thought of the signified sense, indeed to the thing itself (whether it is done in the Aristotelian manner that we have just indicated or in the manner of medieval theology, determining the *res* as a thing created from its *eidos*, from its sense thought in the logos or in the infinite understanding of God)." Jacques Derrida, *Of Grammatology*, trans. Gayatri Spivak (Baltimore, Md.: Johns Hopkins University Press, 1976), pp. 10-11.

intervention, when God gave Moses the Law, the Ten Commandments. These "god wroot" on tablets of stone, and it is this stony law that condemns the adulteress. She is saved only through another act of divine intervention, through "cristes writyng." What is most significant about this passage, however, is the equation made between the act of writing, the "carectes," and Christ's manifestation of his divine nature. Imaginatyf makes this equation three times; each identification becomes more explicit than the last: "God wroot," "poruӡ carectes pat crist wroot," and "cristes writyng saued."

Implicit in this passage as well is the relationship between language and "Clergie," or knowledge. Imaginatyf seems to identify Christ's act of writing with the divine knowledge it reveals: "Thus Clergie pere comforted pe womman." Moving between these extraordinary revelations and the more mundane, the *Vita de Dowel* explores the relationships between language and the cognitive processes through which imperfect man recognizes the divine presence. Language, in *Dowel*, particularly in passus 8 to 12, reflects and even becomes the cognitive processes that *Dowel* examines. It is a vehicle for classification (of ways of life or mental powers), a means of imposing order (the law), and, paradoxically, a means of disorder and deception. More often than not in *Dowel* one cannot distinguish between these uses of language. The phenomenon "is and is not" the essence. The reader comes full circle to the exemplum of the woman taken in adultery. "God wroot," or, more succinctly, the Latin *"Dixit & facta sunt,"* describes the ultimate model of language. God's word, or the logos, results in the creation of both man and the Law. Yet man's language, although created in the image of the logos, is capable of only an imperfect parody of it. The more it strives for perfection, the more it is trapped and frustrated by its own shortcomings.

Langland examines the shortcomings of human language and discourse by returning once again to personification allegory. This time, however, rather than using linguistic signs to explore the external world of moral action (as he does in the *Visio*), he uses them to explore Wille's inner state of moral choice. Even though the dreamer tends to define his journey externally and Dowel as a person (substantive rather than verb), his search becomes an inward journey, an exploration of his own mind. The guides he meets are personifications of his own intellectual activities. As such, the first guides of *Dowel* share his mental limitations as well as his looks, particularly his smugness and belief in established systems and in classifications of knowledge as external guides to salvation. Like the dreamer, these personifications approach Dowel as a problem of definition. Because they are linguistic signs their understanding of the theological and spiritual problems of salvation is limited by their own semantic range of meaning, their own nature as signs. As fragmented aspects of the human psyche, they can give the dreamer only a fragmented view of the reality he seeks, one highly colored by each guide's "hobby horse," his satiric attacks on the vices that most offend him.

The clash in the dreamer's mind between the desire to discover dowel and his preoccupation with and attraction toward an antithetical life of misdoing is realized as satire in the speeches of each of the personification guides. Dame Study, for instance, questions the value of learning in the pursuit of salvation when she harangues the dreamer about its misuse, but her tirade seems all out of proportion to anything the dreamer has said or done. Wille may be argumentative, he may even be too easily seduced by argumentation for its own sake, but he is hardly guilty, at least at the time she rebukes him, of presumption. Her invective (10.49-66) seems less a dramatic response than a projection of the poet's own ironic posture. Satire and invective in *Dowel* are themselves ironically qualified and hence very different from the satire and invective of the *Visio*, where the conventional fictions and images of satire control our responses. Because the *Visio*'s ideals—Piers's primarily—are clearly marked, the satire offers the reader an unequivocal invitation to judge the objects of Langland's scorn by the standards of the opposing ideals; but because at heart satire reflects a preoccupation with the world, with the discrepancies be-

tween *are* and *should be*, Langland in *Dowel* must undercut the
satirist's romantic fiction for the dreamer to move beyond his preoccupation with the temporal, with the conflicts between the actual
and the ideal. Throughout *Dowel*, each ideal or norm is pulled
out like a rug from under the reader's feet. No truth, no moral
judgment, no epistemological vision survives this ironic examination. Each by its nature must contradict itself.

The answers the dreamer receives from Wit, Study, and Clergy
to his question "What is Dowel?" deepen rather than relieve his
dilemma; they return him again and again to invective and complaint and, in so doing, to the irony of repetition. Clergie's lesson
on Dowel suggests the pattern that the other lessons repeat. It
begins, promisingly enough, with faith; dowel "'is a commune lyf,'
quod Clergie, 'on holy chirche to bileue / Wiþ alle þe articles of
þe feiþ þat falleþ to be knowe'" (10.238-39). Clergie calls into
question the necessity of both learning and rational thought for salvation (this lesson is repeated—with a difference—in passus 13,
when Conscience abandons Clergie to follow Patience on a pilgrimage of unknown destination).[11] The truth of salvation must be
grounded in faith: "Fides non habet meritum ubi human racio
prebet experimentium" (10.256). Yet faith itself in the poem is
problematic. It is essential for salvation but cannot be actively
sought. It is at once the cornerstone of the poet's vision and un-
attainable, as the quotation suggests, through human reason, since
it resides precisely in the contradictions between subjective and
objective reality. Writing on faith and the individual in *Concluding
Unscientific Postscript*, Kierkegaard, for whom faith was the central issue of Christianity, notes that faith "is precisely the contradiction between the infinite passions of the individual's inwardness
and objective uncertainty" (*Postscript*, p. 182). *The Concept of
Irony* makes this relationship between faith and the notion of

---

[11]This pattern of repetition and difference occurs frequently throughout
Piers Plowman, creating a kind of structural coherence tht runs counter to
the rather episodic plot.

identity more explicit: "Individuality has a purpose which is absolute. . . . Its activity consists in realizing this purpose, and in and through this realization to enjoy itself, that is to say, its activity is to become *fur sich* [for itself] what it is *an sich* [in itself]" (p. 298). Faith repeats this process of becoming what it is: ". . . faith becomes what it is. . . . In faith the higher actuality of the spirit is not merely becoming, but present while yet becoming" (p. 332). For Kierkegaard faith mediates between man and the Truth, which is for God alone. Yet since this Truth, a transcending of the self, is man's "absolute purpose," he remains ironically trapped. He must try to become what he is not, and in doing so, he reiterates what he is. Faith is the "impossible" exit from this trap, yet, as Kierkegaard says, it can be proved only after death. Man in his quest for faith remains only what he becomes.

In this respect Long Wille's reaction to Clergie's speech—first misunderstanding, then rebellion—becomes a loss of identity, of his Christian grounding, that gives way to what Kierkegaard calls the "sickness unto death," despair. Clergie's attempt to define dowel quickly passes from faith into complaint against the abuses of the clergy. Since such complaints concern themselves entirely with life lived in and for this world, they lead to a suggestion of imminent but earthly reform. However real the abuses Clergie addresses may be, this suggestion creates misunderstanding because the dreamer takes it literally (as is his wont): "'Thanne is dowel and dobet,' quod I, '*dominus* and kny3thode?'" (line 336). Scripture, in her attempt to correct the dreamer's mistake, merely succeeds in arousing the dreamer's presumptuous pride of learning. His debate with Scripture and the ensuing long speech on predestination plunge the dreamer into his first crisis of faith. In his romantic attraction to satire, to the discrepancy between his ideals and his earthly perceptions of the world, he forgets his "absolute purpose," his relation to God. The rebellious monologue that ends passus 10 reveals that, far from actually progressing toward dowel, the dreamer has arrived at an almost nihilistic view of both this world and the next. The constant refrain of invective and complaint that he has heard from his guides directed against the learned and the clergy lead him to question the value of learning, to reject his hosts, and even to deny, presumptuously and despairingly, the role of the individual and good works in salvation.

The question "What is dowel?" has finally been emptied of all its content. Wille's view of salvation undermines the notion of salvation so that it becomes meaningless as a goal or standard of behavior. To him, salvation and damnation are arbitrary, even perverse, fates that have nothing to do with the way men conduct their lives. In the disorientation that necessarily accompanies the dreamer's romantic rebellion and ironic despair, divine providence itself becomes unfair. While such "wits" as Solomon and Aristotle are condemned to hell, sinners like the Good Robber, Mary Magdalene, and David, who all "wrouȝt wikkedlokest in world," are saved. None of the *Visio*'s ideals are left unscathed by the dreamer in this outburst, not even the principle of *ne soliciti sitis* expressed by Piers when he abandons the life of dowel. Yet paradoxically Piers's rejection of rationality and the world is an expression of the highest "trupe" and faith, a recognition of a higher will beyond the human will. Wille rejects rationality because he cannot perceive rationally any such beneficent order. If, as Clergie's and Studie's harangues have led the dreamer to believe, learning is of no more benefit than ignorance, then, the dreamer concludes, divine intention is obscure: "Ther are witty and wel libbynge ac hire werkes ben yhudde / In þe handes of almyȝty god." Out of his despair he fashions a response to what he perceives is life's absurdity by immersing himself in the world and indulging his will. As Kierkegaard suggests, for the romantic ironist "all things are possible" (*Irony*, p. 299). Wille forgets his relation to God and the divine Truth; he becomes "what he beomes."

At the moment of his rebellion Wille looks at his experiences, at the discourse that surrounds him and by which he defines himself (as scholastic philosopher, as dialectician), and perceives only absence. He is confronted by the dilemma of Kierkegaard's romantic ironist:

Our God is in the heavens; he hath done whatsoever he hath pleased; the ironist is on earth and does just as he likes. Still, one cannot blame the ironist because he finds it so difficult to become something, for it is not easy to choose when one has such an enormous range of possibilities. For a change he even deems it appropriate to let fate and accident decide for him. [P. 299]

Throughout the remainder of *Dowel* and all of *Dobet*, Wille responds to this situation by poetically creating himself, assuming the ironic personae he has fashioned for himself—rebel, sinner, penitent, pilgrim, witness. His roles are the trappings of his rebellion.

The climactic eighth vision attempts to reveal the presence behind Wille's experiences, the Word behind the words. His vision is not, however, the vision of the mystic. He does not come face to face with the divine; rather, he views it "through a glass, darkly." Langland surrounds his theophany with a multilayered veil of words that mediate between his human protagonist and the divine presence. At the beginning of this vision the dreamer falls asleep on Palm Sunday to the sounds of "Gloria laus" and "Osanna," the words of the liturgy for Palm Sunday. Indeed, the time frame of the entire vision is similarly controlled by the liturgy for the Easter season. After witnessing the events of Good Friday and Holy Saturday, the dreamer awakens to the Te deum laudamus of the Easter-morning service. Within the vision the events of the Redemption are filtered through a number of verbal screens that interpose themselves between the dreamer and his vision to control and shape it. These include the fictions of the parable, the romance, the synoptic Gospels, and the personification allegory.

In the harrowing-of-hell sequence, narrated by a character named Book, words themselves become dramatic acts, participants in the central act of salvation. The transformation of everyday language into the *verba arcana* of salvation requires the resignification of linguistic signs.

And as Adam and all poruȝ a tree deyden,
Adam and all poruȝ a tree shul turne to lyue,
And gile is bigiled and in his gile fallen; . . .
þe bitternesse þat þow hast browe, now brouke it þiselue;
That art doctour of deep drynk þat þow mayest.
For i þat am lord of lif, loue is my drynke,
And for þat drynke today I deide vpon erþe.
I fauȝt so me purstep ȝit for mannes soule sake;
May no drynke me moiste, ne my purst slake,
Til þe vendage falle in þe vale of Iosaphat,
That I drynke riȝt ripe Must, *Resureccio mortuorum.*

[18.358-60, 363-70]

This speech, Christ's to Lucifer, manipulates signifiers so that
each comes to signify its opposite. Life is brought together with
death; grace becomes guile; Satan's drink of death, through death,
becomes the drink of life. As in the pardon scene, the key words
of Christ's speech—"gile," "lawe," "riȝte," "resoun," "deep," and
"lif"—become divorced from their signifieds and refer only to
their opposites. At this moment irony is mastered in Kierkegaard's
sense, for we witness the negation of negation: "the essence is
none other than the phenomenon, the phenomenon none other
than the essence; possibility is not so prudish as to betake itself
to actuality, but actuality is possibility" (*Irony*, p. 338).

Yet, this resignification of language can represent only a poetic
moment; it can only be a fiction, an attempt to realize in human
terms the mysteries of faith. The necessary distortion of language
that accompanies such a poetic vision strains the conventions that
make language possible at all until all meaningful communication
finally gives way to silence. In his journal Kierkegaard writes:

It is fortunate that *language has a number of expressions for nonsense
and drivel*. Otherwise I would have become mad, for what else does
it prove except all that one said was nonsense. Oh, how fortunate that
language is so developed in this respect: that way one may yet hope
occasionally to hear *reasonable discourse*. [*Irony*, p. 24]

135

Like Kierkegaard, Langland recognizes the Babel latent in his negativity. The last two passus of *Piers Plowman*, ironically entitled the *Vita de Dobest*, illustrates not the life of dobest, but the truth of Kierkegaard's observation: they deconstruct the *verba arcana* of salvation until language becomes nonsense.

The assault on the eighth vision's language begins with the breakdown of the four cardinal virtues, the foundation of the ninth vision's community (19.454-56, 459-74). Through a logic similar to that which transforms signifiers in the previous visions, each of the speakers manipulates language until the words come to have contrary meanings; the cardinal virtues become vices. To the vicory, prudence means guile and deceit; to the lord, fortitude becomes an excuse for bullying; to the king, justice places him above the law. Finally, in a scene that deconstructs the dialectic between waking and sleeping, inside and outside, the personification of Need materializes while the dreamer is awake and undermines *Spiritus temperancie* (temperance) by perverting it to mere expediency and using it to justify stealing. These perversions of language plunge the society of the ninth vision into a moral relativism of the most subversive kind. Language is no longer an expression of social and divine order, but of meaninglessness, of silence that "haunts and jests" (*Irony*, p. 291).

The destruction of Vnite in the final passus parallels the breakdown of linguistic possibilities for signification inherent within personification allegory itself. Turned back upon themselves and their signifieds, the personifications are emptied of meaning: "For contrarious thynges ne ben nat wont to ben ifelawshiped togyder. Nature refuseth that contrarious thynges ben yjoined."[12] Life and Death undergo a transformation that comes dangerously close to negating the words as linguistic signs. In the climactic eighth vision, Life and Death are locked in battle with the sides clearly drawn—Life is identified with Christ and Death with the devil. In fact, Life kills Death through Christ's passion and the harrowing

[12]Chaucer, *Boece* 2.6.80.

136

of hell. In the final passus, however, although Life and Death still struggle, the sides are drawn differently. The spiritual meanings of these terms are gradually stripped away. Death is the scourge of Kynde (nature), Life the henchman of the Antichrist. During the battle Life is on the brink of being killed, of negating itself. A similar process of negation takes place with other personifications. It happens to Coueitise quite ironically from the mouth of Conscience: ". . . wolde criste of his grace / That Coueitise were cristene þat is so kene to fighte" (20.140-41). Even Conscience is afflicted with the linguistic relativism that infects the final passus of the poem with his wish that Coueitise, the signifier of a sin, would act like a Christian.

This process of emptying language of meaning culminates in the entry of the real Antichrists—the friars—into Vnite. With their learning they are finally able to negate language: "Thus he goop and gaderep and glosep pere he shryue / Til Contricion hadde clene foryeten to crye and to wepe / And wake for his wikked werkes as he was want to doone" (20.368-72). The poem's exploration of language and its inadequacies is complete when Contrition leaves off contrition. As a personification and signifier, Contrition can only have meaning as a sign of what it represents—the act of contrition. It must be what it is. Yet is is not. The allegory ceases to mean anything. It gives itself over to the "infinite silence" of irony. The emptiness and the nothingness with which the poem ends reveal and conceal what is most important—in Augustine's words, the paradox between the emptiness of language and the Christian's mandate to preach the Word, to express what he knows, to praise God. In one sense, Langland ends where Kierkegaard does. But his poem does not, and cannot, articulate the way to transcend this paradox—Kierkegaard's leap of faith. It remains written in a language that endlessly and ironically rebels against and confirms its imperfect nature.

5. Drama, Character, and Irony: Kierkegaard and Wycherley's *The Plain Dealer*

DRAMA is fraught with and characterized by the contradictions and discrepancies of imitation. Its actors represent characters, and its characters represent "real" people; its people, in turn, represent types, archetypes, or antitypes; its stage represents a world, or part of one; and the dramatist himself represents any number of possibilities: chance, circumstance, fate, predestination, even Divine Providence. The basis of drama, in this respect, is irony, the metaphysics of paradox described by Sören Kierkegaard in *The Concept of Irony.* Irony is not simply a quality of a given text or performance but the essential condition that makes possible the multiple pretenses of dramatic experience.[1] Its fictions complicate and undermine whatever claims the stage may have to stability or authority, or, in other words, they make Dryden's classically "correct" definition of drama as "an imitation of nature" far more

---

[1] For an argument that anticipates mine (and to which I am indebted) see J. Hillis Miller, "Narrative Middles: A Preliminary Outline," in *Genre* 11 (1978): 357-87. Miller argues that "irony is the basic trope of narrative fiction . . . in the perpetual discrepanc[ies] between author and narrator, or between narrator and character in 'indirect discourse.' . . . All narrative is therefore the linear demonstration of the impossibility of linear coherence" (p. 386).

138

problematic than it first seems.[2] The paradox of imitation, of putting on stage what "both is and is not" (*Irony*, p. 161), raises questions about the nature of drama and the world it tries to reflect; it points also to the dialectics of identity and art so crucial to Kierkegaard's thought. There is a significant overlapping here; the differential natures of irony and drama make it difficult, if not impossible, to discuss one without invoking (if only silently) the other.

The problems of dramatic imitation hinge on several questions: What exactly is being imitated? Does one try to define "nature" as an unchanging ideal or as the inconsistent fiction it often seems? Can it be both? And, finally, how does one describe drama's relationship to the problematics of nature? As reflection or as paradox? These questions are at once crucial and, in any prescriptive sense, unanswerable. "Nature" itself remains elusive. Yet the questions themselves reflect and are reflected in the essential ironies of drama—the "perpetual discrepancies" between playwright and character, playwright and audience, and character and audience that define the genre. Admittedly, these "discrepancies" are unsettling. They complicate any formal definition of drama as imitation and ultimately disturb our convenient assumptions about meaning, communication, and coherence in the theater. Yet such paradoxically is their value. Criticism is always a search for metaphors to inspire or energize a poetics. Those of irony and drama are, I believe, archetypal, describing the fictions that are the genre's bases. And as fictions, as metaphors, they may take us part way toward an implicit (or, in Kierkegaard's sense, "silent") recognition of drama as inherently dialectical, as an ironic con-

[2]On the problems of "imitation" and "nature" in the seventeenth century see Rose Zimbardo, "Imitation to Emulation: 'Imitation of Nature' from the Restoration to the Eighteenth Century," *Restoration* 2 (1978): 2-9; and, Rose Zimbardo, "Dramatic Imitation of Nature in the Restoration's Seventeenth-Century Predecessors," in Robert Markley and Laurie Finke, eds., *From Renaissance to Restoration: Metamorphoses of the Drama* (Cleveland, Ohio: Bellflower Press, 1984), pp. 56-86.

139

founding of the premises of imitation and nature on which it rests.

Few plays deal so suggestively with drama's ironies as William Wycherley's *The Plain Dealer*, a savage, often difficult work that describes itself by its failure to do what dramatic satire is supposed to do: hold a mirror up to nature and improve it. The play is in one sense a satire that celebrates satire's limitations.[3] As such, it reveals some fundamental truths about generic identity and the contradictions and ironies that define it. Wycherley's play often seems less a self-consistent artifact than a reflexive experience that problematicizes the questions of drama and character, art and nature, as it asks them. It points also to the paradoxical existence of drama as, in Kierkegaard's sense, its own archetype, a limit between the concrete and universal, an ironic identification of phenomenon and essence (*Irony*, pp. 180, 231, 240, 264-65). Like Kierkegaard's notion of irony, *The Plain Dealer* interprets only the essential conditions of its existence, the paradoxes of being and not being what it is. In this respect, it is at once original and completely typical of its genre, offering its audience a glimpse of the tensions and discrepancies that sustain the theater's essential fictions of dramatic imitation. It is, to borrow a phrase, just like any other play, only more so.[4]

[3]See Rose Zimbardo, *Wycherley's Drama: A Link in the Development of English Satire* (New Haven, Conn.: Yale University Press, 1965), pp. 98-165. For other representative interpretations of *The Plain Dealer* see Norman Holland, *The First Modern Comedies* (Cambridge, Mass.: Harvard University Press, 1959), pp. 96-113; Virginia Ogden Birdsall, *Wild Civility: The English Comic Spirit on the Restoration Stage* (Bloomington: Indiana University Press, 1970), pp. 157-77; Katharine M. Rogers, "Fatal Inconsistency: Wycherley and *The Plain Dealer*," *ELH* 28 (1961): 148-62; Ian Donaldson, "The 'Tables Turned': *The Plain Dealer*," *Essays in Criticism* 17 (1967): 304-21; and Anthony Kaufman, "Idealization, Disillusion, and Narcissistic Rage in Wycherley's *The Plain Dealer*," *Criticism* 21 (1979): 119-33.

[4]A question that arises here (if it has not already arisen for most readers when they glanced at my title) is, Why Kierkegaard? Why not Derrida or Lacan? In one respect, the purpose of this collection is to explore the validity

Like many other Restoration comedies, *The Plain Dealer* explores an individual's response to his imperfect world but, unlike most, spends as much time laying bare its hero's inconsistencies as it does attacking those of his society. The hero, Captain Manly, is simultaneously a familiar psychological creation and a familiar theatrical type. He is not a classically realistic character but an ironic construct defined by the paradoxes he embodies: either absolute fool and the butt of Wycherley's often grotesque satire or moral crusader and the dramatist's mouthpiece. Manly never becomes one or the other. He does not change or progress as the action unfolds, nor does he represent an ideational conflict as, say, Dryden's tragic heroes do. And he does not confront an overwhelming existential dilemma, not even the one posed by his own contradictory nature. For that matter, Manly hardly seems to have the intelligence or introspection to analyze his behavior. He is, ironically, the sum of all his possibilities. His existence becomes dialectical: the conflicts he embodies are not those between moral man and immoral society but those *within* the individual. Like Horner in Wycherley's *The Country Wife*, Manly is the dramatic "self" as contradiction, an existence that Wycherley seems to find natural enough in a fallen, darkly comic world.

of such questions, to examine the critical enterprise itself as a kind of fiction. The coupling of Kierkegaard and Wycherley inhabits the realm of "what if?" Yet so does reading, so does writing, so does criticism precisely because of—not despite—their temporal, historical natures. Our current critical fictions, our "what ifs?", are irrevocably ideological. In this regard the pairings of Kierkegaard and Wycherley, Kierkegaard and Thoreau, and Kierkegaard and Eliot are *not* ahistorical attempts to read or interpret by Kierkegaard's light. The history they speak to, however, is not a fictional re-presentation of nineteenth-century Danish thought but the history of criticism in its contemporary convulsions. As Paul A. Bové suggests above, Kierkegaard's project poses a radical challenge to bourgeois criticism as an institution. Thus the ironic coupling *Kierkegaard and Literature* is in itself destabilizing; one of its purposes is to see what happens to critical activity if it is perceived ironically, if it rejects the ideological fictions of stability, meaning, reason, and coherence that define criticism generically and politically.

The paradoxes of Manly's character and the interpretative problems they create may come into sharper focus if we look briefly at Wycherley's comic method in his "dedication" to *The Plain Dealer* and then at Kierkegaard's treatment of irony as both an instance—a poetic moment—and a metaphysic. The dramatist's savagely ironic epistle to "Mother B[ennet]," a notorious Restoration bawd, suggests the extent to which problems of judging and interpreting inhere in the play. In his adopted persona of "The Plain-Dealer," as he signed his dedication, Wycherley burlesques conventionally fulsome dedications, using parody and paradox to reflect what he seems to consider an absurd reality:

And this play claims naturally your Protection, since it has lost its Reputation with the Ladies of stricter lives in the Play-house; and (you know) when mens endeavors are discountenanc'd and refus'd, by the nice coy Women of Honour, they come to you, bashful men, of which number I profess myself to be one, though a Poet, a Dedicating Poet; To you I say, Madam who have as discerning a judgment in what's obscene or not, as any quick-sighted civil Person of 'em all, and can make as much of a double meaning saying as the best of 'em; yet wou'd not, as some do, make nonsense of a Poet's jest, rather than not make it baudy: by which they show they as little value Wit in a Play, as in a Lover, provided they can bring t'other thing about.[5]

Wycherley's double entendres and multiple meanings, crammed into nearly every clause, create a patchwork of ironic instability. The satire in this mock epistle is often brutally frank, but it works against so many targets—old fashioned hypocrisy, ignorance, obscenity mongering, fawning poets, dim-witted patrons, "nice coy Women of Honour," misinterpretation—that its implied moral norms tend to get lost in the cross fire. Wycherley's literary parody, in this respect, begins to describe its own essentially ironic form.

[5]All quotations from *The Plain Dealer* are from William Wycherley, *The Complete Plays of William Wycherley*, ed. Gerald Weales (New York: Doubleday, 1965). References are to act and page number.

142

His epistle is not a self-contained, systematic attack but a destabilizing force that extends into the minds of its readers. Ultimately, it undermines the interpretative process itself: "According to the Rules of Dedications, 'tis no matter whether you understand or no, what I quote or say to you, of Writing; for an Author can easily make any one a Judg or Critick, in an Epistle, as an Hero in his Play" (p. 382). Traditional assumptions about "Writing" and understanding seem to become so much hash. In this regard, Wycherley's dedication is less an introduction to *The Plain Dealer* than an initiation, implicating its readers in the processes of interpreting—and misinterpreting—its ironies.

The "Dedicating Poet," then, cancels his bets as he makes them. Irony always implies its opposite, the possibility of an other, and the impossibility of its own coherence. If it insists on anything, it is on its own indirection. In this sense Wycherley's epistle, like the play that follows it, works against itself as well as its ostensible targets, endlessly reiterating and undermining its satiric premises. It becomes a form of repetition, the very experience that Kierkegaard suggests is crucial to the problems of both irony and identity. The dramatist's assertion, *"You . . . Madam, are no more an Hypocrite than I am when I praise you"* (p. 383), underscores his own ironic deception as it questions his stance as satirist. The possibilities it offers are open-ended: either "I am as much as hypocrite as you are" or "in this hypocritical world we are the only honest ones around." There is no hard-and-fast answer here, no one rhetorical meaning to isolate, only the experience of being, as Wycherley entitled his first play, "lost in a wood." His dedication thus poses yet another paradox: although it boils with raucous humor and delights in lambasting hypocrisy, it is essentially static and atemporal, a series of ironic moments that turn inward upon themselves. Its reflexivity both entices the reader to read on and ironically obviates the need for him to go any further—where can one go, after all, beyond repetition? Wycherley's epistle offers only its own pretenses and indirections. It is not a polemic against a corrupt world but a demonstration of satire's limitations, its inability to register the tensions and discrepancies that characterize the experience of irony.

Wycherley's reader, then, as "Judg or Critick" faces problems that cannot be reduced to rhetorical explanations, that are inherent in the process of interpretation itself. These difficulties, though, should hardly come as a surprise—irony, whether narrative or dramatic, resists interpretation. Kierkegaard, for example, claims that irony is the "infinitely correcting moment" (*Irony*, p. 63) that cannot be defined but can be rendered only metaphorically or poetically. His own descriptions of irony are, consequently, paradoxical, circular, and (of course) ironic. Irony is "a nothingness which consumes everything and a something which one can never catch hold of, which both is and is not" (p. 161); "it is a completed standpoint which turns back into itself" (p. 154); it is "the beginning, yet no more than a beginning; it is and it is not" (p. 237); and ultimately it is "infinitely silent" (p. 63). Irony, in short, is an all *and* nothing proposition, an extension of the "perpetual discrepancies" that characterize existence, for Kierkegaard, in a secular, profane world.

The paradoxes Kierkegaard uses to describe irony suggest its significance for the artist. Art is a manifestation of the ironist's "living poetically" (p. 338), a testament to his recognition of his paradoxical existence. This belief underlies Kierkegaard's description of Shakespeare as ironist, a seminal passage in the aesthetics of irony.[6] It is worth quoting at length:

When Shakespeare relates himself ironically to his work, this is simply in order to let the objective prevail. Irony is now pervasive, ratifying each particular feature . . . so that the true equilibrium may be effected in the microcosmic situation of the poem whereby it gravitates towards itself. The greater the oppositions involved in this movement, so much the more irony is required to master those spirits which obstinately

[6]Bert States, in *Irony and Drama: A Poetics* (Ithaca, N.Y.: Cornell University Press, 1971), quotes the same passage but uses it in a different—and illuminating—context. See especially pp. 38-84.

seek to storm forth; while the more irony is present, so much the more freely and poetically does the poet hover above his composition. Irony is not present at some particular point in the poem but omnipresent in it, so that the visible irony in the poem is in turn ironically mastered. Thus irony renders both the poem and the poet free. For this to occur, however, the poet must himself be master over irony. It is not always the case that the poet is master over irony in the actuality to which he belongs merely because he is successful in mastering irony in the moment of artistic production. [Pp.336-37]

Irony, for Kierkegaard, becomes not only a symptom of the artist's living poetically but also a metaphysic, two particular "oppositions" mastered by an encompassing vision. The "poem" itself, in this respect, is not an end but a means to "truth" and "freedom" (pp. 338-39). As an ironic form it exists in a state of actualizing itself, constantly in the process of becoming what it has the visible potential to become, through its "oppositions," repetitions, and changes, through what Derrida (a philosopher greatly, if silently, indebted to Kierkegaard) calls "iteration."[7] This is essentially the open-ended action of "visible irony" being "ironically mastered," becoming "omnipresent" in the work. Irony, in this respect, is a self-generating and self-consuming process that implicates the poet in its existence, freeing him only by undermining his identity outside of his work, by making him in essence an ironic self-creation. The ironist, then, is both creator and part of his creation, both master and ultimately subject of his irony. His freedom is defined, or rather defines itself, only "in the microcosmic situation of the poem whereby it gravitates towards itself," in the reflexive process of irony mastering its oppositions. Thus irony for the poet is, again

---

[7] See Jacques Derrida, "Limited Inc abc . . . ," trans. Samuel Weber, *Glyph* 2 (1977): 190: "Iterability [or repetition] supposes a minimal remainder (as well as a minimum of idealization) in order that the identity of the *self-same* be repeatable and identifiable *in, through,* and even *in view of* its alteration. For the structure of iteration . . . implies *both* identity *and* difference. Iteration in its 'purest' form—and it is always impure—contains *in itself* the discrepancy of a difference that constitutes it as iteration."

paradoxically, both intensely subjective and a means of transcending subjectivity. It offers the artist two temptations: a transcendent freedom and the chance to pursue a hopeless quest for an illusory freedom.

Irony, though, is not masturbatory; it plays itself out as drama and, in this respect, implicates its readers or audience in its dialectical processes. Kierkegaard's recognition of the poet's limited mastery beyond "the moment of artistic production" implies another viewpoint, one capable of judging the artist as well as his work. This perspective is both an outgrowth and an essential condition of irony. In an important sense, irony creates an audience— *its* audience—that "repeats" the poet's dilemma.[8] As in Wycherley's dedication, the reader or spectator is both judge and target, both superior to and implicated in the ironic process. For Kierkegaard, then, the relationship between poet and reader becomes extremely problematic, a repetition of the paradox of "identity *and* difference." Irony leaves its audience in what Ronald Schleifer, in "Irony and the Literary Past" below, calls "the silence of infinite possibilities and nothingness." It offers them two paradoxical alternatives that, in their own way, reflect the dialectic of transcendence and failure that confronts the artist—one may be able to interpret infinitely or not at all. Irony, then, binds the artist and his audience dialectically, implicating each in the other's existence. It comprehends, as it must, both creative and recreative processes: the work itself and what is not the work, the text and what George Steiner calls its "rival text,"[9] its own interpretation.

Metaphorically, at least, Kierkegaard's indirections repeat the

---

[8]On the rhetorical aspect of irony see Wayne Booth, *A Rhetoric of Irony* (Chicago: University of Chicago Press, 1974), especially pp. 1-8, 33-46, 120-36.

[9]See George Steiner, "Critic/Reader," *NLH* 10 (1979): 423-52. In one respect irony blurs the distinctions that it insists on making; this seems the case with Steiner's distinctions between "critic" and "reader." Irony demands *both* distance *and* internalization on the part of its audience, encouraging interpretations precisely because it must frustrate them.

essential paradoxes of dramatic experience. In his view, art becomes the expression of tensions and contradictions within the individual, within human nature itself. His choice of Shakespeare as a "type" of the poet is illuminating; Kierkegaard tends to see the philosophical problems of existence as a kind of internalized drama, a psychomachia of the ironic and secular struggling to actualize themselves as faith. (Such is implicit, at least, in his notion of "mastered" irony.) But drama, like irony, is more than a metaphor; it is the essence of the problem. Kierkegaard's recognition of the "perpetual discrepancies" within the artist's imagination reflects his implicit critique of traditional notions of identity.[10] The poet defines himself not by what he produces but by his living poetically, trying to master the tensions and contradictions of his "actuality." He is both in and of his work. The irony of his existence—the play of "oppositions" within him—is, in a very real sense, his identity.

The paradoxes of Kierkegaardian irony, then, bring us full circle to Wycherley and the problems of nature and imitation. His final two plays seem to delight in undercutting traditional assumptions about both drama and the world it tries to mirror. In essence, Wycherley's ironic characters (particularly Horner in *The Country Wife* and Manly in *The Plain Dealer*) reflect the ironic, contradictory nature of the self. They are not, in this sense, inconsistent dramatic fictions but metaphoric reflections of an inconsistent "actuality," Wycherley's and his audience's. The dramatist's characters, then, become his means of exploring, comically and un-

---

[10]On the contemporary (particularly Lacanian) problematics of identity see Willis R. Buck, "Reading Autobiography," *Genre* 13 (1980): 477-98; and, for a helpful overview, Vincent B. Leitch, *Deconstructive Criticism: An Advanced Introduction* (New York: Columbia University Press, 1983), especially pp. 10-14, 29-32. My uses of "traditional" and "classical" to describe identity and its dramatic imitation approximate Catherine Belsey's in *Critical Practice* (London: Methuen, 1980), although one hardly has to embrace Marxist critiques of the bourgeois self to see their relevance to Kierkegaard, as Bové's essay suggests.

147

systematically, why irony and drama are essential metaphors for, and descriptions of, human nature. This is not, I think, to turn *The Plain Dealer* into an existential philosophical tract or to claim for it a brilliant epistemological originality it may not deserve. In an important sense, drama is inherently self-conscious. It must exist as performance to exist at all. And it is precisely Wycherley's superb sense of the theater that allows him to explore drama's implications as both a metaphor and a mirror for nature. In practice, the playwright seems concerned with probing his audience's (and by implication his own) responses to his demonstrations that the social and human values he portrays in *The Plain Dealer* (among them wit, poise, detachment, love, friendship, and virtue) are often deficient. Wycherley's implicit subject, in this respect, may be an ironic exploration of the social and linguistic myths by which his society sustains itself.

Wycherley's great talent as a comic dramatist lies in his double-edged handling of characters, stock situations, and language. *The Plain Dealer* is at once sharply etched yet disturbingly ambiguous. Manly, for example, embodies the sort of outraged idealism any moral individual (or one who assumes he is moral) is bound to feel when confronted by the world's vice, folly, and hypocrisy; but at the same time he comes close to being a caricature of the foolish, inflexible, and self-important moralist. In the play's opening scene, Wycherley sets Manly's self-righteousness against Plausible's spineless acceptance of social duplicity to suggest something of his hero's contradictory nature. At first, Manly gets the better of the exchange—plain dealing in the sense of bluff honesty is always in fashion—by attacking his visitor's "supercilious Forms, and slavish Ceremonies" and defending his own honor: "Counterfeit Honour will not be current with me, I weigh the man, not his title; 'tis not the King's stamp can make the metal better, or heavier: your Lord is a Leaden shilling, which you may bend every way; and debases the stamp he bears, instead of being rais'd by't" (1.394). Manly's antitheses admit of no middle ground. They become his way of separating himself from what he sees as the cor-

ruption and hypocrisy around him. But his seemingly flat asser-
tions, here as elsewhere in the play, have a way of slipping from
satiric criticism to solipsistic defenses of his own integrity. In his
own way, Manly is as self-dramatizing as Plausible, the fop he condemns for not wearing his heart on his sleeve. The hero's language,
though, one of disjunctions rather than transitions, soon fails him.
By the end of the scene, having castigated the world's double-
dealing, Manly is reduced to speaking the worst of his insults in
asides before he exits, according to the stage direction, "thrusting
out my Lord Plausible." His violence may be what Plausible deserves, but at the same time it reflects Manly's verbal impotence,
his failure to change the world by condemning it. In this respect,
Manly's kicking Plausible down the stairs asks for a double response—the hero seems both social critic and bully.

This "yes-but" effect[11] is typical of the ambiguity that hangs
over Wycherley's hero throughout the play. Manly can be, and
often is, both brutally accurate and outrageously wrong. His attacks are justified in the sense that his society seems as corrupt
as he says it is, but his awareness of its faults is undermined by
his own intolerance, double-dealing, and blindness both to the
vices of Olivia and Vernish and to the virtues (such as they are)
of Fidelia and Freeman. By the time Manly decides to seduce
Olivia, while pretending to be the disguised Fidelia, the audience's
capacity for moral indignation has probably been overloaded to the
point that his scheming offers as good a laugh as his antagonists'
hypocrisy. Ironically, he confirms his assessment of human nature,
becoming both the perpetrator and the target of his satire.

Manly's shortsightedness, however, his knack for undercutting
himself, is neither simply stupidity nor self-deception. As in his
earlier plays, Wycherley in *The Plain Dealer* relies heavily on disguises, eavesdroppings, mistaken identities, and characters falling
over and bumping into each other in the dark. Metaphorically,
these theatrical devices seem to reflect the characters' confusion

---

[11] Weales, *Plays of Wycherley*, ed. Weales, p. ix.

as they try to cope with the deceit and absurdity of a fragmented social world. Their figurative blindness, in this sense, often appears to be less a satiric aberration than an essential of existence in Wycherley's comic universe. The play's major figures, good and bad alike, suffer from congenitally defective judgments. Manly's misadventures demonstrate that he has little idea of what his friends and foes are like; Olivia and Vernish, the play's most ambitious hypocrites, are more successful in deceiving themselves than each other. Freeman and Fidelia, often taken, respectively, as examples of Wycherley's moderation and idealism, do not fare much better. Freeman's pursuit of the Widow Blackacre and her money makes him seem nearly as perverse as she is. He, like Manly, is a product of his society; as it tends more towards the immoral than amoral, so he, too, becomes more acquisitive than pleasure-seeking, more a tolerant part of its duplicity than a bemused critic of its affectations. His repetition of "business" in act 2—"But you have no business anights, Widow; and I'll make you pleasanter business than any you have; for anights, I assure you, I am a Man of great business; for the business" (p. 432)—emphasizes his calculating, almost anti-erotic self-perception as a man on the sexual and financial make. Fidelia has, one imagines, ample evidence of Manly's insensitivity and "downright Barbarity," but clings to her initial assessment of his character: "Sir, your Merit is unspeakable" (I, 399). She sees and does not see, as her unintentionally ironic use of "unspeakable" suggests. Her nature, like Manly's and Freeman's, seems inherently contradictory: the virtuous and selfless lover coexists with the undiscerning teenager suffering from a schoolgirl's infatuation.

The tensions within these characters suggest much about what Wycherley's notion of "nature" entails. The dramatist seems to delight in displaying his figures again and again in familiar, but often troublesome or ambiguous, poses. They take shape through repetition rather than psychological growth, animated by the discrepancies within their natures. They seem to have no past; one cannot imagine Manly, for example, as anything other than a

"Sea-Monster," just as one cannot envision a Widow Blackacre not mired in litigation, an Olivia not scheming and backbiting, or a Fidelia not in disguise following at her captain's heels. The "actuality" of these characters is ahistorical, an extended present that repeats itself in familiar tableaus: Manly insulting the fops and denouncing society's evils, Freeman chasing the Widow, Olivia tormenting Manly, and Fidelia tirelessly demonstrating her love.

Yet these scenes and others like them paradoxically repeat themselves with essential differences. The major characters exist in a state close to what Kierkegaard suggests is "the dialectic of repetion": "What is repeated has been, otherwise it could not be repeated, but precisely the fact that it has been gives to repetition the character of novelty" (*Repetition*, pp. 12, 52). This dialectic, as Schleifer notes, is one of both time and identity, of present versus the past and of the individual against himself. Wycherley's characters, in this sense, are trapped by the repetitions that seem to identify them. They are victims not only of their satiric failings but of their dialectical existences as dramatic figures. Irony, Kierkegaard suggests, "succumbs to itself, since it constantly goes beyond itself while remaining itself" (*Irony*, p. 161). So, too, Wycherley's characters are forever on the way to becoming what they are. Their efforts to live up to their idealized self-images only confirm the discrepancies between what they are and what they imagine they can be.

The paradoxes of character and imitation, though, may perhaps best be rendered metaphorically. In his article below, Schleifer (borrowing both from Kierkegaard and from Saussure) offers this figure to lay the groundwork for his yoking of irony and identity: "Irony . . . is like a piece of paper on one side of which is written, 'Whatever appears on the other side is true'; and on the other side of which is written, 'Whatever appears on the other side is false'." To describe the "is and is not" of dramatic imitation, though, we may have to imagine this paper rotating in front of a mirror that reflects and inverts the writing. Decoding the mirror image of "true-false" does nothing to stabilize its message. We are confronted by yet another "perpetual discrepancy"—that of character, the imitation of ironic identity. This figure may help us recognize what we confront in Wycherley's characters. They represent not deviations from a stable "actuality" but rather the fiction of identity. They assert both their own problematic natures and the problematics of "nature" itself.

The bases of this sort of irony—the paradoxes of Kierkegaard's repetition and Derrida's "iteration"—are, in essence, comic. Bert States, borrowing Kierkegaard's phrasing, argues that tragedy is mastered irony.[12] If so, then the comedy of a play like *The Plain Dealer* lies in its characters' failures to master the "oppositions" of their natures, in what we might call their ironic incompetence. Irony, Kierkegaard suggests, replaces the actual with the ideal and tries to negate the past by idealizing the timelessness of subjective fantasy. In the fallen world of comedy, it becomes a means of comic self-deception for characters who, by their very natures, cannot "actualize" themselves. The more Olivia declares her "aversion" to fashion, wit, men, and the Court, the more hypocritical and grotesque she appears. Hers is, in one sense, a repetitious and fruitless quest to master the contradictions unleashed by her dissembling: passionate woman, dispassionate manipulator. They come to dominate her. The more she strives to outwit others— the more frantic her lying becomes—the more she becomes herself, as Derrida suggests, "in, through, and . . . in view of" her psychological disguises. She embodies, metaphorically, the negation of mastered irony, the surrender to the subjectivity of comic discrepancy.

Manly, too, falls victim to the "oppositions" within his nature that he can neither master nor transcend. Like Fidelia, he sees, but he refuses to change his views on the basis of what he observes or experiences. In act 3 Manly is accosted by several of Whitehall's parasites and rids himself of them by feigning friendship and then asking them for various favors. On a satiric level,

---

[12] States, *Irony and Drama*, pp. 39-54.

he succeeds in exposing their hypocrisy. When the Lawyer hears "in *Forma Pauperis*" and the Alderman learns he is to be bound with Manly "in City security," they both hurry off, freeing the hero, for the time being, from the hypocrisy he hates so heartily. But Manly seems to learn little about either himself or his society by his dissembling. His posing simply confirms what he already believes:

> You see now what the mighty friendship of the World is; what all Ceremony, Embraces, and plentiful Professions come to: You are no more to believe a Professing Friend, than a threatning Enemy; and as no Man hurts you, that tells you he'll do you a mischief, no man . . . is your Servant, who sayes he is so. [3.461-62]

That this speech is directed to Freeman underscores Manly's refusal to see anything that does not fit his radically idealized view of the world. He perceives discrepancies between appearances and natures easily enough, but he does not and cannot see that such contradictions are the essence of his own nature. The paradoxes he embodies—vision and blindness, wisdom and folly, morality and hypocrisy—are reflections of an ironic existence that "is and is not" what it seems. In this respect, Manly becomes (as Shakespeare says of Coriolanus) "a kind of nothing," emptying his actuality of any significance beyond what Kierkegaard calls the "wild infinity" of his subjectivity (*Irony*, p. 335). Olivia, tellingly, taunts Manly for his "spirit of contradiction": "Your Opinion is your onely Mistress, for you renounce that too, when it becomes another Mans" (2.427). Later, in devastating fashion, she sums up his character in a series of antitheses:

> He that distrusts most the World, trusts most to himself, and is but the more easily deceiv'd, because he thinks he can't be deceiv'd: his cunning is like the Coward's Sword, by which he is oftner worsted, than defended. . . . I knew he lov'd his own singular moroseness so well, as to dote upon any Copy of it; wherefore I feign'd an hatred to the World too, that he might love me in earnest. [4.482]

Olivia recognizes that Manly's "singular moroseness" is inherently self-deceiving, though she does not realize that her hypocritical "Copy" becomes her own "Coward's Sword." Her antitheses reflect the tensions within Manly's brand of self-deception. The ironies of his existence master him, making him a part of, and prey to, the society he condemns. He becomes the world's "threatning Enemy" who blusters but does its fools and knaves little harm. Manly ultimately is true to only his "singular moroseness," his subjective vision of "actuality."

But "actuality" itself, like "nature," is an elusive notion in *The Plain Dealer*. Both terms are essentially convenient, even necessary, fictions. They describe subjective perceptions, both individual and social, rather than hard and fast realities. Not surprisingly, then, Wycherley exploits and undermines what they represent—bedrock assumptions about imitation and identity—to characterize the "perpetual discrepancies" between playwright and spectator, and character and spectator, that underlie his play. In the prologue "the Plain-Dealer" announces, "Our Scribler therefore bluntly bid me say, / He wou'd not have the Wits pleas'd here to Day," and goes on to take potshots at "the fine, loud Gentlemen o' th' Pit," "shrewd Judges who the Boxes sway," and "the Ladies" (pages 385-86). This comic antagonism insists on implicating the audience ironically in the "actuality" of the play; they become both the objects of "the Plain-Dealer's" satire and judges of its accuracy. In this sense, they are subject to a "pervasive" irony that reflects the discrepancies within their own natures. If Wycherley holds up an ironic mirror for his audience, what they see are funhouse distortions of their self-perceptions. John Dennis's account of the initial bewilderment of the audience on the play's opening night seems, in this respect, a fair indication of how the play tends to disturb and disorient its spectators or readers.[13] Irony, says Schleifer, "says one thing and means nothing."[14] So, too, drama "means"

---

[13] John Dennis, *The Critical Works of John Dennis*, ed. Edward Niles Hooker (Baltimore, Md.: Johns Hopkins University Press, 1939), 2:277.

nothing beyond the experience it engenders. The "actuality" of *The Plain Dealer*, in this sense, yokes ironically the fictions of drama and nature, of imitation and identity. It "is and is not" what it seems.

Such paradoxes point to the "infinite" silence that lies beneath dramatic language. In his final play (as one might suspect) Wycherley creates an ironic language that turns the conventional dialogue of the Restoration stage against itself and the "actuality" it tries to describe. If his dramatic prose is very much of its time (for example, in relying on antitheses, similes, competing jargons, often fragmented or asymmetrical syntax, and conjunctions that undermine the logical connections they are supposedly making), the uses to which the playwright puts it are not. Language in *The Plain Dealer* is essentially subjective, even solipsistic, seemingly at the mercy of its speakers' idiosyncrasies, obsessions, and pretenses. It insists again and again on its characters' failures to impose their visions of the world on their often chaotic existences. Characteristically, Wycherley's language tends to work against what the audience sees happening onstage: Manly rages against the very faults he ends up committing; Olivia declares her "aversion" to the gossip, sexual intrigue, and fashion mongering that are the sum of her existence; Novel and Plausible corrupt "wit" to self-serving pettiness and invective. Such discrepancies go beyond straightforward linguistic satire to question—and even undermine—the possibility of rational communication itself. Oldfox, exasperated by the Widow's refusal to listen to his verbal advances, voices what seems to be the play's stylistic motto: "All interruption, and no sence between us" (4.471). "Interruption," the borderline between speech and silence, in an important sense is what characterizes Wycherley's dialogue; it reflects the problematic nature of language and communication in a fallen world.

Linguistic corruption extends throughout *The Plain Dealer*, sub-

---

[14]Ronald Schleifer, "The Trap of the Imagination: The Gothic Tradition, Fiction, and *The Turn of the Screw*," *Criticism* 22 (1981): 297.

suming the very real, even meticulous, distinctions that Wycherley makes between different kinds of comic speech. The word, the linguistic sign itself, is undercut to such an extent that it loses whatever claims it might have to signifying objective meaning. Words, from Olivia's "aversion" to Manly's "honesty" and "plain dealing," become arbitrary playthings that are ironically emptied of meaning and at the same time opened to the possibility of infinite meanings. This is Novel's description of "wit":

Talking is like Fencing, the quicker the better; run 'em down, run 'em, down; no matter for parrying . . . no matter whether you argue in form, push in guard, or no. . . . So much for talking, which I think I have prov'd a mark of Wit; and so is Railing, Roaring, and making a noise, Humor . . . where there is Mischief, there's Wit. Don't we esteem the Monky a Wit amongst Beasts, only because he's mischievous? . . . . as good Nature is a sign of a Fool, being Mischievous is a sign of Wit. [5.500-501]

Novel's speech destroys "Wit" as a standard of both language and social behavior. It is not so much that he is "wrong" or his speech satirically flawed (both seem obvious enough), but that his nonsense raises questions of who could conceivably be "right." His definition is laughably inept and self-serving, as Manly and Freeman quickly note; yet their criticism of him cannot transcend the mazes of ironic qualification on which the play's language insists. Manly's attack on Novel and Oldfox—"You have done like Wits now; for you Wits, when you quarrel, never give over, till you prove one another Fools" (5.501)—undermines his own "plain-dealing," cast, inevitably it seems, in the kind of language he claims he cannot abide. In this sense Novel's corruption of "Wit" paradoxically traps the hero as well as himself, even as it sharpens the distinctions between their different sorts of folly.

Novel's "making a noise," then, comically repeats and undermines the language of those characters, particularly Manly and Freeman, who ridicule him. In the process his speech becomes part of the play's ironic fabric, a language of "noise" and silence that offers itself as experience rather than meaning. Ultimately, Wycherley's dramatic language turns upon itself, a reflection of and a vehicle for creating the essential irony of identity.[15] It deconstructs, in Derrida's sense, the dialectic of subjectivity and objectivity, of "inside" and "outside," as it repeats and transforms itself. It becomes a limit between the self and the silence of irony, celebrating its own artificiality, its own essential emptiness.

One must be careful, though, about mistaking the metaphors of repetition and silence for the stuff of dour nihilism. Kierkegaard holds open the possibility that all ironic expression aspires to the transcendence of "mastered" irony, transforming itself into the ideal which it is not. "Mastered" irony "limits, renders finite, defines, and thereby yields truth, actuality, and content; it chastens and punishes and thereby imparts stability, character and consistency" (*Irony*, pp. 338-39). The reflexivity of artistic production, for Kierkegaard, offers at least the possibilities of "freedom," "stability," and transcendence. In this respect, Wycherley's irony in *The Plain Dealer* seems to work in two ways: to underscore the severity of his satiric attack and to allow both the playwright and his audience to distance themselves from the play's corrupt society and Manly's savage diatribes against its vices. At times, *The Plain Dealer's* irony seems to become almost exorcistic, offering at least the hope of "stability" as a counterweight to the kind of dissillusionment that the hero suffers and that all inhabitants of an imperfect world may occasionally feel. Manly can thus be at once a savage critic of "the World" and its biggest dupe, and the audience can empathize with his idealistic posturing while laughing at his failings. Wycherley's irony, then, rebels against its own tendencies toward negation—against its own nature—by offering, for both the

[15]On postmodern views of language and identity see Belsey, *Critical Practice*, particularly pp. 56-84; and Gayatri Spivak, Introduction, Jacques Derrida, *Of Grammatology* (Baltimore, Md.: Johns Hopkins University Press, 1976).

dramatist and his audience, a way of escaping the viciousness of that play's satire.

It may be necessary to emphasize here that, if drama and irony repeat each other, the experience of the theater is hardly that of Kierkegaard's mysticism. It is the nature of drama to insist on the disjunctions between its signs—characters, scenery, costumes, and props—and what they are supposed to signify. The asymmetry of these essential and "perpetual discrepancies" suggests that the comic imitation of a fragmented reality precludes any leap of faith, even as it asks for a suspension of disbelief. In this regard, if drama, like irony, becomes its own archetype, endlessly repeating and returning to its origins in the "discrepancies" of imitation, then it can affirm, finally, only what *The Plain Dealer* affirms: its radical instability and the radical instability it attempts to imitate. Wycherley's play, then, paradoxically resists its own movement towards "mastered" irony; more precisely, it eliminates the middle ground of objective detachment, forcing us into an ironic no-man's-land between the real and the ideal. Ultimately, it ironizes faith itself.

Eliza's role in *The Plain Dealer* is a telling case in point. The conventional critical reaction is to see her as a surrogate for the audience, commenting incisively on but remaining aloof from Olivia's hypocrisy. Birdsall describes her as a "comic realist" who, like Freeman, "offers[s] . . . believable regenerative possibilities."[16] Eliza from this perspective becomes a sensible moderator, an openminded observer whose attack on her cousin's "aversion" to Horner's name, to "China," and to *The Country Wife* serves as Wycherley's warning against false or narrow interpretations of his art. Yet it seems difficult to accept Eliza as a straightforward spokeswoman for the dramatist in a play that insists on its discrepancies and indirections, that undercuts its characters' cherished self-perceptions almost as a matter of course. She, like Freeman, is uncritical of "the World," likening it to "a constant Keeping

[16]Birdsall, *Wild Civility*, p. 176.

Gallant, whom we fail not to quarrel with, when any thing crosses us, yet cannot part with't for our hearts" (2.408). She is in essence, a kind of kept mistress by her society, too much a part of it to "part with't." In this respect, her defense of *The Country Wife* depends less on her own moral propriety than on her willingness to offer herself and her society as targets for Wycherley's satires. Her opposition to Olivia's attack on the play reflects her awareness (the playwright's own, of course) of how accurate its portrayal of folly and hypocrisy truly is—hardly a penetrating perception considering the time she spends in her cousin's company. Eliza's knowledge is rooted in her worldliness. In act 5, while Olivia is denying the goings-on of the previous evening, Eliza implicates herself in the corrupt and farcical world of lust, betrayal, and deception. Her assurance to her cousin, "No, you need not fear yet, I'll keep your secret," and her subsequent advice, "In this Plain-dealing Age . . . leave off forswearing your self; for when people hardly think the better of a Woman for her real modesty, why shou'd you put that great constraint upon your self to feign it?" (5.493), suggest more a cynically tongue-in-cheek acceptance of human frailty than an exemplary moral stance. Eliza in one respect seems to repeat Manly's paradoxical relationship to society, with the difference that her attitude of live and let live replaces his intolerance. She too is both spectator and accomplice; her comic realism gains her little except the company of characters she dislikes but seemingly cannot avoid. In short, the "regenerative possibilities" that she may represent are themselves fair game for the playwright's irony.

Eliza, then, is not a stable character (at least not in the traditional sense) but a reflexive fiction, Wycherley's ironic justification of his art. Her role emphasizes the dramatist's characteristic undercutting of conventions and expectations. At the end of the play one cannot even fall back on the usual system of rewards and punishments—drama finally holds the mirror up to reveal its own paradoxical nature. The one-sided contract between Freeman and the Widow echoes, with a vengeance, the legal satire of act 3.

159

The marriage between Fidelia and Manly seems to punish her and reward him beyond what either of them deserves. Two of the play's funniest lines are undoubtedly Fidelia's justification for her loyalty: "I left . . . to follow you, Sir; having in several publick places seen you, and observ'd your actions thoroughly, with admiration" (5.514), and Manly's outrageous characterization of Freeman as "a Plain Dealer, too" (5.515). If Manly is admirable and Freeman "a Plain Dealer," then the previous five acts of the play have gone for nought. Wycherley's ending flouts what we know, or assume, about the characters and conventions of comedy and the ability of language to describe a stable, recognizable "actuality." Irony at this point seems more a refuge, a comic hall of mirrors, than a transcendent "equilibrium." It mocks what it asks us to accept.

Yet irony, as it undermines classical notions of identity and imitation, subsumes the artist himself. It becomes a kind of silent gloss, Kierkegaard implies, on the problems of identity and artistic creation. The poet, like Socrates in *The Concept of Irony*, becomes his own creation, an actor in the drama of his existence. He actualizes and loses himself in his work; he "is and is not" what he creates. Artistic creation in this respect renders the poet himself a fictional construct, both present within his work and absent from it. What remains is not a coherent, historical "self" but the fiction of self-creation. If his work is its own "actuality," he himself becomes, metaphorically, almost spectral.

Irony is the poet's double-edged sword. For Wycherley it may represent an effort to distance himself from—and master—the tensions and contradictions of his final play. Yet as dramatist he creates not only the play but his role as its creator. Like his characters, like his audience, he remains subject to the constraints and demands of an "actuality" he cannot control but can only imitate; he, too, stands before an "omnipresent" irony that, as Kierkegaard suggests, sweeps all before it (*Irony*, p. 240). The fact that Wycherley signed himself "The Plain-Dealer" to his ironic dedication suggests much about his paradoxical self-perception as both

160

the master and the servant of his work. In one respect Wycherley's assumed "identity" as "The Plain-Dealer" seems almost a deliberate negation of the self as proof of his aloofness from what he perceives as the corruption of society. At the same time, however, this ironic identification underscores the paradoxical position of the artist who finds he is part of the world he feels compelled to satirize. Wycherley "is and is not" "The Plain-Dealer." As Manly is both fool and moralist, so the dramatist is both a detached observer of hypocrisy and its obsessive anatomist. His persona — which Dryden later celebrated (perhaps with unconscious irony) as "Manly *Witcherley*"[17] — becomes, in this regard, an attempt to free himself from both the darker implications of his play and the society it attacks. Yet this task for the dramatist is what the rock and hill were to Sisyphus. That Wycherley wrote *The Plain Dealer* at all suggests that the freedom he sought was essentially imaginative, even romantic, an escape from the oppositions of his final play, from the fiction of identity, and from the "perpetual discrepancies" of his medium.

Signing himself "The Plain-Dealer" to his dedication, then, seems to have been Wycherley's hedge against the absurdities and contradictions of his "actuality" *and* its dramatic imitation. His persona is a fiction that tries to subsume the dialectic of Manly and Wycherley, of creation and creator. But irony, Kierkegaard says, "loves possibility but flees actuality" (*Irony*, pp. 216-17); Wycherley's ironic signature in this sense represents a romantic moment, a possibility of escape that the playwright reiterates even as his play suggests that such fantasies are but another sort of self-deception. Irony, according to Kierkegaard,

is the subjective freedom which at every moment has within its power the possibility of beginning and is not generated from previous conditions. There is something seductive about every beginning because

[17] John Dryden, "To my Dear Friend Mr. Congreve . . ." in William Congreve, *The Complete Plays of William Congreve*, ed. Herbert Davis (Chicago: University of Chicago Press, 1967), p. 123.

the subject is still free, and this is the satisfaction the ironist longs for. At such moments actuality loses its validity for him; he is free and above. [P. 270]

This "satisfaction" may be in one sense the sort of "subjective freedom" that Wycherley seeks. But *The Plain Dealer* itself insists on the power of "actuality," the paradox of the beginnings that can end only in the repetition of "previous conditions." The play's irony, then, is doubly seductive, offering both the "freedom" of transcending "actuality" and the exhilaration of romantic failure. The two, mastery and slavery, are dialectically bound; together they begin to describe the irony of the artist's existence, the paradox of creation itself. Irony celebrates the absolute imaginative triumph of art while advertising its inability to change, in and of itself, the "actuality" it tries to reflect. In this sense the artist can only repeat himself and the paradoxical moment of his self-actualization—he is the subject and hero of his work and also its ultimate silence, its essential mystery. Wycherley's tirade against "Anti-Wits" in the preface to his *Miscellany Poems*, twenty-eight years after his dedication to "Mother B— —," is signed, of course, "The Plain-Dealer."

A postscript: "Manly *Witcherley*" may have taken an ironist's delight in signing himself "The Plain-Dealer," but this act could not resolve the "perpetual discrepancies" that both characterize and underlie his art. Few writers, in retrospect, seem as subject as Wycherley to Kierkegaard's statement that the poet cannot assume that he will be "master over irony in the actuality to which he belongs merely because he is successful in mastering irony in the moment of artistic production" (*Irony*, p. 337). His life after 1676 becomes—ironically, romantically, absurdly—a gloss on and a postscript to the tensions that characterize *The Plain Dealer*. Wycherley's final forty years were marked by his short, unhappy marriage to the Countess Drogheda, lawsuits with her family after her death, poverty, several years in debtors' prison, years of humiliating dependency on his irascible and litigious father, a laboriously composed volume of execrable poetry, and a grotesque deathbed wedding to a young girl, a scene as unsettling as any in his plays. Yet "The Plain-Dealer" seems to have retained much of his ironic attitude: on the errata page of the edition of 1704 of his poems he lists "the whole Book."[18] His attempts to master irony in his final play result in the sort of open-ended standoff that Kierkegaard may have had in mind when he argued that the silence of irony "is that deathly stillness in which irony returns to 'haunt and jest'," (*Irony*, p. 275) and that often "the painful annihilation of the poet becomes a condition for the poetic production" (p. 338). That Wycherley ended his theatrical career with *The Plain Dealer* suggests that his irony sought its end in his early retirement from the stage—his "painful annihilation" as a dramatist—and a subsequent life in which he seemed more its victim than its master.

---

[18]William Wycherley, *The Complete Works of William Wycherley*, ed. Montague Summers (London: Nonesuch, 1924), 3:279.

6. Authorship Without Authority: *Walden,* Kierkegaard, and the Experiment in Points of View

BOTH Thoreau and Kierkegaard feel the necessity to alert their readers to the effort of consciousness by undertaking the most rigorous self-interrogations; both do so in the form of the literary corrective, a provisional writing which reminds us constantly of the writer's experimental authorship. Kierkegaard, particularly in *The Point of View for My Work as an Author,* can help us with the difficulties of *Walden* because no one understands better than he the formal constraints of being a writer aspiring to truth and yet "without authority." Kierkegaard's work justifies his own varied authorial roles by examining how one must undeceive any—including oneself—who believe themselves to be already Christian, a task accomplished only by "bringing to light by the application of a caustic fluid a text which is hidden under another text" (*Point of View,* p. 40). Thoreau does not name disjunct "categories" of authorship, as Kierkegaard does, and yet a rich allusiveness describes his own chosen forms of indirection in generic terms, as literary fictions. Thoreau's self-referential body of allusion refers us, throughout most of *Walden,* to the texts hidden beneath his text, above all to the old, high genres of the ancients with an individual man at the center, whether hero, tragic protagonist, or prophet. (Kierkegaard approves: "If people would only turn back again to antiquity and learn what it means to be a

164

single individual man, neither more nor less—which surely even an author is, too, neither more nor less" *Point of View,* p. 44.) If we see Thoreau's self-conscious mixing of genres and of generic effects as a means of hiding whose multiplicity is analogous in many respects to Kierkegaard's multiple authorial roles, then we can better understand what Thoreau's concept of an ironic authorship has to do with an eternal design that depends for its truth on our perception of it.

If viewed with no sense of the dialectical relation of parts to the whole, many sections of *Walden* appear rich with irresolutions and confusions.[1] *Walden's* self-consciously epic framework, with structural divisions into halves and thirds like those in *The Odyssey* and *Paradise Lost,* frequently seems to both propose and retract an epic seriousness. The text refers disparagingly to a race of human beings who "live meanly, like ants" and to Thoreau himself as a "Human Insect" and yet elsewhere attributes the only sustained epic battle, narrated with high seriousness, to "races" of red and black ants. The passages of epic grandeur respond to those in which Thoreau either mocks his own failed heroism or points to the inappropriateness of epic to a time that may be "but the spring months in the life of the race."[2] But such inconsistency takes on purposefulness as the epic role is both played and observed.

"Where I Lived, and What I Lived For" begins as all epics do, describing the intended quest in terms of the desire for a homeland, the yearning toward a destined place. The tone, however, mocks the yearning ("for I dearly love to talk"), compares the winter's enjoyment to the poet's who "got all the cream, and left the farmer only the skimmed milk" (*Walden,* p. 107), and passes within a single paragraph from the heroic zeal of an Atlas ready

[1]"Dialectical," of course, belongs to Kierkegaard's language, not to Thoreau's, and yet I want to show that Kierkegaard's explanations of the dialectical relation between his own aesthetic and religious works elaborates explicitly on a relation that remains implicit, or densely figurative, in Thoreau.

[2]Henry David Thoreau, *Walden* (New York: Harper, 1950), p.438. All subsequent references refer to this edition.

"to take the world on my shoulders" to the unheroic concession, "But it turned out as I have said" (p. 108). Thoreau's stated purpose, "to brag as lustily as chanticleer in the morning, standing on his roost, if only to wake my neighbors up" (p. 109), identifies his present experiment as another "of this kind," that is, an experiment with a grandly heroic purpose that comes to an end when faced with actual arrival, the permanence of home. He mentions the decision *not* to write an "ode to dejection" because we might well expect it of a saga beginning with an antihero, one committed to boasting about exploits that we have been warned will not lead to arrival but only to the going "round and round" of a lifetime's procrastination. Epic adventure does end with retirement of a sort: when Odysseus goes off to his bed with Penelope, when Aeneas wins the battle for his destined Lavinia, or when Dante attains the vision of fulfillment through Beatrice. Thoreau's epic sections, however, ultimately turn away from the attempt at achieving epic retirement itself, placing it firmly as one trial among many, a merely provisional role.

Thoreau's prose abounds with self-consciously epic gestures that dissolve into ironic exaggerations; frequently epic simile finds itself within a dissonant literality. Thoreau sings, for example, of the "auroral character" of a remembered cabin: "This was an airy and unplastered cabin, fit to entertain a travelling god, and where a goddess might trail her garments. The winds which passed over my dwelling were such as sweep over the ridges of mountains, bearing the broken strains, or celestial parts only, of terrestrial music" (p. 110). The ether soon vanishes with, "The only house I had been the owner of before, if I except a boat, was a tent, which I used occasionally when making excursions in the summer, and this is still rolled up in my garret" (p. 110). Similarly, Thoreau reminds us that epic's *homo viator* always crosses water; looking in his well, he sees that "the earth is not continent but insular" (p. 113). Then the undercutting Yankee adds, "This is as important as that it keeps butter cool" (p. 113). What chance has a landlocked hero, thus undermined, of attaining truly epic stature?

166

So, too, do explicit allusions to Homer both attempt epic seriousness and undercut it. Morning, says Thoreau, "brings back the heroic ages" and throughout *Walden* the sun, morning, awakening,
the robust spirit—all bespeak the energy of epic virtue. A mos-
quito moves him like "any trumpet that ever sang of fame." It was
"Homer's requiem; itself an Iliad and Odyssey in the air, singing
its own wrath and wanderings. There was something cosmical
about it; a standing advertisement, until forbidden, of the ever-
lasting vigor and fertility of the world" (p. 115). Later, in its concern with truth, *Walden* decries fame; even here, the "forbidden"
quality of Homer's "requiem" suggests epic limitation. In "Visi-
tors," Thoreau introduces "Homeric man," a natural man who
thrives in the natural day and who takes wholesome satisfaction in
his own animal spirits. Genuine and unsophisticated, the belief of
"Homeric man" in the straightforward virtues suggests to Thoreau
both the ignorance of a child and "fine poetic consciousness." And
when Thoreau recommends intellectual or spiritual improvement,
"Homeric man" responds only that "it was too late" (p. 197). The
epic hero does not question assumptions about what the virtues
are, and he cannot develop because epic takes for its subject matter
a history already enacted.

Thoreau's rhetoric often simulates the certainty of epic adventure, which promises ultimate safety rather than perpetual trial:
"Weather this danger and you are safe, for the rest of the way is
down hill. With unrelaxed nerves, with morning vigor, sail by it,
looking another way, tied to the mast like Ulysses" (p. 127). When
Thoreau speaks of spending the natural day "as deliberately as
Nature," he envisages the vigor of a reality which asserts, "This
is, and no mistake," and the security of a "hard bottom and rocks
in place" where one might "found a wall or a state" (p. 127). Yet
the conclusion of the epic hero's journey stands in contradistinc-
tion to the self-exposure that both Thoreau and Kierkegaard regard
as experimental and ongoing.

Whatever the attraction of such morning moods, founding a
wall or a state is not the same task as finding oneself, and we

know this in part from chapters like "The Bean-Field" that refer throughout to Thoreau's heroic efforts at growing beans, using a humorously ironic rhetoric to describe a battle of indefinite purpose: "What was the meaning of this so steady and self-respecting, this small Herculean labor, I knew not" (p. 204). He breaks up the "ancient" herb garden so that beans can "go forward to meet new foes" (p. 205). He disturbs with his hoe the "ashes of unchronicled nations" and generally makes himself the Achilles of bean growing: "Daily the beans saw me come to their rescue armed with a hoe, and thin the ranks of their enemies, filling up the trenches with weedy dead. Many a lusty crest-waving Hector, that towered a whole foot above his crowding comrades, fell before my weapon and rolled in the dust" (p. 213). After a flat summation stressing the economics of bean growing (in a work that scorns the profit motive), Thoreau adds, "This further experience also I gained" (p. 216). And there follows a richly metaphoric dismissal of beans in favor of "planting" virtues and a characteristic address to the reader: ". . . but now another summer is gone, and another, and another, and I am obliged to say to you, Reader, that the seeds I planted, if indeed they *were* the seeds of those virtues, were worm-eaten or had lost their vitality and so did not come up" (p. 216). The whole bean experiment takes its place among others as one form of indirection.

When men are "busy about their beans," they forget the relation of parts to whole, of their practical activity to higher truth: "The true husbandman will cease from anxiety, as the squirrels manifest no concern whether the woods will bear chestnuts this year or not, and finish his labor with every day, relinquishing all claim to the produce of his fields, and sacrificing in his mind not only his first but his last fruits also" (pp. 219-20). The heroic strategy of bean growing, its rhetorically epic sweep, gives way abruptly to the higher vision, which sees its narrow particularity: "Shall I not rejoice also at the abundance of the weeds whose seeds are the granary of the birds?" The activity itself, not its fruit, must justify—even glorify—the doing. Here, as elsewhere, an existential experiment linked to genre finds itself surpassed by a more global perspective: truer heroism lies in committing oneself to and then sacrificing the roles one forges for oneself. Such sacrifice suggests the purposeful wit of Thoreau denying his epic structure one of the genre's most salient features, the invocation of the muse. Only the epic that one lives, but cannot write, deserves such an invocation; for the lived epic, "you would not be ashamed to invoke the Muse" (P. 436).

Although explicit allusions to tragedy occur much less frequently than do those to epic, Aeschylus and Shakespeare figure prominently in Thoreau's authorial elite, and he mocks himself as a tragic figure with an often jovial reductionism. He invokes, for example, Hamlet's meditation on stage appearances with "What shall I learn of beans or beans of me?" (p. 204). As in Thoreau's treatment of epic, a seriousness beneath the irony suggests that the analogy between Hecuba and beans signifies more than the lightness of tone would suggest: that tragedy too stands in dialectical relation to the larger experiment in identity.

Thoreau frequently expresses the impulse toward extremism that motivates the tragic hero, a protagonist who chafes at the boundaries and limitations of a culture's ethics. In fact, following one's "genius" allies itself with experience beyond the merely ethical:

If one listens to the faintest but constant suggestions of his genius, which are certainly true, he sees not to what extreme, or even insanity, it may lead him; and yet that way, as he grows more resolute and faithful, his road lies. The faintest assured objection which one healthy man feels will at length prevail over the arguments and customs of mankind. [P. 286]

Kierkegaard too makes self-induced states of extreme consciousness essential to surpassing the merely ethical, and for both Kierkegaard and Thoreau those states are not actual but imaginative. When Thoreau asserts, "We need to witness our own limits transgressed, and some life pasturing freely where we never wander" (p. 419), he echoes Kierkegaard's assessment of imaginative need that his "aesthetic" works fulfill for himself (*Point of View,* pp.

34-43). For Thoreau, imaginative experience makes us witnesses, observers, in a way that provides both the exhilaration of an un- bounded universe and the temptation to transgress known bound- aries: "At the same time that we are earnest to explore and learn all things, we require that all things be mysterious and unexplor- able, that land and sea be infinitely wild, unsurveyed and unfath- omed by us because unfathomable" (*Walden,* p. 419). Thoreau's imaginative experience of the "forbidden" applies perhaps most forcefully to the actions of hunters and fishermen, whose activity his *ethical* sense condemns. However harshly he judges the hunter or fisherman, Thoreau acknowledges a shared desire with him; indeed, he watches in himself an instinct "toward a primitive rank and savage one" (p. 278). He has a thrilling impulse to devour raw flesh and reverences in himself those moods when "no morsel could have been too savage for me" (p. 278).

The desire for raw flesh appropriately alludes to the Bacchic origins of tragedy, how the ripping of flesh, the eating of the god, serves as an analogy for tragedy itself, in which a vicarious violence functions as ritual purgation. The concept of catharsis, however controversial in its particulars, involves experiencing the trans- gression of another as though it were our own, leaving us with a perspective on humanhood that belies superior judgments. Tho- reau understands that, fundamentally, tragedy concerns an indi- vidual beset with the problems of humanness, what it means to be a human being. He recognizes that catharsis affirms a designed order that can sustain belief, even in the act of showing those whom we identify "squashed out of existence like a pulp" (p. 420). And just as Thoreau may transfer tragedy to the realm of nature, so he sees there the ritual sacrifice: "I love to see that Nature is so rife with life that myriads can afford to be sacrificed to prey on one another" (p. 420).

The epic hero represents the promise of his race, a victory over human vulnerability. We never tremble for him because by defini- tion he must triumph. The extremism of the tragic hero involves us in a more fearful identification, and in this, as Thoreau understands, it achieves an "extra-vagance" that epic cannot, a traveling outside oneself in the transgressions of another. The grandeur of the epic voyage must not disguise its limitation: "He who is only a traveller learns things at second-hand and by the halves, and is poor authority" (p. 278). Tragedy paradoxically forges identity through the strongest possible identification, felt and then purged, with some "other." One of the highest functions of literature is that it allows us "to look through each other's eyes for an instant" (p. 11), and this desire inheres in much of *Walden,* particularly in the attitude toward other writers. The first page asserts the difference of another writer's experience, "for if he has lived sincerely it must have been in a distant land to me" (p. 2), and yet the opening of "Reading" proclaims an absolute identification with any who choose to be observers and witnesses of the truth. When we read, when we play the audience to another's life, we raise, like the ancient Egyptian or Hindu philosopher, "a corner of the veil from the statue of divinity": ". . . and still the trembling robe remains raised, and I gaze upon as fresh a glory as he did, since it was I in him that was then so bold, and it is he in me that now reviews the vision" (p. 130).

With considerable subtlety Thoreau relates the case of his own authorship to the case of tragic drama, in which a double or surrogate pushes principle to extremism and enacts the forbidden. Kierkegaard speaks of his pseudonymous roles as a kind of double vision, as though one could attain an observer's point of view on one's own life, and admits that such behavior may appear as insanity to men en masse. Thoreau postulates a like doubleness, one he explicitly relates to tragedy:

I only know myself as a human entity; the scene, so to speak, of thoughts and affections; and am sensible of a certain doubleness by which I can stand as remote from myself as from another. However intense my experience, I am conscious of the presence and criticism of a part of me, which, as it were, is not a part of me, but a spectator, sharing no experience, but taking note of it; and that is no more I than it is you. When the play, and it may be a tragedy, of life is over, the

171

spectator goes his way. It was a kind of fiction, a work of the imagination only, so far as he was concerned. [P. 178]

Kierkegaard, too, sees tragedy as the literary genre that lends itself most readily to paradox, to the doubleness of participant and observer, because, although guilty action demands certain punishment, it leaves the performer blameless.[3] As Thoreau puts it, "The impression made on a wise man is that of universal innocence" (p. 420). Both speak not of literature per se but of life experienced as though it were literature, an imagined duplicity.

It has bothered many that Thoreau preaches "Simplify, simplify" in the act of making such a labyrinthine narrative, admitting even, at its close, that he would be proud to have "attained to obscurity" (p. 429). Defensive comment compares *Walden* to the "scriptures of the nations" and the morning sun:

Some would find fault with the morning red, if they ever got up early enough. 'They pretend,' as I hear, 'that the verses of Kabir have four different senses: illusion, spirit, intellect, and the exoteric doctrine of the Vedas'; but in this part of the world it is considered a ground for the complaint if a man's writings admit of more than one interpretation. [P. 429]

Certainly Thoreau thrives on enigma and can as roundly chastise an audience, a readership, as can an Old Testament prophet. And the extent of that seemingly authoritative and scriptural voice, overtly sermonizing to its readers, has then and now drawn forth charges of arrogance and egotism, if not of self-aggrandizing heresy. Yet taking offense too easily ignores the reason why a book that so often simulates such a prophetic, scriptural ring should comment with such regularity on its own lack of authority, its own nonscriptural status.

[3]Kierkegaard refers, like Thoreau, to ancient tragedy; in fact, he sees modern tragedy's "guiltiness" as a distinguishing, and unfortunate, characteristic. See especially "The Ancient Tragical Motif as Reflected in the Modern," in *Either/Or*, 1:137-50.

When Thoreau addresses spiritual questions, he tends to acquire a tone of lyrical prophecy that comes as close as any other to the enigmatic density of scriptural revelation. But he makes clear that writing scripture and living the sacred are different, though related, processes. Thoreau presents Zoroaster, for example, as a wise man who answered the ultimate questions "by his words and by his life." The hired man in Concord possesses a religion characterized by "silent gravity and exclusiveness," whereas Zoroaster invented worship because he humbly acknowledged the universality of the questions he answered, like all other wise men, "according to his ability" (p. 142; Thoreau's fondness for citing from all the "Bibles of mankind" may suggest a pantheism roundly condemned by Kierkegaard; yet Socrates and Zoroaster live their wisdom in a similar manner, alert, self-conscious, and inventive). Quickly and characteristically, however, Thoreau turns from Zoroaster and an explicitly religious declaration to a topical New England, from the deepest self-exposure to easy sermonizing. The individual's most difficult "reading" gives way to a touted concern for the institutions of reading: schools, universities, and libraries. Such abrupt transitions humble Thoreau's own "scripture," which so often drops its prophetic, elevated tone with a noticeable suddenness, emphasizing its relation to that other Scripture of "the workman whose work we are": "We are the subjects of an experiment which is not a little interesting to me" (p. 177). How reminiscent this is of Kierkegaard's constant awareness of "the fact that it was not I that played the part of master, but that another was Master" (*Point of View,* p. 69).

Thoreau's scriptural flights may be suddenly and ironically dropped, or they may identify themselves as chosen revelations, imagined or dreamed truths on which to model one's life. At the end Thoreau urges the imaginative leap of faith: "If you have built castles in the air, your work need not be lost; that is where they should be. Now put the foundations under them" (*Walden,* p. 436). Thoreau never suggests that laying those foundations means reading his book. Although he senses that works of genius are "sacred, and to be read with reverence, as the works of nature are studied," he also understands that "there are few instances of a sustained style of this kind."[4] Both Thoreau and Kierkegaard choose tonal qualities that often simulate those of a familiar ministerial tradition, but for both, the vulgarity of the sermon lies in its assumption of religious authenticity, the presumed distance of a speaker from his audience. The sermonizer accepts the notion of the flock and its shepherd; he administers but does not try to convert his congregation to the ministry. As Stanley Cavell has noted,[5] *Walden* does the opposite, frequently challenging its audience to lay it down and take up their lives. He who has a revelation can write and read his own scripture; epiphany makes its own text.

Walden does not, I think, pretend to *be* the American New Testament, to be scripture as such.[6] Yet it wears the scriptural voice with the seriousness that experiential choice always means to Thoreau. That is, he may temporarily suspend disbelief in his own lack of authority, may urge the need for multileveled exegesis, but he also reminds us repeatedly that even the natural world offers veiled revelation ("We are not wholly involved in Nature") and that *lived* religious consciousness stands in dialectical relation to the work that is *Walden*. We should not doubt the sincerity of Thoreau's acknowledgment: "I never dreamed of any enormity greater than I have committed. I never knew, and never shall

---

[4]Henry David Thoreau, *A Week on the Concord and Merrimack Rivers* (Boston: Ticknor and Fields, 1868), p. 396.

[5]See Stanley Cavell, *The Senses of Walden* (New York: Viking, 1972), pp. 47–48.

[6]Cavell's *The Senses of Walden* remains the deepest examination of *Walden*'s self-referential, metaphoric discipline but tends to read *Walden* as a work most fundamentally about writing. Cavell's "recurrent form of doubt" seems to me perhaps his greatest insight (and ultimately more convincing than the argument that *Walden* becomes what it promises): "The form of doubt is caused partly by the depth of the book's depressions and the height of its elevations, and, more nearly, by the absence of reconciliation between them, which may seem evasive or irresolute of the writer—as if we have been led once more only to the limits of one man's willingness to answer, not to the limits of the humanly answerable"; ibid., p. 108.

know, a worse man than myself" (p. 101). Indirectly *Walden* addresses Thoreau's own "private ail" in all its sermonizing *and* in all its boasting. When, therefore, Thoreau claims scriptural complexity with: "It is a ridiculous demand which England and America make that you shall speak so that they can understand you. Neither men nor toadstools grow so" (p. 427), we should imagine Kierkegaard explaining that "all doubly reflected communication makes contrary interpretation possible, and the judge will be made manifest by his judgment" ("Supplement," *Point of View,* p. 156). Kierkegaard suffers "times when I could not make myself intelligible to myself," and Thoreau acknowledges that, "for the most part, we are not where we are, but in a false position. Through an infirmity of our natures, we suppose a case, and put ourselves into it, and hence are in two cases at the same time, and it is doubly difficult to get out" (*Walden,* p. 428). For Kierkegaard the goal may be the scriptural one, "to call attention to religion" or "to wake my neighbors up," but the attempt must be undertaken "without authority" (*Point of View,* p. 151). The scriptural experiment, though not sustained, makes author and reader aware of multiple meanings, of the fact that we "read" our lives according to some chosen interpretational strategy.

Thoreau's experiments in genre comprise what Kierkegaard would see as the indirections of the "aesthetic" author, one who soars with poetic effusions only to be reduced through a heavy irony (or a flatly assertive Yankee understatement). Deeply confessional tones of voice assert truths, often with messianic force, which subsequent tones of voice retract, undercut, or rebut. Yet from this very combination of lyricism and reductionism the self learns much that can be incorporated into the religious life; every generic experiment ends as a lesson in consciousness. Kierkegaard speaks of the need for religious consciousness to move away from the poetic, to "evacuate" the poetical: "The religious agreed to this elimination but incessantly spurred it on, as though it were saying, Are you not now through with that?" (*Point of View,* p. 84). Thoreau means much the same thing when he transfers poetic sensibility to the author's life. The author's true poem is not the written text but "what he has become through his work."[7] Thoreau's generic roles, like Kierkegaard's pseudonymous ones, represent both failure, an ironic distance from the ultimate goal, and also some metaphoric truth about the *way* to approach the eternal. *Walden* presents itself as failed epic in its address to men en masse, its attempt to awaken a race when salvation needs must be individual, but asserts that taking life as an epic struggle keeps it from slipping back into the ordinary, the commonality of the "well-beaten path." Homeric man assumes his place in nature and finds simple renewal in the day's cycles. So too does tragic vision fail by creating a doubleness that detaches the self from identity, but such vision offers experience of the universally human, the continuity beneath the changing self. Tragic man removes himself from nature to become a witness and a vicarious participant in its deaths and rebirths. And *Walden* must fail as scripture because it claims no authority, not even an author superior to others in moral stature. Yet the attempt at scriptural man opens Thoreau to nature's multiple meanings, to the potential revelations and parables to be found everywhere one looks. Kierkegaard assumes points of view to demonstrate how they pale before the religious attitude and how only successively more stringent negations can aspire to sublimity. Thoreau, whose "Poet" fishes for food rather than contemplating heaven, describes a similar process when he says, "And we are enabled to apprehend at all what is sublime and noble only by the perpetual instilling and drenching of the reality that surrounds us."[8] For both, the authorial experiment directs experience toward the absolute, and these experiments in identity spur the discovery of what part of the self abides, because from each adopted point of view the self gains some understanding of the relation between the real and the eternal.

Kierkegaard's treatment of his own authorship explains what the

[7]Thoreau, *A Week on the Concord*, p. 363.
[8]Ibid., p. 70.

176

paradoxical involvement in the writing and reading of a life has to do with religious consciousness. Poetical and ethical stages of experience help eliminate the illusions that hinder religious consciousness because they teach the superfluity of pleasures and rewards as well as the irrelevance of worldly virtue (following ethical rules). The paradoxical activity of authorship (my life as text) provides a paradigm for self-realization in the context of the eternal. According to Kierkegaard, the dialectical relation between parts and whole, between writing and reading, involves the author in a kind of willful suspension that simulates the leap of faith made by religious consciousness. The eternal can be grasped only through our active expectancy of it, just as our activity as writers and readers of *the text that is our life* involves us in a perpetual expectancy of the ultimate book (*Edifying Discourses,* 1, 7-33). The process of *Walden* does more than reduce a "fact of the imagination" to a "fact of understanding" (p. 12). Like Kierkegaard's "Choose thyself," Thoreau's "Explore thyself" proposes a committed, passionate inwardness that asserts particular, chosen truths, although the author is fully aware that revelation is always partial. *Walden's* later chapters stress the ultimate limitation of such chosen possibilities, as usual in the context of nature:

Our notion of law and harmony are commonly confined to those instances which we detect; but the harmony which results from a far greater number of seemingly conflicting, but really concurring laws, which we have not detected, is still more wonderful. The particular laws are as our points of view, as, to the traveller, a mountain outline varies with every step, and it has an infinite number of profiles, though absolutely but one form. Even when cleft or bored through it is not comprehended in its entirety. [P. 384]

Indeed, *Walden's* "Conclusion" begins "Thank Heaven, here is not all the world" and specifically acknowledges the provisional nature of all points of view: "The universe is wider than our views of it" (p. 422). Thoreau urges belief in a "solid bottom everywhere," though experience offers only the "bogs and quicksands of society";

177

daily life becomes all surface, all changes of clothes and acquaintance with "a mere pellicle of the globe on which we live" (p. 438) when it loses consciousness of eternal truth as its end.

Thoreau's activities, all "allegories and measures of each other,"[9] most often stand as tropes for writing and reading, both necessary adjuncts in the work intended as an experiment and as corrective revelation in the direction of the eternal. One of *Walden*'s most dramatic transitions occurs after "Reading," a paean to the comradery afforded by the literatures and tongues of all the ages, when Thoreau begins "Sounds" with: "But while we are confined to books, though the most select and classic, and read only particular written languages, which are themselves but dialects and provincial, we are in danger of forgetting the language which all things and events speak without metaphor, which alone is copious and standard. Much is published, but little is printed" (p. 146). As so often in Thoreau, a surface incongruity ("confined to books" leaps forward) emphasizes a hidden continuity. "Particular written languages" stand in direct opposition to the experiential, universal language of that book, isolate and singular, to which the previous chapter leads us: "How many a man has dated a new era in his life from the reading of a book. The book exists for us, perchance, which will explain our miracles and reveal new ones. The at present unutterable things we may find somewhere uttered" (pp. 141-42). "A" book, any book written by a particular author in a particular tongue, intimates immortality in the form of "the" book, definite and sublime. And immediately juxtaposed to a chapter on the reading of books lies this chapter devoted to the sounds of an articulate Nature, which exhorts: "Read your fate, see what is before you, and walk on into futurity" (p. 146). "Reading" a fate means treating life as though it were a text and choosing successive interpretational strategies by which to live. It might well be Kierkegaard admonishing us to imagine a coherence, a fate, and then to suspend disbelief and act as though the imagined were truth.

[9]Cavell, *The Senses of Walden*, p. 60.

Kierkegaard declares that from the first he regarded himself "preferably as a *reader* of the books, not as the *author*" (*Point of View,* p. 151). At the same time he asserts an equivalence between this literary activity and his "own upbringing and development." When Kierkegaard speaks of himself as "hardly more than a poet," (p. 155) and Thoreau abjures the discipline of poetry in favor of reading a future, they show the primacy of self-correction implicit in the service they offer their readers. Kierkegaard speaks of overcoming the aesthetic and Thoreau of reading a life, but both refer to the paradoxical relation between writing and reading. A Don Quixote might choose to create his life as though it were a book, or a later Äxel might live life to put into a book, but Thoreau and Kierkegaard make the book secondary to the activities of writing and reading; they take their places as scribes and readers of their own development. Writing a life commits one to choosing a possibility, regarding everyday activity with the intensity and self-consciousness of an author; reading a life implies seeing possibility in the context of other "books," particularly that of the ultimate book that cannot be written.

In *Walden* the relation between writing, reading, and any ultimate authorial intent remains teasingly buried in the work's figurative undertext. Yet the chapter on "Reading" helps us by putting forward an ideal "reader" who strongly resembles Kierkegaard's ideal of the writer who becomes primarily a reader of the text he writes to subsume merely poetic consciousness into the religious consciousness that, he argues, has always been his goal. Of course, no very taut analogy exists between Kierkegaard's aesthetic and ethical experiments and Thoreau's generic ones. Thoreau's self-conscious pantheism sees religious consciousness as an end, not Christianity per se, and his paeans to the present moment show less concern than does Kierkegaard with an enslavement to aesthetic pleasure. Whatever his dark side, Thoreau does not emphasize suffering, so characteristic of all Kierkegaard's "stages of the way," and is therefore less inclined to adopt roles of a ridiculous or inferior stature. Yet the relation of points of view to the whole,

179

whether the whole of *Walden* or the whole of a prior authorship, suggests an illuminating sameness in difference regarding the authorial activity itself.

Kierkegaard makes us regard his authorship in the light of the truth that "the supreme paradox of all thought is the attempt to discover something that thought cannot think" (*Fragments,* p. 46). Thoreau places the same paradox in the context of writing when he says: "The volatile truth of our words should continually betray the inadequacy of the residual statement. Their truth is instantly *translated;* its literal monument alone remains" (*Walden,* p. 428). The truth of particular words can only dimly approximate universal truth as a kind of translation. Kierkegaard knows that the most we can do is direct experience toward the absolute; Thoreau remains "convinced that I cannot exaggerate enough even to lay the foundation of a true expression" (p. 428). The troublesome close of *Walden* offers no finished, created identity for us to admire (certainly no boasting Chanticleer). Rather, it addresses the problem of ending an existential experiment by claiming only this as learning:

. . . that if one advances confidently in the direction of his dreams, and endeavors to live the life which he has imagined, he will meet with a success unexpected in common hours. He will put some things behind, will pass an invisible boundary; new, universal, and more liberal laws will begin to establish themselves around and within him; or the old laws be expanded, and interpreted in his favor in a more liberal sense, and he will live with the license of a higher order of beings. [P. 427]

The activity itself validates the experiment, even though identity within a changing self can only be an imagined futurity.[10] The absolute paradox explains why *Walden* so appropriately ends not on

[10]My emphasis here neither contradicts nor disallows Thoreau's devotion to the sensuous life, his all-but-omnipresent delight in the surfaces of things. In Thoreau the revelations of a constantly changing nature relate to the great cycles of life, as does the particular to the universal, in terms of the authorial

a note of closure or self-fulfillment but with paragraphs heralding a future resurrection. Its famous last paragraph reads: "I do not say that John or Jonathan will realize all this; but such is the character of that morrow which mere lapse of time can never make to dawn. The light which puts out our eyes is darkness to us. Only that day dawns to which we are awake. There is more day to dawn. The sun is but a morning star." How well the "but" of the last sentence suggests eternity in a book containing so many ecstatic hymns to the sun. Like Kierkegaard's revealed and explicated roles, Thoreau's failed genres function as self-acknowledged indirections that formally demonstrate their author's paradoxical relation to a sublimity expectantly and passionately awaited.

In their particulars, then, Kierkegaard's and Thoreau's points of view offer no easy correspondences. Yet as those points of view relate to the whole, to a passionate expectancy of the eternal, they deserve abundant mutual explanation. And their sameness in difference should help us see beneath the surface arrogance of Thoreau's bragging Chanticleer to an underlying text whose most fundamental subject is self-deception. Thoreau's goal, like that of other transcendentalists, stands firmly in the realm of the ideal, but the method of attaining the goal, one's writerly and readerly activity, stands firmly in the realm of the dialectical and the experimental. And this fact does much to explain why self-glorification and self-deprecation cohabit in almost every chapter and inform the texture of the whole.

Richard Rorty's sense of Kierkegaard as an "*intentionally* peripheral" philosopher seems insightful in this context, for it hits upon the antisystematic quality shared by this most literary of philosophers and this most philosophical of littérateurs, their common dread that "their vocabularies should ever be institutionalized."[11]

---

activity. Phillip Gura discusses this paradoxical sense of Thoreau's "transcendence" in terms of philological theory in "Henry Thoreau and the Wisdom of Words," *New England Quarterly* 52 (1979): 38-54.

[11]Richard Rorty, *Philosophy and the Mirror of Nature* (Princeton, N.J.: Princeton University Press, 1980), p. 369.

For, in its totality, *Walden* ironically documents its own failures, demonstrates in its own form the inadequacy of any single tradition, past or present.[12] Its ultimate focus rests not on the experiment of Walden pond but on the experiment of which we ourselves are the subject, our difficult, individually forged relation to "the workman whose work we are" (p. 177). A transcendentalist's Kantian goal dresses itself in an authorial self-consciousness whose continuous deconstructions ask for association with the later Wittgenstein or the later Heidegger. Kierkegaard, insisting on his ironic relation to both Hegel and Kant, calls Thoreauvians to attention precisely because his concept of authorship isolates in his own work what makes Thoreau so hard: a capacity to throw so much personal authority, so much eloquence and high seriousness, into parts that stand in ironic relation to the whole, such that even the most dynamic, lyrically authorial "present" stands harshly judged in the context of an absent and ideal futurity.

---

[12]Like Kierkegaard, Thoreau has less fondness for modern genres than for ancient ones, often punning on "novel" to reinforce his boredom with the genre. An argument might certainly be made that Thoreau purposely simulates novelistic character as well as the ancient genres he so overtly admires, especially since *Walden* frequently chafes at its own dullness. But Thoreau's condemnation of the novel makes it a less interesting genre to the undertext taken as my subject here. In *Walden* all the ancient genres have virtues to recommend them, but the novel epitomizes the interest of surface, and nowhere else does Thoreau wax more contemptuous than in disdaining both the novelist and his audience: "The next time the novelist rings the bell I will not stir though the meeting-house burn down. 'The Skip of the Tip-Toe-Hop, a Romance of the Middle Ages, by the celebrated author of the "Tittle-Tol-Tan," to appear in monthly parts; a great rush; don't all come together.' All this they read with saucer eyes, and erect and primitive curiosity, and with unwearied gizzard, whose corrugations even yet need no sharpening, just as some little four-year-old bencher his two-cent gilt-covered edition of Cinderella,—without any improvement, that I can see, in the pronunciation, or accent, or emphasis, or any more skill in extracting or inserting the moral" (*Walden*, p. 75).

7. Irony and the Literary Past: On *The Concept of Irony* and *The Mill on the Floss*

K IERKEGAARD'S dissertation for the degree of *Magister Artium* on the concept of irony stands as both a seminal work in that author's production and an important document in nineteenth-century thought. Not only does the explication of irony comprehend his "whole authorship" described in *The Point of View for My Work as an Author,*[1] setting forth concepts that are central to his aesthetic and religious writings but it also describes the emergence of self-consciousness as a *problem* to literature, philosophy, and theology. Kierkegaard's concept of irony, then, is an essentially literary "concept," which, coming at the beginning of his career, involves his "whole authorship," his "philosophy" itself, in literature and language. In order to problematicize what he calls "the individual" and his own particular concern, it addresses the problem of identity; as we shall see, the individual and irony are implicated in one another, repeat and undermine each other. Kier-

---

[1]This work is important as a point of departure for any theoretical discussion of irony and fiction. Here Kierkegaard explains the method of "indirect communication" that he utilizes in his work. This method is basically that which he saw in Socrates, and in this work he refers to himself as the "Magister of Irony" (p. 57).

183

kegaard's concept of irony, then, is an early version of what Jacques Derrida has called "deconstruction": it calls into question traditional rhetorical and metaphysical assumptions—assumptions based on traditional notions of identity—and, in so doing, calls into question its own Christian grounding.

The point of my presentation, however, is not to demonstrate the affinity between Kierkegaard's concept of irony and Derrida's concepts of difference and play. These affinities (especially if one reads *The Concept of Irony* with "La Différance" in mind) will occur without rigorous demonstration. Rather, I hope to read Kierkegaard against himself: after all, the procedure of delimiting something "against" itself—a procedure that "deconstructs" the dichotomy of outside-inside and the very notion of self-identity itself—is, as I hope to show, the procedure of Kierkegaard's irony. Still, Kierkegaard offers as a model for his concept of irony a description that Derrida might have chosen in modifying Ferdinand de Saussure's differential definition of identity.[2] Saussure has said that the relation of the signifier to the signified is like the relation of two sides of the same piece of paper. Kierkegaard describes irony in similar yet radically different terms. Irony, he suggests, is like a piece of paper on one side of which is written, "Whatever appears on the other side is true," and on the other side of which is written, "Whatever appears on the other side is false."[3] Such an image leaves the mind spinning: each signifier

[2]Derrida touches on his relationship to Saussure in "Différance'" trans. David B. Allison, in *Speech and Phenomena* (Evanston, Ill.: Northwestern University Press, 1973) and in *Of Grammatology*, trans. G. C. Spivak (Baltimore, Md.: Johns Hopkins University Press, 1976). For a short discussion of Saussure's treatment of identity see my article "The Poison of Ink: Modernism and Post-War Literary Criticism," *New Orleans Review* 8 (1981): 241-49.

[3]When I wrote this example, I clearly remembered its appearance in Lee Capel's introduction to *The Concept of Irony*. Looking for the reference, however, I found that it was written in the margin in my own hand. The example Kierkegaard gives brings out more clearly the signified's transformation into its opposite, even while it obscures the fact that it is indeed the process of signification that he is talking about: "The entire dialogue," Kierkegaard writes,

refers to another signifier in a never-ending rotation of the paper, *mise en abyme.*

In the first part of this article, then, I plan to remain relatively close to *The Concept of Irony* in my discussion of Kierkegaard; by this means I hope to gain a wider view of his thought and the literary problems he defines. Even here, however, I will probably be further from the text than might at first glance seem appropriate to a study of this nature. I can only plead in extenuation that, in using Hamlet, I am following Kierkegaard's own use of Socrates as a point of departure for *The Concept of Irony.* Kierkegaard's text, as Lee Capel notes in his introduction, parodies his own teachers and scholarship itself; that is why he wrote in Danish (*Irony,* pp. 29-30). Thus in his dissertation Kierkegaard quotes his teachers with approval and then goes on to show that his approval is based on the fact that they make characteristic mistakes; he uses their own premises and arguments against them, and he parodies the whole scrupulous enterprise of academic writing by putting his most effective arguments and demonstrations in the notes. Finally, he examines Socrates at great length to discuss (silently) his contemporaries and Christ. I hope, then, that my choice of George Eliot, a writer of vastly different temperament from Kierkegaard's, to examine the literary consequences of his analysis of irony, will present the usefulness and pertinence of Kierkegaard's thesis, even if the relationships between these texts —like the relationship of Kierkegaard to Derrida—is by and large

"remind one of the well-known dispute involving a Catholic and Protestant, which ended with each convincing the other, so that the Catholic became Protestant and the Protestant Catholic. . . ." (p. 93). "One sees in this," Kierkegaard adds in a note, "the possibility of an infinite dispute in which the disputants are at every moment convinced without either of them at any moment ever having a conviction. Only this correspondence between them remains: at the moment A is Catholic, B becomes Protestant, and at the moment B becomes Catholic A becomes Protestant." For *mise en abyme* see J. Hillis Miller, "Stevens' Rock and Criticism as Cure," *Georgia Review* 30 (1976): 5-33, 330-48.

presented in silence, each being an imagined prototype and example of the other, a moment of repetition.

On *The Concept of Irony*

Kierkegaard's conception of irony is both similar and dissimilar to the common notion of irony. In irony, Kierkegaard writes, "the phenomenon is not the essence but the opposite of the essence" (*Irony,* p. 264). In other words, irony is the apparent disparity between language (phenomenon) and meaning (essence). Kierkegaard contrasts this definition with the common notion of the ironic figure of speech: "The ironic figure of speech," he writes, "cancels itself out, however, for the speaker presupposes his listeners understand him, hence through a negation of the immediate phenomenon the essence remains identical with the phenomenon" (p. 265). Kierkegaard's irony, on the other hand, is not a means of communication but a means of negating communication; it questions and problematicizes the very disparity (dichotomy) between speech and meaning: "It pertains to the essence of irony not to unmask itself" (p. 85); "Irony [is] infinitely silent" (p. 63).

Kierkegaard contrasts the silence of irony with the "infinitely eloquent" systemic, or speculative, discourse, and throughout his study he repeatedly contrasts the Word and Silence. In these terms he distinguishes between the dialectics of Plato and Socrates, examining and questioning:

One may ask a question for the purpose of obtaining an answer containing the desired content, so that the more one questions, the deeper and more meaningful becomes the answer; or one may ask a question, not in the interest of obtaining an answer, but to suck out the apparent content with a question and leave only an emptiness remaining. [P. 73]

This distinction directs attention to the double nature of language. Language can be seen as corresponding to its "essence," transparently referring to the world, the presence of the signified; or it can be seen as essentially self-referential, referring only to itself (to a signifier) and thus drawing attention to the silence which lies behind it, which it "speaks." Kierkegaard does not discuss language in these terms (they refer "back" to Saussure and Derrida), yet he does note Socrates' method of abstraction, the progressive emptying of language of any referential content until it remains an empty shell. Kierkegaard sees in *The Symposium* the basic method of Socrates as ironic:

Love is emancipated more and more from the accidental concretion in which it appeared in the preceding discourses and reduced to its most abstract determination. It exhibits itself not as the love of this or that, for this or that, but the love of something which it has not, i.e., as desire, longing. . . . Desire, longing . . . , [however,] is the negative aspect of love, that is to say, the immanent negativity. . . . This determination [of love] is also the most abstract, or, more concretely, it is the abstract itself, not in the ontological sense, but in the sense of lacking content. . . . [Socrates'] abstract is a designation utterly void of content. He proceeds from the concrete and arrives at the most abstract, and where the inquiry should begin, there he stops. [Pp. 82-83]

This is the "infinite negativity" of irony. Irony "devours" the answer by turning "back into itself"; "by no longer having anything to do with the World" it negates the validity of experience (pp. 154-55).

Before turning to the ramifications of this notion of irony, we should look for a moment at the silence that Kierkegaard sees as its basis. "We might say," he writes, "either it is the word that creates the individual, or he is begotten and engendered by silence" (p. 67). Irony itself can be seen as a paradox, the playful expression of the desperate fact that there is nothing to express, "a standpoint which continually cancels itself," continually "erases" itself: "It is a nothingness which consumes everything and a something which one can never catch hold of, which both is and is not; yet it is something in its deepest roots comical. As irony conquers everything by seeing its disproportion to the Idea, so it also succumbs to itself, since it constantly goes beyond itself while remaining itself" (p. 161). The paradox that irony expresses is just that "which both is and is not." It is the paradox of the "nature" of the individual—of identity—continually being yet always becoming. This is what Kierkegaard is striving to come to terms with in this book, and, indeed, in his "whole authorship." The standpoint of irony is essential to the individual, to subjectivity—"Irony is itself the first and most abstract determination of subjectivity . . . and with this we have arrived at Socrates" (p. 281)—yet irony cancels itself out and, with itself, the individual. In *Point of View* Kierkegaard talks about extremes of loneliness, and, despite the self-assertive tone of that book, a terrible anxiety concerning his own identity and concerning the misunderstanding that his subjective (that is, ironic) works encounter underlies his discourse. He is at once the agent of "divine governance" and "nothingness," the teacher of Christianity and a spy (*Point of View,* chap. 3). The ironist Socrates, he writes elsewhere, has "a tragic fate," even if his death "is not essentially tragic" (*Irony,* p. 288). The silence of irony "is that deathly stillness in which irony returns to 'haunt and jest'" (p. 275); it is the silence of infinite possibilities and nothingness: the paradox of the individual.

This is not to say that irony is not comical at its deepest roots. Rather, irony stands between the "speculative" nothingness that arrives at something in a logical, systemic way and the "personal" nothingness that results in despair (p. 286). This middle term stands between the word and silence (hence the "comedy" of incongruous juxtaposition), yet I would suggest that for Kierkegaard the pressure of despair is the greater. In *Fear and Trembling* he writes: "If there were no eternal consciousness in man, if at the foundation of all there lay only a wildly seething power which writhing with obscure passions produced everything that is great and everything that is insignificant, if a bottomless void never satiated lay hidden beneath all—what then would life be but despair?" (p. 30). "In man," however, eternal consciousness meets

188

"an historical point of departure" (*Fragments,* title page), and the comic paradox is restated. *The Concept of Irony* already hinted at these formulations in its discussion of the relationship between personality and irony: "As certain as it is that there is much in existence which is not actuality, and that there is something in personality which is at least momentarily incommensurable with actuality, so also it is certain that there resides a truth in irony" (p. 270). Personality is irony as it straddles the worlds of phenomena and essence, and it is no accident that Kierkegaard marks the "inception" of irony in a personality, Socrates.[4]

In this regard, for orientation, we might turn to *Hamlet* and look for a moment at T. S. Eliot's important essay on that play, "Hamlet and His Problems." Eliot finds the play an "artistic failure" precisely because of the incommensurability between the emotions of "Hamlet (the man)" and "the facts as they appear."[5] It is this incommensurability, Eliot argues, that has led such critics as Coleridge and Goethe to use Hamlet to realize their own art or to "discover" Shakespeare himself in the play. Eliot's essay is salutarily deflating, yet he does not draw out the implications of his reading. Like Socrates, Hamlet is an ironical personality continually juxtaposing the ideal (significance: what he desires) and the actual (the facts as they appear: what he does), and emptying the actual

[4]This "personal" definition of irony is parallel to the "personal" definition of faith expounded in *Fear and Trembling*: "Either there is an absolute duty to God. . . /or else faith never existed, because it has always existed, or, to put it differently, Abraham is lost" (p. 91). Inception is necessary to both of these concepts because both are ontologically linked to freedom, and what has always existed is necessary and not free. This metaphor of "inception" links Kierkegaard's argument to the temporality of the "maieutic" function of discourse we have discussed in the Introduction. See *Philosophical Fragments*, pp. 92ff., for Kierkegaard's analysis of the relation between necessity and freedom. As we shall see, however, these freedoms are diametrically opposed: the freedom of faith is positive, while the freedom of irony is "infinitely negative."

[5]T. S. Eliot, *Selected Essays* (New York: Harcourt, Brace & World, 1964), pp. 121-26.

of meaningful significance (or objective correlation) in the face of what Eliot calls his "inexpressible" emotion. This emptying creates a void that critics fill with their own art or theories about Shakespeare. Yet, rather than failing, *Hamlet* becomes an ironical success, creating in that void the possibilities of infinite meanings. Eliot formulates a paradox in his discussion of Hamlet's madness that is close to Kierkegaard's conception of irony: "For Shakespeare it is less than madness and more than feigned."

This will be better understood if we turn back to Kierkegaard. From the foregoing we can see that irony is nothing but a standpoint for personality that looks in two directions: "Irony is the beginning, yet no more than the beginning; it is and it is not. Moreover, its polemic is a beginning which is equally a conclusion" (p. 237). Irony "hovers" between the universal and the concrete (pp. 180, 240), it is a limit rather than a manifestation (p. 231), and in a temporal sequence it presents and problematicizes the momentary: the continually being yet always becoming present moment that is the border and hovering limit between past and future.[6] And as a mere limit it is necessarily empty.

From another point of view the emptiness of irony, the nothingness (silence) it expresses, can be conceived as infinite possibility. "All things are possible for the ironist," writes Kierkegaard (p. 299), because every actuality is negated—irony "loves possibility but flees actuality" (pp. 216-17). The contemporary ironist for Kierkegaard was the romantic (p. 292), the poet who, by virtue of the infinite negativity of irony, is absolutely negatively free in total possibility, recurring originality:

---

[6]In *Point of View*, Kierkegaard divides his literary production into "aesthetic works"—"ethical works"—"religious works," categories corresponding to those of *Fear and Trembling* (subjectivity—resignation—faith) and to those of *Repetition* (recollection—irony or "shrewdness"—repetition). These categories, especially those of *Repetition*, suggest that irony corresponds to the borderline "present" in the temporal sequence past—present—future. Such "correspondence," however, is at best problematical: the borderline of the present blurs as it marks these distinctions.

The outstanding feature of irony . . . is the subjective freedom which at every moment has within its power the possibility of a beginning and is not generated from previous conditions. There is something seductive about every beginning because the subject is still free, and this is the satisfaction the ironist longs for. At such moments actuality loses its validity for him; he is free and above it. [P. 270]

The romantic ironist is free to choose any role because he is not bound to the actual "rich man, poor man, etc." (p. 299). But this is just the method of Hamlet's madness. He says that he is not what he seems to be, though he assumes the roles of grief and mirth, madness and lucidity. He says that he cannot speak ("But break, my heart, for I must hold my tongue"), yet he fills the play with his continuous play with words: puns, banter, and even serious soliloquy, all of which press always towards the "inexpressible." He even makes himself the limit between being and non-being — in his mind he hovers over existence — and speculates on, in Kierke-gaard's words, "the infinite possibility of death" (p. 117). Because he does not act, Hamlet is repeatedly "momentarily" free, yet his freedom is an ironic negative freedom separate from the world.

Hamlet's relation to the past is of special interest in this regard. "Irony," Kierkegaard writes,

has no past. This is due to the fact that it sprang from metaphysical investigations. It had confounded the temporal ego with the eternal ego, and as the eternal ego has no past, so neither does the temporal. Insofar as irony should be so conventional as to accept a past, this past must then be of such a nature that irony can retain its freedom over it, continue to play its pranks on it. It was therefore the mythical aspect of history, saga and fairy-tale, which especially found grace in its eyes. Authentic history, on the other hand, where-in the true individual has his positive freedom because in this he has his premises, must be dispensed with. . . . Irony did the same [that is, lifted it off the earth] to all historical actuality. With a twist of the wrist all history become myth, poetry, saga, fairy-tale — irony was free once more. [P. 294]

Hamlet does not mythologize the past, but he does empty it by continually dwelling upon himself: he is constantly "forgetting" the past. In dialogue he refers ironically to the past, rendering it in understatement and silence, and his soliloquies center on himself and express his own double mind.

Hamlet empties the past in his all-encompassing doubt. His present inability to act is founded ostensibly on his questioning of the veracity of the ghost's report, and throughout the play his relation to the ghost is duplicitous in its nature. In his dead father —Hamlet, whose name he repeats—he finds his "premises," his necessary duty to the past that bears his own name, and yet he simultaneously denies the authority of the past both by his inaction and by his "play" with it in the present, freely repeating it in a drama, and without freedom repeating it in the murder of Polonius, "A bloody deed! almost as bad, good mother, / As kill a king and marry with his brother."

Such repetitions are central to Kierkegaard's thesis: it is the constant urge or irony to negate the past by making it present, by repeating it in myth, saga, or fairy tale; irony discovers itself to be the origin, the "beginning," the archetype, of the past. This is accomplished in the creations of types or archetypes as modes of explanation for the present as well as the past. Such creation is an ironic movement: types and archetypes are "present" only insofar as they negate actuality by repeating an ideal realm. Yet it is ironic in another way as well: irony (and Kierkegaard's thesis) renders repetition problematic even as it asserts it. Irony, Kierkegaard writes in his *Journal,* "seeks to see constantly a new side of repetition": "The dialectic of repetition is easy," he adds in *Repetition,* "for what is repeated has been, otherwise it could not be repeated, but precisely the fact that it has been gives to repetition the character of novelty" (pp. 12, 52). This "ease" is the ease of the problematics of time—the problematic of identity itself —that govern the never-easy relation of past and present and disturb the "ease" not only of repetition but of any grounding of experience: consciousness, understanding, interpretation, all forms, repeated and new, of repetition. That is, these repetitions of the past are repetitions with a difference:[7] Hamlet's comparison of the murder he commits with that of his uncle at once empties his own act, sucking out its significance as it asserts it by replacing it with a prior event, while it distorts (replaces) the ghost's version of the past. Irony discovers novelty in repetition and, in so doing, confuses repetition and creation, conclusion and beginning.

In the notion of repetition we have arrived at the crux of Kierkegaard's conception of irony and, indeed, of his whole authorship. For we have seen that the concept is predicated on the notion of the individual, on Socrates' absolute relation to the concept and, implicitly, on the possibility of "the true individual." Socrates is "true" to his premises insofar as the disparity of his character can be conceived under the category of irony. "In this way," Kierkegaard asserts, "I have secured the possibility of being able to explain the disparity among these three conceptions [of Socrates: those held by Xenophon, Plato, and Aristophanes] by another conception of Socrates corresponding to this disparity" (pp. 183-84). This Kierkegaard accomplishes by conceiving of Socrates as *essentially* disparate (that is, ironic), which the *phenomenal* disparity of his life repeats. Insofar as this is true, in Socrates irony is "mastered." Such "mastery," however, is at best momentary: irony by definition is the disparity of phenomenon and essence, and the moment of their correspondence is, like the reading of our piece of paper, the moment of a new disparity; the impossible notion of "essentially ironic" sets it all spinning again. Irony "both is and is not."

[7]Derrida explicitly describes the problematic of repetition in "Limited Inc abc . . . ," trans. Samuel Weber, *Glyph* 2 (1977): 162-254; he is discussing language and uses the term "iterability": "Iterability supposes a minimal remainder (as well as a minimum of idealization) in order that the identity of the *selfsame* be repeatable and identifiable *in, through,* and even *in view of* its alteration. For the structure of iteration . . . implies *both* identity *and* difference. Iteration in its 'purest' form—and it is always impure—contains *in itself* the discrepancy of a difference that constitutes it as iteration" (p. 190).

Here we are returned to the notion of the individual, the problem of identity. The individual for Kierkegaard is just the paradox implicit in this conception of Socrates: the "true" individual repeats his essence, constantly becoming what he already is. It is the paradoxical formulation of this conception that leads Kierkegaard to say, "No authentically human life is possible without irony" (p. 338). In *The Concept of Irony* he defines faith in terms very close to these:

True actuality becomes what it is, whereas the actuality of romanticism merely becomes. Similarly, faith is a victory of the world, yet it is also a struggle; for only when it has striven has it been victorious over the world, although it was victorious before it had striven. Thus faith becomes what it is. . . . In faith the higher actuality of spirit is not merely becoming, but present while yet becoming. [P. 332]

It is significant that this definition is of faith and not of the individual per se, because it is faith that allows the paradoxical statement of individuality, the assertion of presence, of absolute purpose. Elsewhere Kierkegaard speaks directly of the individual, and here we can see the importance of faith to his conception:

Individuality has a purpose which is absolute, therefore, and its activity consists in realizing this purpose, and in and through this realization to enjoy itself, that is to say, its activity is to become *für sich* [for itself] what it is *an sich* [in itself]. But as the average person has no *an sich* but becomes whatever he becomes, so neither does the [romantic] ironist. [P. 298]

The absolute purpose, of course, is the individual's relation to God (in whom he finds his "premises"), or faith to the faithful man (his *an sich*). Yet this *an sich,* which Kierkegaard unironically calls Being or "eternal consciousness," is an eternal and archetypal category. Without this archetype and the faith that recognizes (constitutes) it, the individual becomes merely ironic, becoming in meaningless repetition.

This, I believe, would be Kierkegaard's conception of Hamlet (the man). The essence of Hamlet is not irony but his relation to his "premises," to his father and to God (the possibility and ground of faith and purpose). The essence of the individual, his premises, is the recognition that he does not possess wholly the freedom of beginning, that he is not altogether originary, that his very individuality—his identity—is problematically not simply his "own," not simply "itself." Hamlet plays out his own drama, but he "forgets" the dramas of Laertes and Ophelia, which seem merely to repeat (with a difference) his own. Because he fails to recognize himself outside himself, to recognize that he is a repetition (of his father, King "Hamlet"), he is mastered by irony and repeats his uncle (King Claudius). Socrates can be authentically ironic because he precedes the "Absolute Moment" in history when faith (and purpose) became possible (Christ's incarnation), and also because irony has "world historical validity" (that is, purpose) as a moment in the movement toward faith: it creates the subjective, the individual, as a legitimate category. Kierkegaard goes so far as to compare Socrates to John the Baptist (p. 280) and, negatively, to Christ (p. 53). The distinction between Socrates and Hamlet (the man, the "romantic ironist") is of ultimate importance in our reading of the play and our understanding of Kierkegaard. It is significant to the play because without an authentic being all of Hamlet's actions (which are, in fact, nonactions) break down into meaningless repetitions: Hamlet remains about to become his father's avenger.

In the last chapter of *The Concept of Irony,* however, Kierkegaard discusses mastered irony, and he specifically refers to Shakespeare as a master who uses irony for his own purposes. Irony for Shakespeare becomes a moment in the total realization of actuality, and it is used more or less in proportion to the possibility of expressing the actual (p. 336). Past and future are one for the artist, standing as he does ironically in the present: "Actuality in this way acquires its validity—not as a purgatory, for the soul is not to be purified in such a way that it flees blank, bare, and stark naked out of life—but as a history wherein consciousness successively outlives itself, though in such a way that happiness consists not in forgetting all this but becomes present in it" (p. 341). Mastered irony does not forget: Shakespeare remembers the past and makes it present in *Hamlet* in just the way (dissimilarly) that Hamlet repeatedly forgets and empties the past and actuality itself in his self-conscious poses. Perhaps the central ironic scene in *Hamlet*—though "central-ironic" is another impossible notion—is Hamlet's rehearsal of the players. Afterward Hamlet dwells once again upon himself, his "originary" individuality:

> What's Hecuba to him or he to Hecuba,
> That he should weep for her? What would he do
> Had he the motive and the cue for passion
> That I have? He would drown the stage with tears.
> [2.585-88]

Shakespeare draws attention to the fact that Hamlet (the man) is immobilized by his own constant play acting and posing by which he repeatedly displaces himself, that his repetitions merely signify his becoming what he becomes. Yet what he becomes is (by another conception corresponding to this disparity) what all along he is: a romantic ironist living possibilities, a figure in a play. The language of this scene contains the past and future of *Hamlet* (the play) within itself, the metaphor of the play becomes ("both is and is not") the literal fact.

It remains, however, to reconcile this reading, if I can, with that of Eliot. Here we might look at Kierkegaard's discussion of tragedy:

When the great perish in this world this is tragedy, but poetry reconciles us to this by showing us that it is the true which is victorious. It is in this that the exaltation and edification consist. We are not exalted by the destruction of the great, we are reconciled to its destruction by the fact that truth is victorious, and we are exalted by its victory. If, however, I see in tragedy merely the destruction of the hero and am exalted by this, if in tragedy I merely become conscious of the nothingness of human affairs, if tragedy pleases me in the same way as comedy: by showing me the nothingness of the great as comedy shows me the nothingness of the small, then, manifestly, the higher actuality is not yet present. [Pp. 334-35]

In these terms *Hamlet* fails as a tragedy precisely because "the facts as they appear" lend no necessity to its bloody end: we can imagine Hamlet going on endlessly, repeating endlessly those matters that with himself he too much discusses, too much explains. The end of the play, I would argue, is arbitrary and accidental: again Hamlet is caught in a "play" which, ironically, he does not see to be deadly business.

Yet the arbitrary ending is altogether necessary if we see the play as basically (essentially) the dramatization of the romantic ironist. Here, the absence itself of "the higher actuality" is the element of truth, but now it is the truth negatively conceived: the play is ironical. Like Socrates, Hamlet has "a tragic fate," yet his death "is not essentially tragic" because his death is an objective correlative to his essential inability to express himself meaningfully throughout the play: his last wish is the same as his first, to be "explained," and his last word is "silence." Thus the play is not "an artistic failure," as Eliot asserted, but a failure as tragedy: at the same time Eliot failed to distinguish and distinguished too minutely between the character and the play.

The distinction between the character and the play brings us back to a consideration of Kierkegaard that is vital to our understanding: the distinction he draws between Socrates and the romantic ironist. Socrates is the point of departure for the "infinite eloquence" of speculative thought found in Kierkegaard's dissertation. We have to decide either that Socrates did, in fact, master irony and that the dissertation is a discourse on the individual (repetition-faith-religion) or that the whole dissertation is a discourse on silence (alteration-irony-romanticism), as the early characterization of Socrates implies, and that irony turns once again on itself to undermine its own conclusions, the possibility of its being mastered altogether. Kierkegaard himself alludes to these choices in *The Concept of Irony* and tries to have them both: "As for the

197

manner in which [Socrates' irony] manifested itself, we must say that it appeared partially as a mastered moment in discourse, and totally in its complete infinity whereby it finally swept away even Socrates himself" (p. 240). Yet the only way he can have both is by allowing himself a "total" perspective in which the mastered moment is only "partial" within the scope of his view, the scope of a prior (and thus repeated) reading: Socrates becomes for Kierkegaard what Hamlet has been for us with our knowledge of the end of the play at the beginning. Mastered irony forgets nothing —nothing, that is, except its own beginning: it forgets that it has no past. Kierkegaard, then, needs God (a ground, a "past," a premise) to provide the "absolute purpose" of actuality and thus the possibility of the true individual, an eternal consciousness in history. Yet this presence while yet becoming—of God, of faith, of Being itself—is indistinguishable from the "mythic," susceptible to that twist of the wrist which, Kierkegaard argues, is the essence of the romanticization of consciousness, the ironist's relation to the past.[8] The final irony of this work, then, is that the authentic

[8]Early in the dissertation Kierkegaard contrasts Socrates and Christ, and in the first thesis appended to his dissertation he notes: "I. The similarity between Christ and Socrates consists essentially in dissimilarity" (p. 349). The dissimilarity is that while the Gospels "merely reproduced the immediate image of Christ's immediate existence," Xenophon had to deal with a man "whose immediate existence means something 'other' than it appears"; and while John saw the "immediate divinity" of Christ, Plato had to create "his Socrates through poetic activity, since Socrates in his immediate existence was wholly negative" (pp. 52-53). Yet insofar as Socrates is what he becomes, namely, the master of irony, his otherness is his identity, and his negativity is his positive content; and insofar as Christ is the Absolute Paradox, namely, that he is both God and Man (and thus archetypal man), what he is appears only when it is mediated by faith.

Of the Platonic "image" Kierkegaard says: "But when the image permeates more and more, when it is able to accommodate within itself more and more, it then invites the spectator to find repose in it, to anticipate a pleasure which the restless reflection might perhaps lead him to after an extensive detour. Finally, when the image acquires such scope that the whole of existence becomes visible in it, then this becomes the regressive movement

irony of Socrates can be conceived only from the vantage of faith, which itself can be viewed ironically. Thus any judgment of the authenticity of irony must necessarily undermine itself; irony indeed sweeps all before it.

Yet this, of course, is not—cannot be—the "final" irony. *The Concept of Irony* presents a theory of fiction that recognizes the complicity of the opposites it presents: repetition-alteration, faith-irony, religion-romanticism. The very method of *Irony* demonstrates this theory: parody, extended citations in altering contexts, the confusion of "theme" and detail by the use of (peripheral) footnotes to make (central) arguments. All are instances of "repetitions" that are different; they instance the complicity of repetition and alteration, the inside and the outside, the *problem* of identity itself. Identity in time, Kierkegaard knew, can be understood only under some notion of repetition, and only faith, he felt, could realize and validate that repetition of identity. Such faith, however, need only be negatively (one might say ironically) conceived to produce a theory of fiction: *the willing suspension of disbelief* that suspends (but not altogether) the silence behind speech, the meaningless becoming behind identity, the metaphor behind the literal.[9] *Irony,* by using Socrates as a negative meta-

toward the mythical. . . . The image so overwhelms the individual that he loses freedom. . . . " (p. 135). In these terms, the "extensive detour" of the dissertation describing Socrates leads us back to Christ, and the dissimilarity between Christ and Socrates breaks down. More important, insofar as the image leads to mythology it contains in itself the same mythologizing tendency which Kierkegaard sees as romantic irony's relation to the past. He sees this as a flight from freedom, the romantic's flight from his true self (and from repetition—faith—religion). Yet since this flight depends upon the reality of the "true individual"—depends upon a posited faith (repetition—religion) that recognizes (constitutes) identity—which is itself the acceptance of freedom, we are lost in a tangle of contradictions, *mise en abyme*, the tangle, I will suggest, of fiction.

[9]From what I have said of *Hamlet*, it is only a short step from Kierkegaard's religious justification of experience to Nietzsche's aesthetic pronouncement in *The Birth of Tragedy*, trans. Francis Golfing (New York: Anchor Books,

phor, a dissimilar repetition, of Christ, locates and dislocates (so that it "hovers") such a theory in the play between the gaiety of its faith and the anxiety of its despair. In a sense, a fictional sense, its faith *is* ("and is not") its despair, expressed, as *Irony* argues it always is, in irony.

On the Resistance to Irony

Toward the end of *The Mill on the Floss,* George Eliot interrupts the narrative to present an extended and allusive meditation on the relation between character, destiny, and tragedy:

We have known Maggie a long while, and need to be told, not her characteristics, but her history, which is a thing hardly to be predicted even from the completest knowledge of characteristics. For the tragedy of our lives is not created entirely from within. "Character," says Novalis, in one of his questionable aphorisms,—"character is destiny." But not the whole of our destiny. Hamlet, Prince of Denmark, was speculative and irresolute, and we have a great tragedy in consequence. But if his father had lived to a good old age, and his uncle had died an early death, we can conceive Hamlet's having married Ophelia, and got through life with a reputation of sanity, notwithstanding many soliloquies, and some moody sarcasms towards the fair daughter of Polonius, to say nothing of the frankest incivilities to his father-in-law.

Maggie's destiny, then, is at present hidden, and we must wait for it to reveal itself like the course of an unmapped river: we only know

---

1956): "Only as *aesthetic phenomenon* is existence and the world forever *justified*" (pp. 33, 64). Moreover, it is a short step to Nietzsche's notion—again an attempt to realize and validate identity—of the eternal recurrence of the same. This step, short as it is, steps around a self-present God, replacing (but not altogether—here, too, are manifestations of repetition) a reading of God's signatures in the world with the simple act of reading, archetypal repetition with the figure of eternal recurrence, identity with fiction.

that the river is full and rapid, and that for all rivers there is the same final home. [Bk. 6, chap. 6][10]

This passage is important because it raises questions on whose answers any interpretation of the novel must rest, questions, indeed, which concern the whole enterprise of narrative. For literary narrative seeks to create some relationship—or at least the illusion of relationship—between destiny and time, consciousness and experience.

That this passage describes Maggie Tulliver and her predicament by speaking about others (Hamlet, Novalis, "we") is a matter to which I shall return. Nevertheless, Maggie in many ways repeats Hamlet. Her "characteristics" consist of a constant urge to flee from the world and from herself. In an early incident in the novel, when Maggie cuts her hair, we can see this urge to flee from the conflicts of the world in her attempt to transform herself physically, and this instance can stand for the repeated actions of the heroine in the novel:

She had thought beforehand chiefly of her own deliverance from her teasing hair and teasing remarks about it, and something also of the triumph that she should have over her mother and her aunts by this very decided course of action: she didn't want her hair to look pretty, —that was out of the question,—she only wanted people to think her a clever little girl, and not find fault with her. [Bk. 1, chap. 7]

The novel constantly depicts Maggie's longing to be well thought of and "to be loved" (bk. 6, chap. 2), and what this longing comes to is the wish for the recognition of her inwardness, her "character," her imaginative concept of herself. Maggie's eyes project this inwardness throughout the novel, and everyone who sees her is struck at once by her dark eyes. They remind Philip of "the stories of princesses being turned into animals," and the narrator himself says, "I think it was that her eyes were filled with unsatisfied

---

[10]*The Mill on the Floss* (2 Vols.), Cabinet edition (Boston: 1900). All references are to this edition: they are noted in the text by book and chapter.

intelligence, and unsatisfied, beseeching affection" (bk. 2, chap. 5). This longing without an object (merely "to be known" in the abstract), this mute intelligence, contrasts Maggie with her brother Tom, who, like the Dodson side of the family, which he resembles, is basically purposeful and unimaginative: he is altogether social.

Yet it is just the inwardness of Maggie that engenders interest. Comparing Maggie with an abstract well-bred young woman, the narrator concludes, "If Maggie had been that young lady, you would probably have known nothing about her: her life would have had so few vicissitudes that it could hardly have been written; for the happiest women, like the happiest nations, have no history" (bk. 6, chap. 3). Individual history consists of unhappiness, and Maggie's unhappiness arises largely in the *disparity* between her own conception of herself and the conception of her by others. To herself she is a "clever little girl," yet it is her "destiny" that her cleverness never receives the approval with which she thinks it will be met. Perhaps the most abrupt disillusionment she meets with in her childhood occurs when Mr. Sterling says that girls have "a great deal of superficial cleverness; but they couldn't go far into anything. They're quick and shallow." Maggie "had hardly ever been so mortified. She had been so proud to be called 'quick' all her little life, and now it appeared quickness was a brand of inferiority" (bk. 2, chap. 1). This attitude toward women is first voiced by Mr. Tulliver, who congratulates himself for marrying a woman who is not too "'cute," and remarks, concerning Maggie, that "an o'er-'cute woman's no better nor a long-tailed sheep" (bk. 1, chap. 2). Maggie's cleverness creates a situation in which she is out of place; it gives her ambitions and desires that can never be fulfilled. From one vantage point Maggie's inwardness can be seen as an effect as well as a cause of her unhappiness, and what I have earlier called her flight from the world into herself can be seen as an attempt to participate actively in creating her own destiny in a world that imposes a narrow destiny upon women. Cutting her hair, not to be pretty but to be recognized as a person, is an apt symbol of her childish protest of the imposition of roles upon her.

In other words, Maggie's life and her unhappiness can be viewed as the social violation of a woman who is forced into an imaginative life because there simply is no place for a woman alone, let alone a "clever" woman, in her world:

While Maggie's life-struggles had lain almost entirely within her own soul, one shadowy army fighting another, and the slain shadows forever rising again, Tom was engaged in a dustier, noisier warfare, grappling with more substantial obstacles, and gaining more definite conquests. So it had been since the days of Hecuba, and Hector, Tamer of horses: inside the gates, the women with streaming hair and uplifted hands offering prayers, watching the world's combat from afar, filling their long, empty days with memories and fears: outside, the men, in fierce struggle with things divine and human, quenching memory in the stronger light of purpose, losing the sense of dread and even of wounds in the hurrying ardour of action. [Bk. 5, chap. 2]

Later Maggie herself makes this same observation to Philip: "I begin to think that there can never come such happiness to me from loving: I have always had so much pain mingled with it. I wish I could make myself a world outside it, as men do" (bk. 6, chap. 7). Maggie's unhappiness, her homelessness in the world is based on the fact that circumstances deny her a world to act in, forcing her back in upon herself, while at the same time they deny her that inward self.

In this novel, however, Eliot seems less concerned with a commentary on social life and the situation of women than with the more general predicament of Maggie.[11] She is more concerned with memories and fears, with consciousness, than with either Maggie's or Tom's confrontation with society. Maggie's story is again that of Hecuba, with whom Hamlet compares himself: both

[11] This despite some important feminist approaches to the novel. See Elizabeth Weed, "*The Mill on the Floss*: or The Liquidation of Maggie Tulliver," *Genre* 11 (1978): 427-44; and Mary Jacobus, "The Question of Language: Men of Maxims and *The Mill on the Floss*," *Critical Inquiry* 8 (1981): 207-22.

are in a world where loss is inevitable and action impossible, and the protagonist has only the past and the future.

Maggie's response to her unhappiness is a further turning inward, an imaginative refashioning of the world; ultimately it is her imagination itself that is in opposition to the world: "Maggie's was a troublous life and this [refashioning of her little world into just what she would like it to be] was the form in which she took her opium" (bk. 1, chap. 6). Most often her imaginings lead her to a mere "forgetting" of the world (frequently in the form of losing herself in art): she forgets Tom's rabbit (bk. 1, chap. 4), forgets her fishing while "looking dreamily at the glassy water" (bk. 1, chap. 5), drops her cake while she studies a print of Ulysses (bk. 1, chap. 9), spills Tom's wine in her enthusiasm for the music box (bk. 1, chap. 9), forgets her father as she dreams of Walter Scott (bk. 4, chap. 13), forgets the social situation as Stephen tells her a story (bk. 6, chap. 13), and ultimately loses herself in the flood: "In the first moments Maggie felt nothing, thought of nothing, but that she had suddenly passed away from that life which she had been dreading: it was the transition of death, without its agony—and she was alone in the darkness with God" (bk. 6, chap. 5). In all these instances Maggie is abruptly brought back into the actual world; her forgetfulness precipitates a crisis that brings the world all the more emphatically back into her consciousness.

In these returns, unlike Hamlet she cannot hover over the world and appear to participate in it with "a light and graceful [verbal] irony." Rather she strives continually to find a place for herself in the world, and her intercourse with the world is neither light nor verbal: she takes herself seriously. This depiction of Maggie tends to resist the denial of the world, of "history," implicit in her standpoint in relation to the world by emphasizing the positive nature of her negative stand: the emphasis is on the seriousness with which she regards herself and her escapes rather than the unseriousness basic to her denial of the world that those escapes entail. Her life is seen as pain, both by herself and by the narrator, and her denial is expressed in compensatory imagination.

204

Maggie's intercourse with the world is not characterized solely by imaginative escape, however. While her dreaming seems on first glance comparable to her father's madness, in her active striving to find a place for herself she does more than go to bed silently as her father does. Rather she is continually trying to make her inward life free of the restraints of "reality," negatively free through denial, so that her character might indeed be her destiny. Thus her intercourse with the world, while basically nonverbal, still remains in essence the self-centered irony of Hamlet: she strives, like him, to assert herself, to have her character shape her destiny. Her attempts to find a place for herself are active repetitions of her flight into imagination: like Hamlet, she assumes roles. Cutting her hair, fleeing to the gypsies, and meeting secretly with Philip are all "pranks" that she plays on reality, albeit pranks that she takes seriously, with the utmost intensity. The most explicit of these active refashionings of the world is her "enthusiasm" for *Thomas a Kempis* and her egotistical renunciation:

For the first time she saw the possibility . . . of taking her stand outside of herself, and looking at her own life as an insignificant part of a divinely guided whole. . . . With all the hurry of an imagination which would never rest in the present, she sat in the deepening twilight forming plans of self-humiliation and entire devotedness; and, in the ardour of first discovery, renunciation seemed to her the entrance into that satisfaction which she had so long been craving in vain. She had not perceived—how could she until she had lived longer?—the inmost truth of the old monk's outpouring, that renunciation remains sorrow, but a sorrow borne willingly. [Bk. 4, chap. 3]

Maggie's period of renunciation shows clearly the paradox inherent in her situation: the renunciation of the actual world in order to find a place in the world for the self. Yet the place Maggie finds is outside herself, outside the world. Maggie is seeking freedom to assume her character, to realize her imaginative conception of herself as a part of the world so that, as the narrator says, she might give "her soul a home in it." There is a contradiction in this en-

205

deavor that transcends the social situation of women out of which it is born: the imaginative self Maggie seeks to fulfil can be fulfilled only outside the world, so that Maggie's inability to rest in the present is her inability to rest in the world.

Thomas a Kempis is called "a voice from the past," and it is out of the past that Maggie seeks to create her future. Throughout the novel the moral dilemma for Maggie is the choice between the "voice" of the past and her present feeling, what the narrator calls the relation between "passion and duty" and defines in terms of time (bk. 7, chap. 2). This, too, is why Maggie's dreaming is so often called "forgetfulness." More specifically, her choices in relation to Philip and Stephen are defined as choices between the past and the present. When she explains to Stephen why she cannot marry him, she says that she is held by her "memories and affections" and that to stay with him "would rend me away from all my past life has made dear and holy to me" (bk. 6, chap. 14). Her alternative to Stephen is a vision of the past: "Home,—where her mother and brother were,—Philip,—Lucy,—the scene of her very cares and trials,—was the haven towards which her mind tended,—the sanctuary where sacred relics lay, where she would be rescued from more failing" (bk. 6, chap. 14). This home for Maggie is purely imaginative; it is really a vision of a desired future created from a past that never existed, that is merely an illusion. When Maggie reaches "home," she meets rebuke from her brother and a general ostracism that nearly forces her back to Stephen. Never in her life has her home provided her with those things for which she returns.

Throughout the novel Maggie has been seeking this envisioned home. In an early passage, after Tulliver has lost his money and Maggie has argued with Tom, she is described in terms that bring all of her "characteristics" together: her cleverness, the dreamy pleasure she takes in music, the yearning that her eyes signify, and her need for a "key" to life that would make the world comprehensible:

Maggie . . . was a creature full of eager, passionate longings for all that was beautiful and glad; thirsty for all knowledge; with an ear straining after dreamy music that died away and would not come near to her; with a blind, unconscious yearning for something that would link together the wonderful impressions of this mysterious life, and give her soul a home in it. [Bk. 3, chap. 5]

More specifically, this home is her image of the mill on the Floss, her home of the past. Throughout the novel Maggie's "affections" identify and link her with the past. Her constant love for Tom, even though he neither understands her nor provides her with sympathy, stems from the fact that, as she tells Philip, "the first thing I ever remember in my life is standing with Tom by the side of the Floss, while he held my hand: everything before that is dark to me" (bk. 5, chap. 1). Her affection for Tom grows, as the narrator says, from an early life where "objects became dear to us before we had known the labor of choice, and where the outer world seemed only an extension of our own personality; we accepted and loved it as we accepted our own sense of existence and our own limbs" (bk. 2, chap. 1). This primitive love is of the past before language, before the conscious self begins to make distinctions in the world. It is the time that Wordsworth's "Intimations of Immortality" nostalgically describes, the time beyond time when the child verges on nonbeing, the silent presence of undifferentiated being. This is an image of a world that answers the self, seems its very extension, yet does so because that self, extended beyond itself, lacks identity: an image, that is, of the "mythic" past, which is not of the past at all. The memory of standing on the Floss with Tom "remembers" that borderline between existence and nonexistence: it is death without its agony.

The fulfillment that Maggie longs for is thus the avoidance of consciousness itself. Memories and fears are the elements of Maggie's unhappiness, yet they are also the elements of consciousness, the past and the future: for Maggie visions of the past and future are interchangeable. Yearning for the loss of self-consciousness, which is itself the basis of such yearning, Maggie cannot rest in the present—cannot retrieve that "presence" which, if it occurred

207

at all, was present on the basis of the absence of her (conscious) self—but must always seek to be somewhere else and, indeed, to be someone else.

Maggie's final reunion with Tom bears this out. In her last awakening from a dream during the final flood, Maggie cries "in the dim loneliness": "'Oh, God, where am I? Which is the way home?'" (bk. 7, chap. 5). The way home is death, in which Maggie at last reconciles duty and passion, memory and the present, the other and the self; death is the home she has been seeking. The family traditions in this novel substantiate this sense of "home": the most important aspects of kin relationships for the Dodsons center on funeral rites and wills. In *The Mill on the Floss* one's duty to one's family is, in large part, fulfilled by dying.

Such yearnings and self-contradictory impulses create particular problems for the narrator even as they create an image of his art and task. Insofar as Maggie presents the disparity between character and destiny, the narrator must both sympathize with her and depict her contingency, the accidents and "history" that make her what she is. That is, the narrator is faced with the contradictory tasks of sympathy and distance in his depiction of Maggie; he must depict both her character and her destiny in a language that is distanced as well as close, defining as well as sympathizing: the language of irony. In *The Mill on the Floss,* however, the narrator is constantly resisting irony in relation to Maggie. One form of this resistance has already been alluded to: the narrator strives to take Maggie seriously, and as he does so, he strives against our reading. This seriousness is a way of identifying with (and identifying) Maggie, a way of closing the distance necessary for irony.

Central to this identifying resistance of the narrator is his own relation to the past. Throughout the novel the narrator interpolates passages in which he identifies his own past with that of Maggie. The most obvious of these is the first chapter, in which he "remembers" the Dorlcote Mill. He identifies with Maggie most often, however, in associating the past with (present) affection to justify Maggie's lifelong attachments (bk. 1, chaps. 5, 7; bk. 2, chap. 1).

Passages such as these have led critics to complain that Eliot was identifying herself with her character, and these passages would in part corroborate that assertion. Yet identification works more toward a sympathetic reading of Maggie in this novel than toward an elegiac celebration of the past.

Sympathy is a central concern of George Eliot: she is always striving to find those beginnings, that "primitive love," in which people are joined, communities established, "enthusiasms" of self-lessness possible. In a way, this is what the duty of the past is to Maggie, in contrast to the passion of the moment. Eliot turns to the past to find those links between people—for the Dodsons the past of family tradition, for Maggie the past of childhood, for the narrator the past of the remembered mill. Yet as this novel shows, the past of sympathetic union, the *identifying* force of the past, in both senses of the word, is illusory and recedes as we approach it, until the vision of union becomes a visionary past of nonbeing. The sources of love and sympathy, *The Mill on the Floss* seems to imply, move backward toward the edge of time as if to say that those qualities which allow for the most genuine human sympathy are in themselves the least characteristic of conscious humanity: mute, blind, unconscious. There is a terrible irony in the epigraph (and epitaph) of the book, "In their death they were not divided," because it expresses the logic of the novel's vision of sympathy and love: only in extreme selflessness is extreme union possible; only in death can Maggie and Tom be reconciled, the "past" retrieved. The contradictory definition of identity the novel offers—self-identity grounded in identification with someone or something else—questions the very identities of the heroine and the narrator. And since their identities (their differences) are determined in large part by the temporality of the novel, the literary past of the narration itself, this contradiction both determines and undermines the fictional enterprise.

The problematic nature of sympathy and identity can be seen most clearly, I believe, in the stance the narrator exhibits toward the characters. There is a double edge to those passages of recollection mentioned above, because, while they justify Maggie's (and the narrator's) present affections by means of the past, they also empty them of present significance. As the narrator says, "Very commonplace, ever ugly, that furniture of our early home might look if it were put up to auction," yet "the loves and sanctities of . . . memory" (bk. 2, chap. 1) hide its present state. Narrative comments on the action also have this double effect. In the reference to Maggie's renunciation inspired by Thomas a Kempis, quoted above, the narrator interpolates a rhetorical question ("How could she [see] until she had lived longer?") which attempts to undercut the ironic viewpoint for which Maggie's egotistical renunciation necessarily calls. Yet this sentence calls attention to her lack of self-awareness even as it apologizes for it. Moreover, it enlarges the distance between the narrator and his subject, even as it is pushed toward identification, by calling attention to the temporal difference between them: it moves sympathetic identification to the "past" (when the narrator was an adolescent, "before" the novel) and replaces it in the novel with identifying difference. On the next page, in a similar movement, the narrator ironically "apologizes" for the absence of irony in his work:

In writing the history of unfashionable families, one is apt to fall into a tone of emphasis which is very far from being the tone of good society, where principles and beliefs are not only of an extremely moderate kind, but are always presupposed, no subject being eligible but such as can be touched with a light and graceful irony. But then, good society has its claret and velvet carpets. . . . : how should it have time or need for belief and emphasis? But good society, floated on gossamer wings of light irony, is of very expensive production: requiring nothing less than a wide and arduous national life condensed in unfragrant deafening factories. . . . This wide national life is based entirely on emphasis,—the emphasis of want. . . . there are many among its myriads of souls who have absolutely needed an emphatic belief. . . . Some have an emphatic belief in alcohol, and seek their *ekstasis* or outside standing-ground in gin; but the rest require something that good society calls "enthusiasm," something that will present motives in an entire absence of high prizes . . . —something, clearly, that lies outside personal desires, that includes resignation for ourselves and active love for what is not ourselves. [Bk. 4, chap. 3]

Here is another call for sympathy that undermines itself. The equation between religion and gin (earlier, Maggie's imagination was called her "opium") points to the illusory nature of emphatic belief even as the narrator is striving for a sympathetic understanding of such belief. Underlying this passage is the narrator's use of the criteria of good society to dissociate himself from enthusiasm even as the rhetoric of the passage is directed ironically and bitterly against the foundations of such criteria and against irony itself. Thus the narrator is left without a standpoint outside his work; he is left, as it were, hovering over it.

This passage also creates an important commentary on Maggie's dilemma: Eliot recognizes the human need for the creation of a "standing-ground." This necessity is based on the fact that human beings have a sense of a relationship between character and destiny in which destiny somehow fulfills character; that is, it is based on the human apprehension that things are more meaningful than they appear to be, meaningful in some personal and ultimately transcendental sense. It is this transcendental sense, the apprehension of destiny, that requires a "standing-ground." Thus we see in this passage that all are given some ground: even good society has the resting place of irony, comfortably endowed with velvet carpets, yet hovering self-deceptively on "gossamer wings" above the painful actuality at the base of its "goodness." So too the narrator has an ironic standpoint outside the novel, yet it is lighter than the irony of good society, and it takes him further. For this passage also indicates that an "outside standing-ground," whether it is "enthusiasm" or the sense of self-complacency and disdain for "unfashionable families"—or even something discovered in art—is a human illusion, an aspect of consciousness that cannot be fulfilled. Consciousness must dissociate itself from the world to achieve its "character," and when the world is too emphatic, it cannot;

211

then it must find a standing-ground outside consciousness itself. Either way, lightly or emphatically, the world is lost, all is swept away. In the former, as we see in the narrator, consciousness undermines its own standpoint; while in the latter, as we see in Maggie, consciousness desires its own destruction. This is why, I believe, Maggie's vision of a happy future is a vision of a time before consciousness, before irony. Maggie's vision itself seeks to resist the very standpoint that produces it: it seeks to resist consciousness.

The predicament of the narrator is the same as Maggie's. Just as she seeks to become unconscious in order to find a place for herself in the world, so the narrator must speak in terms different from what he means in order to speak at all. Irony is necessary even in an attempt to resist irony:

It is astonishing what a different result one gets by changing the metaphor! . . . It was doubtless an ingenious idea to call the camel the ship of the desert, but it would hardly lead one far in training that useful beast. O Aristotle! If you had had the advantage of being "the freshest modern" instead of the greatest ancient, would you not have mingled your praise of metaphorical speech, as a sign of high intelligence, with a lamentation that intelligence so rarely shows itself in speech without metaphor,—that we can so seldom declare what a thing is, except by saying it is something else? [Bk. 2, chap. 1]

The novel is constantly calling Maggie "something else," offering metaphors for Maggie in the form of parallel types and archetypes. Yet all these types seem to undermine themselves. This process recapitulates the method of the novel, which invokes a fictional past, for the reader as well as Maggie, to understand the present. Typing is the method of narrative; it creates patterns or the illusion of patterns amid the unmapped flow of events: it asserts significance in repetition, character in historical destiny. Thus in the novel Maggie compares herself to the witch in the story of the witch trial she recites to Mr. Riley (bk. 1, chap. 3); she likens herself to dark heroines in novels (bk. 5, chap. 4); and throughout the novel she identifies herself with the legend of Saint Ogg (bk. 1, chap. 2).

212

Such an identification occurs in Maggie's dream when she is with Stephen, and this is important in relation to the larger question of narration and the literary past as well as to the novel's formulations of types for Maggie:

She was in a boat on the wide water with Stephen, and in the gathering darkness something like a star appeared, that grew and grew till they saw it was the Virgin seated in St. Ogg's boat, and it came nearer and nearer, till they saw the Virgin was Lucy and the boatman was Philip, —no, not Philip, but her brother, who rowed past without looking at her; and she rose to stretch out her arms and call to him, and their own boat turned over with the movement, and they began to sink, till with one spasm of dread she seemed to awake, and find she was a child again in the parlour at evening twilight, and Tom was not really angry. From the soothed sense of that false waking she passed to the real waking. [Bk. 6, chap. 14]

In this dream Lucy is identified with the Virgin who in the legend blesses Ogg because he did not "question and wrangle with the heart's need" (bk. 1, chap. 2). Thus Maggie, who in many ways repeats the Virgin with her "heart's needs," is able to identify and sympathize with Lucy, whom she herself has wronged. More important, however, than the sympathy and guilt that Maggie's dream reveals is the narrative progression of her dream. The "false waking" of the dream is characteristic of Maggie throughout the novel: she transforms memory into her own desired dream world. Here again Maggie wakes up into her own past—and again it is a past that did not exist: as a child, Tom really did get angry.

In this dream, too, we can see the significance of Maggie's repeated urge to drift. The syntax of her dream, like her floating adventure with Stephen, drags her along as one thing follows another, not so much in any order as in a relentless temporal succession joined by "thens" and "ands." In narrating the dream, telling is drifting, and events, not interpretations, are of the highest importance. Nevertheless, interpretation comes to Maggie without effort, as if to say there can be no remembered event without interpretation: she wakes to the "terrible truth" that "she was alone with her own memory and her own dread" (bk. 6, chap. 14).

Memory and dread, the lot of women, and, more important, the past and future that are the "substance" of consciousness, face her now as she recognizes "the clew to life" that she had lost, "renunciation." Drifting is the opposite of consciousness, yet upon waking Maggie remembers the meaningless successiveness of her dream vision in the language of morality—morality, as we have seen, conceived in terms of time. Renunciation is the choice to order her life and follow sympathy rather than self, memory rather than desire; it is the choice to make the past, and passing time itself, meaningful. The past events in the dream—Saint Ogg, Tom, Philip, Lucy—all come into Maggie's conscious mind to determine her future. Yet this past is in some essential way only an illusion, truly a dream, and hardly "past" at all: renunciation, after all, when it is (can it be?) *chosen* is closer to the interpretations of consciousness than it is to the successiveness of drifting. If memory and dread—the past and the future—are the "substance" of consciousness, they are also "present" in consciousness, even if this "presence"—the "borderline" consciousness itself—is determined by their absence. Maggie is still trying to find that impossible "home" where sympathy and self can be joined, "identity" realized.

Irony, George Eliot knew, is not enough: narration demands more, even if it is an "enthusiasm" for irony that sustains its telling. Maggie's choice (renunciation?) to make the past meaningful is also the choice of the narrator and the novelist, the choice to discover a human image in a past that is gone. Like Maggie, the narrator is a dreamer, and for him too the distinction between telling and dreaming is vague. Chapter 1 opens with the narrator as "rapt" in the scene he depicts as Maggie is in the movement of the mill. Moreover, the opening scene itself is the narrator's dream of himself standing on the stone bridge that will be washed away by the flood at the end of the novel. Toward the end of the chapter he says, "Before I dozed off, I was going to tell you what Mr. and Mrs. Tulliver were talking about, as they sat by the bright fire in the left-hand parlour, on the very afternoon I have been dreaming of" (bk. 1, chap. 1). Yet in the novel there is no "before": in chapter 1 all we have is the narrator's dream. Just as the narrator resists (presents?) irony in an attempt to create a sympathetic vision of his subject, so he speaks of a "before" to create a sense of reality for his novel. Yet the novel itself betrays that attempt. It literally sweeps away the bridge which is the narrator's standpoint, and his rapture, his love of moisture, and his attachment to the peaceful, "remembered" home in this first scene identify him with Maggie and with her inability to establish any authentic relationship with her world. The first scene sets the tone of the narrator's memory, yet it is the antithesis of this scene to which the novel builds: the book ends in flood, not order, chaos, not discrimination; it ends in silence and darkness.

Still in the course, the drift, of the novel the narrator offers a final archetype for Maggie, implicit in the quotation with which I began, the type of Hamlet, rendering her a tragic heroine and giving her a truly literary past. In a passage discussing Mr. Tulliver, which uses terms very close to those in which he discusses Hamlet, the narrator remarks that "Mr. Tulliver had a destiny as well as Oedipus, and in this case he might plead, like Oedipus, that his deed was inflicted upon him rather than committed by him" (bk. 1, chap. 13). Destiny, in the language of Kierkegaard, is just that being which one always is yet is always becoming (repeating), and in the context of the novel this passage must be read ironically: Tulliver might plead to the contrary, but he did call his destiny down upon himself in his attempt to stem the industrialization of England as well as in his choice of a wife. Tragedy, George Eliot wrote elsewhere, is the necessary conflict between two goods, the "valid claims" of the individual and those of the general polity.[12] In Tulliver's case it is the conflict between his familial pastoralism (including choosing a woman not "o'er-'cute" for his wife) and Britain's emerging industrialism, the past and the present.

When the hero's past is conceived negatively, however, as in

[12]George Eliot, "The Antigone and its Moral," in *Essays*, ed. Thomas Pinney (London: Routledge and Kegan Paul, 1965).

215

the cases of Maggie and Hamlet, his destiny does seem arbitrary in ways that Tulliver's does not. Maggie's past, unlike her father's, is simply a denial of the present, and we can imagine her, like Hamlet, having "got through life with a reputation of sanity, notwithstanding many soliloquies." In *The Mill* her valid claims are only negatively described as the yearning for some vague affection, understanding, home, the yearning for an illusory "past" uniting self and sympathy, character and destiny. The only way to give Maggie a valid claim on some good, to render her life tragic, is to transform these negative qualities into positive qualities of type: to make an imagined past represent the inwardness of personality against the outwardness of "reality." Thus much of the novel attempts to establish prior types (literary archetypes) for Maggie— innocent, saint, dark heroine, tragic figure—even while they are undermined by her repeated quests to lose herself and her extreme lack of self-awareness throughout her history. The narrator emphasizes Maggie's lack of awareness of herself as he tries to mitigate it, and in so doing he undercuts his attempt to render her life as tragedy. Yet her fate is tragic, as is the predicament of its prose narrative that attempts to discriminate between destiny and character and to discover sympathy in a world of indifferent things and events—a world adrift, without purpose, lacking anything more than a historically contingent destiny. But it is a tragic fate only because it is arbitrary, as all endings are, despite the fact they all arrive at the same final home. Like the opening image of the river's flow, the typing of narration is a mode of verbal assertion that ironically—now in the full force of the term—disguises (reveals?) itself as discovered (imposed) pattern; it is an attempt to discern growth and archetypal significance in repetition, the method, in the madness of unmapped events, of consciousness and irony.

The Contributors

Paul Bové is a critic and literary theoretician. His latest publication is *Destructive Poetics*. He is associate editor of *boundary 2* and associate professor of English in the University of Pittsburgh.

Laurie Finke is assistant professor of English in Lewis and Clark College in Portland, Oregon. She has published articles on Chaucer, Shakespeare, and eighteenth-century drama and has edited *From Renaissance to Restoration: Metamorphoses of the Drama* with Robert Markley.

Louis Mackey has published many studies of Kierkegaard, including *Kierkegaard: A Kind of Poet*. He is a professor of philosophy in the University of Texas at Austin.

Robert Markley is assistant professor of English in Texas Tech University and editor of *The Eighteenth Century: Theory and Interpretation*. He is coeditor of *From Renaissance to Restoration: Metamorphoses of the Drama* and also has published on eighteenth-century drama, literary theory, and the history of science. At present he is pursuing the rhetoric of restoration comedy.

Ronald Schleifer is associate professor of English in the University of Oklahoma and the editor of *Genre*, He has published widely on romantic and modern literature and literary theory and has edited *The Genres of the Irish Literary Revival.* His most recent work is a translation, prepared with Alan Velie and Daniele McDowell, of A. J. Greimas's *Structural Semantics*, for which he wrote the introduction. His *Rhetoric and Form: Contemporary Genre Theory and the Yale School,* coedited with Robert Con Davis, will appear in 1984.

George Stack is professor of philosophy in the State University of New York at Brockport. He has published widely on Kierkegaard, including *Kierkegaard's Existential Ethics* and *On Kierkegaard: Philosophic Fragments.*

Carole Anne Taylor is assistant professor of English in Bates College. She has published widely in American studies and literary theory and is coauthor of *Roland Barthes: A Bibliographical Reader's Guide.*

218

Index

Abraham (patriarch of Jews): 7, 38
Aeschylus: 169
Alienation: 26, 33-34, 36-38;
within bourgeois culture, 41, 44,
46, 49-52, 54-55
Allegory: 129, 134, 136-37; see
also *Piers Plowman*
Androgyny: 95
Anonymity, in bourgeois society:
48-49
Antichrist: 137
"Antigone and its Moral" (George
Eliot): 215
Aristophanes: 193
Aristotle: 133
Artistic self-creation: 160-61
Athanasian creed: 125
Atomism: 31-32; see also alienation
Audience: in drama, 146, 154-58;
and irony, 154, 157, 158
Augustine: 119, 128, 137
Authentic existence: 58, 59, 68, 74,
77; see also Kierkegaard, Sören
Authority: problems in authorship,
164-82; see also Kierkegaard,
Sören; Thoreau, Henry David
Autobiography: 12

Barthes, Roland: 17
Being: 60, 61, 85, 115, 194, 198;
ideal versus actual, 76
Bentham, Jeremy: 32, 52
Birdsall, Virginia Ogden: 158
Boesen, Emil: 38
Bonaparte, Louis: 41

Capell, Lee: 185
Cavell, Stanley: 174
Character: 15, 40, 43, 138-39, 151,
159; as imitation, 152 ff.; versus
play, 197; in *The Mill on the
Floss*, 201; and consciousness,
211; see also *Plain Dealer, The;
Hamlet*
Choice (in Kierkegaard's philosophy):
10, 19, 71, 72, 214
Christ: 55, 61, 78, 97, 124, 127,
135, 136, 185, 195, 198-200
Christianity: 12, 29, 34, 78, 111,
131, 188
Coleridge, Samuel Taylor: 189
Concept of Dread, The (Kierke-
gaard): 31, 73, 83
Concept of Irony, The (Kierkegaard):
4, 5, 9, 16, 21, 113; idea of self

219